THE CUPPA TREE

KEZ WICKHAM ST GEORGE

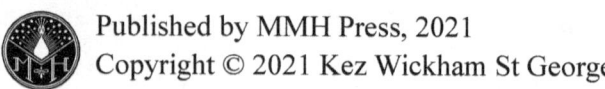 Published by MMH Press, 2021
Copyright © 2021 Kez Wickham St George

All rights reserved. No part of this book may be used or reproduced by any means, graphic, electronic, or mechanical, including photocopying, recording, taping or by any information storage retrieval system without the written permission of the copyright owner except in the case of brief quotations embodied in critical articles and reviews.

This is a work of fiction. Names, characters, businesses, places, events and incidents are either the products of the author/s' imagination or used in a fictitious manner. Any resemblance to actual persons, living or dead, or actual events is purely coincidental.

Because of the dynamic nature of the Internet, any web addresses or links contained in this book may have changed since publication and may no longer be valid. The views expressed in this work are solely those of the authors and do not necessarily reflect the views of the publisher and the publisher hereby disclaims any responsibility for them.

Cover: Dylan Ingram
Interior: Chelsea Wilcox
Editor: Dannielle Line

National Library of Australia
Cataloguing-in-Publication data:
The Cuppa Tree/MMHPress

ISBN: 978-0-6450966-6-8 (sc)
        978-0-6450966-5-1 (e)

DEDICATION

To Tim, Wendy & Jordan Husband
Thank you for being a huge part of my family.
Thank you for the holidays we spend with you wherever you are in this big wide world. Thank you for loving me as your aunty, an honour I cherish.
'You Become What You Believe.'

KEZ

PROLOGUE

The small fire lit outside my little home on wheels, halfway across the Nullarbor Plain, casts orange flickers and shadows upon our faces. I raise my cup of billy tea to the sky in gratitude. 'Thank you,' I say out loud.

'Amen to that!' is echoed by Eric, Doll, and Gordi as they, too, lift their tin mugs as a sign of respect.

These are my fireside companions for the night; all of us travelling through the Australian outback, all of us mesmerised by the universal light show on display.

Yes, I am travelling once again, and the fine red dust that coats my skin and my hair is pure joy to me. The cold wind of the night desert wraps its frosty mantle around my shoulders. And I wait to once again be part of the words, stories, poems, and descriptions I've heard or been told of an Australian desert at night.

Well, my friends, they have it right. Admiration for the world's glow sits deep in my chest as I wait for the universal sky show. The last of a deep sunset covers the scrub-covered land, where intense mauves are sinking into the night sky like a deep bruise upon Earth's soft face. The night sky comes suddenly upon us as the last white streak of an aeroplane flying to far-off countries fades away in the distance. And finally, the myriad dance of stars twinkles overhead, no longer concealed by the acrid smoke and yellow fog blanket that covers the city we left behind. Out here they shine faithfully every night. Most people in the city jungle fail to notice them, their days packed with the busyness of life.

I'd never thought this was in my future, especially now being in my mid-sixties; yet here I am, strong in all ways. And I am so incredibly grateful for what I have. Lessons from the past have been well learnt; some were unwanted but appreciated, and they too have been taken on board in my journey of life. My future now investigates unknown adventures once again, this time with my new travel companion, Gordi. The miles have slipped away along the long Nullarbor Plain. Thankfully, so too, has some of the stress enveloping me since returning home from New Zealand. This is my new home, a fourteen-foot motorhome, and hopefully, a new way of life.

I think about my life and all the lessons learned, and I realise looking for a personal perspective is fruitless; the vastness of what lies before us shows just how small our worries and stresses in life are. Although they may seem huge at the time; in the bigger picture they are but a tiny part of the universe. I was once told that *'each of us creates our own universe around us, when we should be creating it inside of us.'* I cannot add to this, as I feel it is so true.

But I digress; for this story starts nearly two years ago after I returned to Australia from New Zealand. My daughter Rae had been through so much her first marriage had failed her second child was due, I'd also entered the Wearable Arts Festival in Mandurah. It took three months of diligent sewing, pinning, cutting, and painting to make my Avatar dragon warrior art piece. Jess, my grandson and warrior model (who else would I ask?), loved it and strutted his stuff across the stage. The Wearable Arts folk also asked if I would once again design and make the floral arts presentation for all six category winners. I'd also been invited to organise another art exhibition event, exhibiting with two other artists. Four large canvas were to be completed for this exhibition. I was also a full-time carer for my little family of two. To say there was some stress in my life at that point is an understatement, as you will find in my story of The Cuppa Tree.

CHAPTER 1

I longed for just one good night's sleep, but the stress had returned. Stress for me, I realise, seems to have this funny way of popping up as soon as I have turned off the last light. All I wanted to do was lie down in a huge rubbery lump and cry myself to sleep. But as I willed my body to relax, my muscles still aching from the stress of the past months, I needed to give my emotions down time and myself permission to let go. It felt as if I'd been standing to attention nonstop. But the mind is a different matter, and my mind this night had other plans. It went in constant circles. My face ached with the tension of holding back unspoken words of reproach to my family, headaches now formed a constant throb in my neck and temples. I knew I looked awful with grey-blue rings around my eyes, the mirror every morning showing me that within the depths lay a deep and foreboding weariness. None of my family or friends had any idea of the turn of events that would propel me into my decision to go on the road again.

But let's go back to the beginning: my homecoming.

It hadn't been all bad. The early days following my return to Perth after a year away had been brilliant. I spun many a travel yarn over dinners with friends and we laughed over the videos I'd taken. Jess hid his head among the couch cushions, embarrassed his nana was cavorting in front of the camera. I enjoyed my small claim to fame as a solo traveller, with friends and family saying 'Ooh' and 'Aah' in all the right places. It felt wonderful to be home again, settled in Rockingham once more, and even better, my small family of two, soon to be three; now lived permanently with me.

Immersing myself once again in the art scene in Rockingham, I joined every exhibition with a fresh piece of work. My photos from the far north of Western Australia and New Zealand providing fresh inspiration for my own art. Plus, I'd joined the Rockingham Arts Council and the local volunteer brigade who helped at all exhibitions held by the Rockingham Council. Busy was not the word I would use to describe it. It was pure joy to be part of such a buzzing art world, and I felt like I'd rebooted my life.

I started a new life for myself whilst I was still travelling, and I'd also written a novel about my experiences in New Zealand. I fictionalised some and added a lot of humour. As with every author, my book was part of me, and it contained a lot of my personal life during this period. Impulsively, I called and pitched the book to a publisher; a daunting experience in itself. I never expected a signed contract to arrive so soon, or the publicity it generated.

They asked me to meet with the publishing house representative, Mike. The young man arrived with a flourish; professional was written all over him. Mike's enthusiastic and charming banter immediately drew me in as he put me at ease and pumped up my ego.

'I can see you're a writer, Tara!' he exclaimed as he flipped through the draft of my four hundred pages of handwritten manuscript.

The warning lights should have gone off when he patted his pockets after ordering coffee and cake.

'I seem to have left my wallet at home!'

I still ignored that warning twinge in my chest. I was floating happily on my ego, inside a pink balloon of what a fantastic writer I was, so I offered to pay for both our coffees. By the time the bill was delivered to our table I'd signed a contract, agreeing to deliver the first typed draft in three months. And although I knew this would take time and a lot of work, I was over the moon that Mike thought my adventure novel was worth publishing.

Before he left me at the café, Mike confirmed my book would be fully edited, proofread, and well marketed through an agent saying, 'I can almost hear Europe asking for more.' He expected my novel to sell well; he thought it was quite different from other travel literature because of its being so personal. Mike opened his arms to me, and I stepped into a cloud of spicy aftershave.

He almost purred. 'Tara. you're going to one of my best authors yet, I'll make sure of that.' Then calling out as he crossed the street, 'Next time, it's on me, Tara!'

With complete faith in him, I worked diligently getting the manuscript just right, spurred on by Mike's motivating phone calls. 'Keep going, Tara.

Everyone here loves your book,' and 'I have read part of it and could not put it down,' at which my shaky ego would breathe a sigh of relief.

After I sent the first draft by email for editing, Mike's staff informed me he was in Singapore on business. However, in his notes he'd requested I post by mail the manuscript, to have it printed double-sided on A4 paper, with each page physically signed by me. This I did, though I was confused why; but he was a publishing house representative and knew much more than I did. Or so I thought.

Two weeks later, the first eight chapters of the manuscript arrived back on my doorstep with 'please restructure' or 'rephrase,' written in red on every page. There were marks in red circling small errors. I looked down at the big red marks on most of the pages announcing changes or improvements to be made and sighed. Once again, I followed Mike's instructions, but I could feel my intuition kicking in. A small voice in my head would play over and over.

'Tara, you have paid over four thousand dollars to have this work done for you, so why are you doing all the correcting?'

It felt wrong. The next morning, I phoned Mike; he quickly dismissed my questions, even going so far as saying, 'If you are going to be insulting, I will not work with you.'

This confused me as I was only asking questions, not hurling insults; but Mike knew how to turn on the charm, declaring again how he loved me and my book.

'Just keep going, Tara; it is going to be a great hit.'

So why was my gut churning?

I was soon to find out. The blinkers soon came off. A few days after I rang Mike, a friend called in. She'd just read one of the books this company published. She was indignant on behalf of the author.

'Tara! It was awful! This publisher is pure rubbish; quit while you can.'

My tummy rolled over as I thought of ways to have any of the money refunded. Mike was always either away, busy, or else did not answer or return my calls. There didn't seem to be a lot I could do other than to keep going. Keep the communication if possible open and friendly, being aware of Mike's charm. Seeds of distrust were starting. I felt awful; obviously his comments to me about being a good writer where just banter to gain a paying client.

Questions were now piling up. I began investigating. On his web page, thirty or more books were listed as published, I rang one of the advertised authors. To my horror, I was informed this in a loud voice.

'Don't mention that prick's name to me, he's nothing but dogshit.'

I then got a rundown on how Mike sweet-talked her into paying another ten thousand dollars to start him off in the movie world. Apparently her book was a bestseller in Spain and a movie company there was interested in buying the manuscript for a screenplay. She'd been so delighted with this news, she'd agreed to source the money from her superannuation. Two years had passed since then. Her mistake was putting the money straight into his bank account. She trusted him; he was her trusted publisher, right?

I heard her heart break over the phone; I felt the hot tears behind my own eyes, but I'd nothing to offer her. I could not apologise for another's ignorance or dishonesty, but listened as she poured out her story to me, ending with 'I hope you've not been hoodwinked by this piece of shit.'

I said I was fine, thanked her for her time, put the phone down and let the tears flow for us both. What was I to do? I decided I would be smart, to keep writing, making weekly phone calls to Mike to enquire how it was all going. After two weeks, I was informed by his message service that Mike was working overseas. My friend who'd first delivered the news about Mike also made enquiries through her son who was employed in a computer detective business.

His news was all bad. Apparently, Mike was the owner, not just a representative of the publishing house. He'd a reputation for being 'shonky,' 'a thief' and 'a liar.' I felt disappointed and blamed myself for believing this charmer. I'd read about this kind of thing happening and it hurt to think maybe I fitted the stereotype of a typical older woman, a little lonely and a sucker for a gorgeous smile and compliments.

CHAPTER 2

My brain went into overdrive. It was time to rethink: 'How do I get my novel back? How do I get my money back? What do I do now?' My family and friends who'd been so supportive of me all the way through the process now shook their heads and offered advice, but nothing helped. It gutted me Mike had played me for a sucker. I realised I'd fallen hook, line, and sinker for his effusive charms. My Intuition no longer a whisper, yelled at me, 'I warned you!'

To add to my troubles, problems were brewing with my daughter Rae and my grandson Jess, and I needed to relegate all stressful thoughts about my book and the shonky publisher to the back burner. My family now needed me. I needed to focus on them, so my phone calls to Mike dwindled down to once a fortnight, while his phone calls to me became almost non-existent. When we conversed, he continued to string me along and confuse me, lying constantly.

During one phone call Mike casually said, 'I am an accountant now, not involved with publishing. You'll have to deal with management.'

I knew it was all lies, which only added salt to the gaping wound. A charismatic crook had shafted me, and now I'd no idea where it was all going to end. I realised I would have to leave it alone until I could give it more energy, because for now, my family was far more important than my ego.

Baby preparations had begun with a vengeance; Rae told me an early delivery was predicted. The midwife was a Eurasian lady with golden dusky skin and beautiful dark almond eyes. A Muslim, her headscarves were as colourful as her demeanour was exuberant. Narina was exotic in every way, and she fascinated me. She confirmed the baby's head was in place, her announcement accompanied by much arm waving and shouting as her heavy accent became a jumble of mixed languages. I think it was the one time I let my guard down and giggled. From where I stood, she looked like a exotic circus troubadour announcing the next show, her wide multicoloured sleeves billowing softly through the air. Rae and Jess both frowned at me, but they could not see her from where I was standing.

Jess and I decided to paint the nursery a dusky green. Rae, who was feeling bulky and awkward, bought all the baby furniture online while I sewed cream coloured net curtains to block the bright sunshine that streamed into this small room. It seemed like only yesterday I'd decorated this room for Rae. Once we'd finished the room, all three of us stood back, satisfied with the results. Jess was now a tall, slim young teenager, all of thirteen. He was developing a voice that was deepening each day he moved towards adulthood. But he was still just short enough for me to slip my arm around his waist, his head resting just under my chin.

'It's time to move the baby furniture in,' Jess announced with authority. He was becoming much like Russ, his Granddad. Pride swelled my chest for the young man before me. I watched as he muscled the bassinet and changing table into the room. I treasured every moment of our time together, partly because I'd this strange gut feeling that things were about to change.

Lately, as I watched Jess daydreaming, often a scowl would flick across his face. I would enquire if there was anything wrong, he would shrug.

'Nothing's wrong, I'm bored.'

One night when Rae went to bed early, Jess suddenly felt the need to explain what he foresaw as his future if he remained living with us. He saw himself as Mum and Nana's little boy who would be forever treated like a child, his opinions looked on as nothing more than silly. He said he felt we were always going to be the adults in this situation. What he really meant to say was Rae and I were control freaks; but he was too polite. He saw boarding school as his salvation. I sat listening, trying to swallow the words. Boarding School? Where on earth had that idea come from? Jess jumped up and rushed into his bedroom, then raced back into the loungeroom, his face bright red with excitement, his arms full of paperwork.

'I've done some research on this Nana.' He plonked a big pile of brochures in front of me on all the schools that provided accommodation for boarders.

I was impressed with Jess's boarding school presentation. He produced the brochures, the research on costs; he had approached his teacher about boarding colleges and even collected information off the internet he thought might help his case.

From my vantage point, I could see his reasons were valid. Jess felt he was being smothered between two mothers; he felt he'd to ask our permission to be a young man and wasn't allowed to make his own mistakes. Rae, hearing the noise, joined us, and was now laying on the couch reading the brochures while I sat in the lazy boy chair next to her. It all read so beautifully, the photos of the grounds and buildings were gorgeous, so much was on offer, the best education, sporting opportunities and the rest. However, I knew deep down Rae could not afford any of this and neither could I. The fees were exorbitant.

At the thought of our mounting expenses and Jess wanting to leave home, Rae suddenly burst into tears. Jess got up off the couch with a big sigh and skulked out of the room mumbling 'Not again' under his breath. Rae and I sat there mute.

'This sucks!' he yelled, then slammed his bedroom door.

I made the obligatory cup of tea, Rae's hiccoughing sobs somehow annoying me as well. If only I could yell, 'This sucks!' But adults don't do that, do they? I took Rae a cup of tea and a packet of tissues. I took my cup of tea and headed outdoors into the back garden where I could always feel Russ's presence amongst his ferns.

'Families are never easy, are they?' I muttered to myself and the sky, and I swear I could almost hear Russ chuckling in agreement. 'This too shall pass' was my mother's wise advice, so I added that to my thoughts of Mike, my book, Jess, boarding school, and Rae, who was not having a pleasant pregnancy. She was nauseated, bloated, and there was the threat of toxaemia if she did not rest, and if she kept worrying.

Rae was emotionally fragile and tired most days. I knew if I dared criticise her, there would be tears and mood swings for the day. Peace, I decided, was the ultimate objective for the remaining weeks until my new grandchild arrived. During this time, I also became amazed at how much a small baby needed, and the cost! I couldn't remember it ever being so exorbitant back when Russ and I were starting a family. I wanted to suggest shopping for second-hand furniture, but Rae was so proud of her efforts regarding online shopping that I knew the last thing she needed was my opinion. This was her only way of contributing, so I did what any good mother does. I shut my mouth.

CHAPTER 3

The day came when the nursery was finished; clean, and smelling of baby powder, and all three of us stood huddled in the doorway admiring our work.

'Thanks, guys,' Rae whispered as tears formed in her eyes then spilt down her pale face.

She'd already filled the dresser drawers with all the online baby shopping. I picked up a little outfit, once again the feeling of gobsmacked was there. Had babies shrunk since the days when Rae or Jess had been in my arms? Were babies really this tiny? Rae smiled as I held up the tiny stretch and grow suits and she laughed as she saw me catch sight of the jaw dropping prices.

She'd chosen names. Rose for a girl, after Rae's grandmother, and, if the baby was a boy, it would be Russell, after her father.

'Mum, you don't mind if I called him Russell after Dad, right?'

The name *Russ* caught in my throat. It floated around in my mouth, and it tasted of loss and love, of memories and laughter. It seemed years since anyone said my husband's name out loud. How could I possibly say no to that request? I was too moved for words, and quietly nodded. Russell it was. Jess wanted to name him 'Ripper,' and since no amount of reasoning could dissuade him, I suggested that might be the baby's nickname. My arms went around Jess, his arms went around me; we both felt the emptiness of that moment. Burying my face in his hair, I whispered, 'Love you, kiddo.' That was all I could muster.

The early phases of Rae's labour were textbook. She'd chosen a hospital birth, so when she came into my room at one in the morning.

'Mum, my waters have broken.'

We both leapt into action. We called the maternity ward at Rockingham

Hospital and they gave us instructions on timing the labour pains. It all went beautifully. Once the contractions were ten minutes apart, I woke Jess, who amazed me with his calmness. He helped his mum into the car, making sure her small suitcase was in the back seat. Then he added a pillow, books, drinks, and snack bars for himself and off we drove to the emergency department.

The orderlies put Rae into a wheelchair and sped us to the delivery theatre. Rae smiled as Narina asked, 'Who is coming in to hold Mum's hand?'

Her laughter careening down the over bright hallway as she looked straight at me. There was no way in hell I was going to miss out on seeing my grandchild being born.

Jess cringed and said, 'Urk! Not me!' Finding a two-seater couch to curl up on, he was happy to let the female brigade take over. 'Let me know when my sister's born,' he mumbled and closed his eyes.

'Did I just hear him say sister? Do we have a psychic in the family?'

I soon forgot my questions in the excitement of childbirth, which, to me, has always been the miracle of all miracles.

Rae became tired early on; Narina said the baby's slowing heartbeat showed it was under stress! A surgeon was quickly called in to perform a caesarean birth. My poor daughter's face went grey with pain, her eyes fixed on mine.

'Mum, if anything happens you will keep Jess with you, won't you?'

I nodded, but it shocked me to think she would even think that way.

'Nothing is going to happen, honey. You're going to be fine,' I reassured her.

They asked me to stand beside her top half, the rest of her body draped in a sheet. Her hand clung to mine tightly, but there was no way around it. The medical team decided they could not proceed with an epidural; she needed a full anaesthetic. The rest was a waking nightmare for me, Rae's hand slipping from mine, tubes and machines now attached to her body. Those eyes that trusted me only a minute before were now closed with tape. I watched as the doctors removed the tiny blue baby out of my daughter's body, quickly wrapping it in a silver foil blanket and placing tiny oxygen tubes into the smallest nostrils I'd ever seen, nurses now doing their utmost to help the babe in its first moments of life.

I watched, frozen now as they struggled to revive Rae; the machine that once pleasantly bleeped with her heartbeat now screamed 'Emergency!' as she flat lined. I could not take my eyes off that straight line as the theatre suddenly exploded around me with tubes, lights, orders, and counter orders. Narina held onto me as the medical team physically fought off death. I could hear my voice chanting, 'Please don't take my girl!' I kept chanting my prayer as everyone around me fought to save Rae's life. When I heard the heart monitor give off a faint beep, and then another beep, and another, I fell to my knees and thanked God. Narina once again pulled me close.

'Have faith Tara, have faith, the baby is okay but tiny,' she said, obviously worried.

In all the craziness of what happened with Rae, I was a little dazed. I'd forgotten about the little one. Even with the tumultuous events of the last few minutes, how could I have forgotten about my grandchild? I was mesmerised as I peeked into her bassinet. Rose was perfect, wrapped in a pale pink blanket, a halo of ginger fuzz crowning her tiny head. She was a picture of pure peace, long ginger eyelashes on pale cheeks, tiny pink rosebud lips, she was perfect.

I whispered, 'Hello Rose, welcome sweetheart.'

The theatre nurse allowed me one quick cuddle, placing Rose in my open arms. The smell of the newborn baby filled my nostrils, her little mouth was making a small mewling sound. I felt my heart skip a beat. My granddaughter was beautiful. Placing a quick kiss on her soft cheek, I found it hard to let go as I placed her back into the warm nest of silver blankets. The lights were turned on over the bassinet, tubes and wires were monitoring her weak heartbeat. I'd never felt so damned helpless in all my life. The surgeon finally announced all was fine with Rae; he'd closed her up. I felt my body relax and realised it was my job to tell Jess what happened. I walked out of the theatre and Jess jumped out of his seat.

'Well?' he shouted. 'What do we have? A Russ or a Rose?'

Without answering, I slumped beside him, hot tears and stress taking over my body. My arms went around my grandson. Jess struggled to understand my despair.

'Nana, what's happened?'

I knew I was scaring him. 'Your Mum has had a hard time, Jess. Everything is fine now, but baby Rose is very small and weak.'

Jess and I clung to each other, both of us needing to be held tight. There are times I really dislike being the adult, having to be the strong one emotionally, and this was definitely one of those times.

It was well after dawn when we arrived home, the sun just caressing the sky. I tucked Jess in bed and made myself a cup of tea. When I finally sat down in Russ's old rocker chair in the conservatory, I allowed myself to completely let go. The tears fell, unhindered. I wrapped my arms around my body, rocking myself with weariness. Russ would have loved Rose so much. It was then I felt a hand on my shoulder. I looked around, half expecting Jess to be standing there, but there was no one in the room but me. I'd had a similar experience once before when life's problems had become too overwhelming.

Today I needed help to carry on being the senior adult in this family. 'Thanks Russ,' I said out loud to the shadows in the room , though I felt certain that somehow, somewhere, if he knew what was going on, he would be there with me.

It was late morning the next day when I woke. I ached all over. I was not used to sleeping in a chair. Jess was asleep on the bean bag beside me, the sadness of what happened written on his face.

His waking words were 'I want Mum to come home.'

I wanted to say, 'So do I, Jess. I want it all to be better.'

Instead, I said, 'Soon, Jess, as soon as she is able to walk around.' If only I'd known what the future held in that moment, I would not have uttered a word. My heart ached for us all.

The day dragged on into night as both of us waited for a call that said Rae and baby Rose could have visitors. At two am my mobile phone trilled, Narina's voice trembling as she told me that our precious baby Rose passed away an hour ago. . It tore me in two. It's hard to understand the grief that engulfs you when you experience the death of a child. I could not cry. I could not do anything to make it better. Rose had gone. I'd held her and kissed her just once in her short life. Neither her mother nor her big brother Jess had seen her. Jess sobbed his grief out in my arms while I remained dry-eyed. I was numb.

The knot of grief stayed like a blob of glue on my chest. I chose a plain small white coffin and bought a small sweetheart rose to sit on top of the coffin lid. I invited two people to the hospital chapel, Jo and Narina, to join Jess and me. No music was played, it was so quiet. The morning sun shone through the blue and green stained-glass window as the minister gave a short sermon. I have no idea what he said, my mind was caught up in the dust motes softly swaying around the room.

Soon I was back home, Jo was making me a cup of strong tea which was tasteless in my state of grief. Narina stayed at the hospital and sit with Rae for a while. Through the funeral, through it all, my spirit stayed still inside my physical shell, a shell that now moved solely on autopilot. All I remembered was the minister saying I could collect the ashes in a week. The morgue would ring and confirm a date.

They performed many tests on Rae. First, I was told she had the baby blues; then she was diagnosed as suffering from chronic depression. They advised Rae needed more than what the hospital medical staff could provide; perhaps a psychologist was needed? More tests were to be done. In the days I visited, I would tell her stories of her childhood as I brushed her hair and washed her hands and face. Jess would read to her too, tell her all about his day. Seeing her so unresponsive was crushing to us both. She never inquired about her baby, Rose, or asked how Jess was. She just stared out the window, completely and utterly devoid of any emotion. To be honest, some days I envied her.

CHAPTER 4

The surgeon suggested relocating Rae to the mental health ward in the hospital where she could be given the appropriate medications. In his opinion, he considered counselling would not do me any harm either. None of it made any sense to me. I felt there was something else wrong, but like a robot I did what I was asked. They were the professionals, and if they could help Rae, then I could be of help by making sure I was mentally and emotionally strong. So, I dialled the many numbers suggested, and finally found a psychologist who was available, a Ms Frost.

Her secretary booked a meeting for me the following week. It arrived quickly. I walked into her office and was asked to wait.

'Ms Frost will be with you soon.'

Looking around the office, it reminded me of a tacky bedroom, stuffed with odds and ends. Eclectic furniture pieces included a two-seater couch and one overstuffed chair, both covered in a light brown velvet material. A small desk sat in the middle of the room, with photos in silver frames of Ms Frost on a horse and on a yacht. In the corner of this dark room was a tall lamp that glowed a molten orange, showing off a fringe of glass beads. At the base of the lamp sat a dried flower arrangement, or perhaps the flowers were long past their use by date. The smell of heavy poppy perfume permeated the air.

Ms Frost sayshayed into the room and greeted me. Pale-skinned, and dressed in a hot pink leather jacket a tad too tight along with a too short skirt, she was not at all what I expected. Twinkling jewellery shone in every nook and cranny of her round body. A huge, silver jewelled dragon wrapped itself around her left wrist while sparkling gemstones in rings on her small chubby little fingers. The bracelets on her right arm clinked and jangled as she reached up to tie back her platinum blond hair with a gold diamante clasp.

I had to look away as her breasts seemed uncertain whether to stay confined within the leather jacket, or to pop out for a breath of fresh air. When she sat in the overstuffed chair and crossed her legs, I noticed she wore killer high heels, also sprinkled with diamantes on the insides of her stiletto heels. Ms Frost was the twinkling star in this sad little office. All we needed was lights, music, and action. I could almost hear the clapper board.

'Hello, dear,' she said, her voice sounding like sticky warm treacle. 'Please sit down. My name is Jade,' she oozed.

She extended her hand to shake mine. Long fuchsia pink fingernails curled around my hand; her grasp was also warm and sticky. Ms Frost immediately instructed me that I was not to ask questions until she'd finished talking. Instantly, I could feel my cheeks flushing at this young thing talking down to me. Whenever I tried to answer her, she waved her pen at under my nose saying, 'Remember the rules dear, no talking, till I've finished.'

Her demeaning attitude and condescending voice went on and on, mainly about her fees. 'IF' she took me on as a client, then once more about the fees. I was finding it hard to breathe, the room had no fresh air in it. Then the bombshell.

'We, the medical team and I think you should take your daughter home into more familiar surroundings.'

It seemed Rae's medical team had discussed my/our case without my permission; I felt anger rising with a sense of relief, as it is such a different emotion to grief and numbness. She must have sensed the change in my attitude because she quickly put the pen down and sat back in her seat as I rose from mine. For the first time in several weeks, I let rip. I don't have a nice temper when riled, but her attitude was shocking, and I snapped. Ms Frost, as she preferred to be called, was no help at all. From where I stood all she cared about was whether her long acrylic nails matched her outrageously skimpy outfit, and, of course, her fees.

I hit out verbally. 'Listen here, young lady just who do you think you are? I'm a prospective client, and you will not insult me by talking to me in that manner. Nor will you discuss 'this case' as you put it, with anyone, including the medical team, without my permission. Do you understand? I came here for assistance for my own emotional health, not my family's. You, Ms Frost, are rude and improper. You have no idea of empathy and no idea of professional dress nor conduct. I will be reporting you to your superiors, and I, not you, Ms Frost, will consider if your professional skills are worthy of being my counsellor. And if I find this conversation has gone beyond this room, you will not work in Rockingham again, do you understand me?'

I marched out of that sickly sweet room into the reception room, informing her secretary I would not be returning. Was that a smirk I saw appear on her face? Outside, I gulped in the fresh air. It tasted of the sea and sunshine; it had never felt so good.

I wanted to see Rae, whether they permitted me to or not. Walking down dimly lit hospital corridors has always given me the creeps. Tiny blinking, beeping lights, the silent halls, the smell of anaesthetic—is it any wonder why that people feel sick in hospitals?.

Rae had been freshly washed; her hair hung in damp tendrils around her neck. She looked so young and vulnerable. I wanted to wrap her up and take her home, but common sense prevailed. The duty nurse must have seen me enter and immediately informed the medical team caring for Rae. No sooner had I sat down to tell Rae my daily news, avoiding anything about my recent encounter with *Miz Frost,* than the ward doctor arrived.

'Tara.' She offered her slim hand. 'Dr Portia Munroe; I'm here to help assess Rae's condition.'

This young Eurasian woman was no older than Rae, and I liked her instantly. Her attitude was one of professional empathy. I studied her white smile on golden skin, her longish brown hair carefully tucked up into a neat chignon. It all spoke of consummate skill and professionalism. She looked at me seriously with large hazel eyes as her warm hand gently held mine.

'The medical team and I are doing all we can to understand what has happened to Rae and how we can assist her to recover,' she said in low, soothing tones.

It didn't make much sense. All I could hear were snatches of phrases like 'small cerebellum stroke' and 'take her home.' Once again, feelings of anger rose around me like a wave.

Portia continued. 'If you feel you cannot cope, I understand. I'm talking about a facility that will care for her until she is fully functional, and her medications stabilise her more. It's up to you.'

Portia and I sat there holding hands. Tears slipped uncontrollably from my eyes. I couldn't believe what I was hearing.

'I can't put her into a health care facility, that's silly; she's just your age!' I moaned.

Portia looked into my sad eyes.

'She will receive much better care there than we can deliver here. Rae will have care twenty-four hours a day.'

Portia's large hazel eyes gazed into mine and I let her wrap her arms around me.

'Tell you what: why don't you go home and think about it, then ring me and let me know if you have a plan.'

Her hand patted my back, as if to calm a child.

'We only want the best outcome for Rae.'

I believed right then that this woman was sincere; she brought a real calmness to my situation.

'Here is my card, Tara; call me tomorrow if you wish, we can meet and talk again.'

Portia had somehow turned that one nut or bolt that makes everything click into place. I knew what I needed to do. As I left the hospital, calmness set in, though I still could not quite put my thoughts into words. I rang Narina, thanking her for her part in healing Rae, her empathy, and her concern: 'Please send me your invoice and I will pay with in the week.'

I'd dropped Jess at his Auntie Jo's home for the afternoon while I had been at Ms Frost's rooms. It was time to collect him and go home. I was parking my car outside Jo's driveway when it all became clear. The confusion had gone, and I knew what I needed to do to protect my family.

CHAPTER 5

Jess was out the back fixing a birdhouse that had come down during a summer storm. We sat in the conservatory and watched him as he put together pieces of wood and hammered nails, total concentration on his face. I saw before me a young man who'd grown so tall; his muscles were firming up, and he'd lost that little boy look. He was a teenager. When did that happen? Jo sat opposite me, passing me a cup of tea.

'Want to talk about it?' she asked.

My friend knew me too well, and she knew that if I could 'spit it out' it would help me better understand my own thoughts. I took a deep shuddery breath, and then it all spilled out.

'I want to bring Rae home, Jo. I intend to hire a nurse who deals with this sort of problem, but she is not going to go into any facility of any kind; it just feels wrong.' Portia's words rang in my head now *'Go home and think about it.'* It was exactly what I needed to do. I needed to make some phone calls, meet with Portia again, and make a plan.

Jo invited us to join her and her family for a dinner of fish and chips on the beach. Safety Bay beach had always been my retreat for any problem solving, and as I walked up and down the shoreline chatting to Jo, ideas bounced between us both. Jess and the other children were playing on the sand, building big, wonky-sided sandcastles. These were the kiddies Jess had grown up with, and they were all mates. Seagulls screamed at me as I tossed the last of my half-eaten meal into the water for them to eat. Small waves, which were now tinted a pinkish-mauve matching the brilliant sunset sky, washed up and over my feet. We watched as the sun glinted on the water and turned the sky into a shade of the deepest apricot before the last of its rays sank below the Indian Ocean.

I ached for my daughter to join us here on the beach, to be running around with her son, yelling out to me as she usually did to 'get off your bum and join us!' Part of my family jigsaw was missing. Jess ran up to me, whooping and hollering at the seagulls. He threw back his tanned face and sun-bleached head as he gave a big belly laugh. There was a beautiful freedom at the beach at twilight when there were only a few people around. Jess wore a huge smile on his face as he shouted for me to pay attention to his cartwheels.

Suddenly he stopped g and a look of horror crossed his face.

'I forgot all about Mum and Rose just now.'

Tears replaced laughter, and I hugged him tightly.

'Jess,' I said firmly, 'I have a plan, and it just may work.' It was time to make it all come together for us both; it was time I stood firm and put into place what had been rattling around in my head for days. I had to bring Rae home where she belonged and find someone who could help me nurse her. I knew there was a lot to do, so I would get busy while it was still clear in my mind. As we drove home that night, I explained my idea to Jess.

'Yahoo!' he crowed. 'Mum's coming home!'

I couldn't yet envision all that the move would entail, nor did I bother to explain what had to be done, as I couldn't. I was flying by the seat of my pants. This was not something I knew could be taken on board lightly, but my daughter needed to be coaxed back into the real world. And the best place I knew to do this was at home with family and memories.

It took four weeks to get ready for the move. They admitted Rae into a stroke ward until they cleared her, and there were a huge number of phone calls to be made before the hospital would be happy with my arrangements. Once they knew of my plan, they agreed to have her release papers ready to sign. Dr Portia Munroe was now my medical advocate and friend, and they offered me a social worker to help me sort through the insurance and social security papers. Jo and Millie, another close friend, became my personal counsellors, both offering their help in any way they could. I switched bedrooms with Rae as my room had the ensuite and faced the gardens. I'd always relied on the sun to wake me. Now I hoped it would brighten Rae's morning and help aid her recovery.

The door to the nursery remained closed. It was still too much for me; the knot of glue still stuck to my heart. My memories of Rose were bittersweet. I'd put a small photo of her beautiful baby face on my phone that Narina sent before they'd placed our baby in her coffin. My new bedroom afforded views of the sunset. I placed a large cane chair by the windows so I, too, could have some time out, watching the birds as they settled into their nooks and crannies as day turned to dusk. This was the calming time for my soul, as the world outside my window settled itself to sleep.

I advertised for a professional physiotherapist. This, along with Portia's expert guidance, made me feel safe and less overwhelmed. We interviewed six possible therapists together until we found the one who I felt would become part of our family. Shortly afterwards, an A4 envelope was delivered by courier. It was from Gordi O'Halloran, an older man well into his sixties who was a trained physiotherapist, medical nurse, certified massage therapist, not to mention an acupuncturist, kinesiologist, and herbalist.

Gordi's credentials and certificates bulged out beneath his application letter to me. However, it was not his degrees or certificates that got him the job; it was that he wanted to meet Rae before he accepted. No one else bothered to ask. To them, it was just a job. His empathy showed clearly in his eyes, and in his melodic, gentle voice as he greeted her. The way he placed his hand on her head like he was blessing her, convinced me that he was the one. Gordi had a lingering Scottish brogue and a pedigree that fascinated me. He was a Scots/New Zealander who'd emigrated with his folks when he was just ten years old. The brogue was still there, inflected in certain words.

In just three short days after our interview, Gordi moved in to begin work with Rae. A quiet, solid looking, tall, and pleasant man, he became an immediate magnet to Jess. I never knew just how many questions a teenager could ask, but Gordi handled himself well as Jess rattled on nonstop, never showing any signs of impatience with him. If anything, it was me who kept interjecting, saying, 'Jess, stop, later.' 'Jess, enough for now.'

Tiredness ruled every movement of Rae's life; indeed, we now had our own sleeping beauty. We felt as though she would soon get up and ask, 'Want a cuppa, Mum?' Or pat my arm or give me a quick hug as she walked past, as though everything had righted itself and she was back to normal. Funny how all the little things you don't think of every day suddenly become so important in your lives together. We just hoped the road to wellness had begun for my daughter.

They gave Gordi and I instructions on how to care for Rae. On waking,

Gordi would make himself some kind of fruit and vegetable mix in the blender, then from eight till ten in the morning he would work with Rae. Afterwards, he would wander out into the kitchen and make himself a large fruit and fibre breakfast. Gordi took good care of his body and those of his clients. He believed he could not help anyone if he were not in one hundred percent health himself, and it showed in how he cared for himself and Rae.

Gordi administered Rae's medication, provided massages, and exercised her limbs. While he mixed nutrients with juices for her breakfast, I would get Jess his breakfast and off to school, did the housework and dealt with any messages. By midday, it was my turn to be with Rae. I would read to her and tidy up around her room and often I had this feeling that just behind those closed eyelids she was intently watching us; she was just too tired to respond. While I did these little things for Rae, Gordi would go out into the garden or practice his yoga. He even had Jess try out some exercises. I'd practiced yoga on and off for years, so if I'd some time to spare, I would join him. Sometimes all three of us would be out there, erupting into fits of laughter as either Jess or I crumpled over into a heap. It bonded us well, and Gordi quickly became part and parcel of our little family.

It was important for my health that I kept doing what was important to me and looking after the family. I once again took up mentoring young writers, while continuing with my artwork and trying to find the whereabouts of my novel. It was also important that I 'go out and play' with my friends, gathering experiences for my blog. Staying home 24/7 was not going to help any of us. I'd discussed this with Gordi when we talked about his responsibilities.

He had agreed, saying, 'Hearing you talk about your day full of interesting goings on will certainly help Rae.'

Gordi asked Jess to do the same. He, too, was encouraged to tell Rae about his daily activities in the hope it would help bring her back.

There was another new thing that Gordi did that Jess and I quickly came to appreciate. While I cooked the dinner, Gordi would sit with Rae in her room, strumming his guitar. It reminded me of my Maori friends back in New Zealand, who would often serenade the family after dinner. I was overcome with a sudden rush of love and affection. The first time I heard Gordi play, I stopped washing the dinner dishes just to stand and listen. A deep longing washed over me then, and a part of me wished I were back in

New Zealand.

I quietly made my way down to Rae's bedroom and listened through the door as Gordi began strumming the song, 'Killing Me Softly.' Peering through the doorway I saw Gordi as he sat on the side of Rae's bed playing the guitar, peaceful and calm. Right then and there, I knew I'd made the right choice with Gordi. I quietly left Rae's bedroom feeling emotionally lighter than I had for a long time.

From that moment on, whenever Jess or I heard the guitar being strummed, we told each other it was relaxation time. Guitar time became a special time, not just for Rae, but for all of us. It was a healing time. I could see the stress leave Jess's face and I felt my body relax one muscle at a time.

Rae was slowly improving week by week. She could now form simple words, her tongue slurring. My heart overflowed with love for her; whenever she looked me in the eye and slurred, 'Mum,' I left her room crying. Christmas was just a month away and was accompanied by the usual hype on the telly and in shops. Tinsel and baubles decorated every shopping centre windows and outlets, and Jess had already put up a string of small silver and gold bells across his mum's bedroom window. We were warned not too much excitement, so we left it at that.

CHAPTER 6

Jess made a long shopping to-do list and at the bottom of the list was written, BIG CHRISTMAS TREE in capitals. He was so excited and full of energy about Christmas, for it meant holidays, presents and a school break. Jess ordered the tree on the internet. The photo online showed a mid-sized tree, and shortly after an email arrived confirming our tree was ready for collection from a Christmas tree farm near Busselton.

Gordi returned to his own home in New Zealand for two weeks over the Christmas break, so I enlisted the help of a long-time friend of ours, Mack. He was happy to help us out. Mack had the perfect Ute for the job, whereas my little Ford Festiva would not have coped. Busselton was a two-hour journey from Rockingham, so I made up a picnic hamper for Mack and Jess and off they went on a blokes' day out to pick up the tree.

By the time they returned, the sun had set. They both struggled through the front door with one massive green monster tree, their smiles as big as the tree itself. It was still wrapped up in netting and its pointy end bent over as it touched the lounge ceiling. Jess and Mack fitted the tree into the tree clamp and Mack gave an invisible air trumpet fanfare to the cutting of strings as the long leafy branches escaped, filling half the room. The look on Mack's face was so funny, I had to laugh along with them, realising it had been a while since I'd even used these facial muscles.

Jess ran around literally throwing tinsel and baubles at the tree, so I invited Mack to stay for dinner as thanks for his help.

'There's enough food here to feed an army,' I explained.

'Great! I've got an appetite the size of one!' Mack replied, eagerly agreeing to the invitation. It was nice to have a man in the house who was not there for any other reason but to visit as a friend, not speaking medical terminology; someone with no advice on what to do for Rae.

Both males consumed a large amount of food, for which I was most grateful. It was nice to feel they appreciated my cooking, not simply consumed by a ravenous teenager. Jess wandered off to watch TV, while I thoroughly enjoyed having an adult conversation with Mack. Oh, how I'd missed that! Mack had already been in to see Rae and wished her a Merry Christmas, so after dinner I invited Mack to join me in a wee tipple. We sat back with our brandies, comfortable in each other's company, and watched Jess as he placed a few gifts under the tree.

Every year I put together a basket of packaged food for the Salvation Army, and this year was no different. Jess spied the basket and hauled it over. Seeing Jess struggling, Mack knocked back the brandy and offered to drop it off the next day for me. He enquired where Rae's nurse was. He must have heard about Gordi through the local gossip train, common in all small towns.) So I told him what Gordi was doing for us. 'He's such a blessing!' I added, thinking that it was such a pleasant feeling to relax and openly discuss my world.

'Yes, but you're paying him to be Rae's nurse. That's his job. You are actually the one who is responsible for them all. It all falls on your shoulders. Let's face it, Tara, a lot of folks would have stuck their loved one in a home by now.'

Wow, Mack's assumptions took me by surprise.

'Would you not take one of your family into your home and try to help if you could?'

Mack shrugged his shoulders. 'Not all of us are like you, Tara.'

He saw the look in my eyes and moved to reassure me.

'Sorry, love, I didn't mean to upset you. We all know how much your kids mean to you.' Mack got up to go home. 'Night, Jess, see ya round buddy,' he called.

'Thanks for your help, Mack. Merry Christmas,' Jess yelled back.

At the front door Mack pointed to where Jess had placed some tired old plastic mistletoe, then looked at me, hopeful for a Christmas kiss. I granted his wish, and stepping forward, I even allowed him a light embrace. His moist warm brandy flavoured lips closed over mine and his body moved in closer, his hands curling into the back of my hair, cupping my face.

Suddenly I wanted to relax into this man's embrace and let whatever could happen, happen. Our lips were now exploring each other's, and when his hands lightly brushed my nipples, it felt wonderful. In fact, my body's reaction surprised me. But the timing was all wrong. Mack sensed my hesitation and grinned, winking at me as he stepped outside.

'Call me if you need anything.'

'You cheeky bugger,' I replied, deep down wanting to giggle like a naughty teen. Instead, I said, 'Go home, Mack.'

When Gordi asked for the Christmas week off, he'd shown me what exercises Rae needed to do. Today she was sitting by the Christmas tree in her wheelchair, just having finished her leg exercises, when Mack drove up to collect the Christmas basket for the Salvos. I offered him cake and coffee, but he caught me off guard in the kitchen, clearly demonstrating he'd different ideas. As I plugged in the jug, Mack pushed me up against the kitchen bench.

'Want a little more of last night?' he asked, his face just inches from mine. His breath stunk of stale booze and his face was unshaven. His lips puckered up for another kiss and I felt his hand fumble up the leg of my shorts. I felt insulted.

'Why, you dirty old man! Get out!' I said, smacking his hand away.

Mack stuttered, 'But, last night?'

I pushed him away and brusquely answered, 'One huge mistake!' Mack slunk out of the house. 'And don't come back, ever!' I yelled at him. I looked across at Rae, who answered my look of horror with a slow smile.

'Oh, Mum; only you!' she slurred.

I got the giggles at what it must have looked like to her. 'Sorry Hon, I guess he got the wrong idea last night, I was being silly and allowed Mack a quick kiss under the mistletoe.' I need not have bothered explaining, as Rae was once again staring out the window in a world of her own.

It was just the three of us who woke up on Christmas Day and opened the presents. I warmed up the custard and the mince tarts, but no one was hungry. The sparkle of Christmas had left, I did not care if we celebrated or not. My Russ was not here, and neither was the baby who we all thought would share this day with us. Jess put a beautiful silk scarf around Rae's neck, his present to his mother.

Rae tried to wrap her arms around him as he whispered, 'Merry Christmas, Mum.'

'Merry Christmas, Honey,' I said, passing Rae the gift of perfume I knew she loved most. Jess loved his new iPad, and I loved the red crystal earrings Jess bought me. It was a Christmas Day, but a day full of long silences, sad feelings. It was hard to swallow the dinner I'd cooked for us all. And it was even harder when friends popped in to wish us season's greetings.

They all left quickly when picking up on the fact that in our house, there was little to cheer about. Gordi called to wish us all a wonderful day. I was almost at the point of asking him to please come back when my ego took over, forcing a cheerful note or two out to wish him a wonderful Christmas too.

I found that last week without Gordi exhausting. Upon noticing the grey circles forming around my eyes once more, Jo stepped up to the plate once again.

'Hey, Tara, how about we take Jess with us to Bunbury for a week?'

Jess's eyes lit up. 'Can I, Nana?'

At first, I pretended to hum and haw about the idea, saying, 'Oh, I don't know, Jess. What about me? What will I do without you?'

His eyes immediately dulled. 'Oh, that's right, Mum,' he mumbled, looking despondent.

'Go and pack your case, silly! Give your mum and I a hug and a kiss. We'll both be fine.' As I watched them drive off, though, I had to stop myself from calling out, 'Stop! Take me with you!'

CHAPTER 7

The truth was, it seemed as if all the fun and company we used to have at Christmas had gone. Now it was just Rae and I inside an empty house, the lounge looking as though a whirlwind had just passed through. Tinsel decorations spilled from the tree to the floor, cold cups of tea and plates full of uneaten cake and crumbs were sad reminders. Rae asked if I could help her back to bed, which I did, thinking I would watch some TV or have a 'nana nap' myself, but a sudden urge to be busy took over. I took down all the decorations, cleaning the kitchen benches and tipping out all the leftovers, throwing out all the leftover pudding, pies, and shortbread, until all signs of Christmas were gone.

I struggled to dismantle the tree, though it felt good taking out all my frustrations on an inanimate object. Finally, I dragged it outside and threw it on the wood heap in the backyard, ready to use as winter firewood. I was over this Christmas stuff. I threw the stupid tinsel in the bin, the twenty or so baubles were soon added to the pile of stuff I was chucking out, I felt like a Grinch, muttering 'I hate Christmas.'

The only ornaments I kept were the ones with Russ, Tara, Jess and Rae written on them. I wrapped these in tissue paper and found an old shoe box, carefully laid them inside, taping the lid down. Then I made myself a promise, no more Christmases until this family was together and as normal as possible. I shoved the shoe box onto the top shelf in my wardrobe, piled a whole lot of winter clothes on top, and closed the door.

The rest of the decorations went in the bin. Jess used so much sticky tape on the walls and windows, I religiously removed every inch. Then I smiled at a memory of the Christmas after Russ and I were married. I was merrily taping Christmas cards to the walls when he saw me. I got an hour's lecture on damage to the paint. Using my feminine charm to shut him up worked a treat when we were young.

The vacuum cleaner did a splendid job of cleaning up anything left behind. I replaced the small coffee table that had been where the tree stood, filled a large vase with water, went outside and cut myself a mix of fresh roses, popping them into the vase. I then tackled each room that still reminded me of Christmas and took down everything that looked bright and cheerful. Once finished, I made a bacon sandwich for myself and an apricot and yoghurt smoothie with ice for Rae, muttering to myself as the smoothie whizzed 'Merry fuckin' Christmas.' Then for some insane reason looked over my shoulder to see if anyone was listening.

I helped Rae to drink the smoothie, washed her face and hands, and told her we loved her. She settled down for a sleep soon after, and I took my bacon butty outside.

It was so peaceful, yet I could still feel the anger inside me. I was pissed off at God, at the angels, and everyone else I could think of. When I looked up into the night sky at the stars blinking in their own Morse code, realising all I really wanted for Christmas was for Russ to be beside me, watching Rae become herself again. I wanted to see the joy in her eyes as she witnessed her son, Jess, full of Christmas spirit. I wanted to hear her burst out laughing at the silly Christmas jokes her father would read. To see her walk through the lounge with a beautiful baby in her arms, once again so full of youth and say, 'Merry Christmas, folks.' It was not to be. All the love and best intentions in the world could not change the emptiness of this house this year.

I woke feeling a lot better. After a quick bite of toast, I mixed up the protein powder the hospital had given me with some banana goop for Rae, making sure she was fed, washed, and comfy. Her exercises could wait till the afternoon. I cleaned the inside of her bedroom windows, chatting away to her, when I noticed she was slurring her words more than normal. I put it down to tiredness. It had been a big day for her yesterday. Until the sound of the bed shaking alerted me Rae was having a seizure.

I dived for the phone. As the ambulance screamed into my driveway, Rae was in serious trouble. The seizures would stop for a moment, then start up again. Her back arched involuntarily; her face pulled into a rictus. The ambulance raced her to the hospital, where thankfully the doctors and nurses got her seizures under control with medication. Suddenly Portia appeared.

'Tara, I'm so sorry. It's not good,' she warned. I looked at Portia, , and said the silliest thing. 'But it's Christmas!'

Portia led me to the waiting room while Rae's medical team did their best to control her seizures. I watched a succession of doctors coming and going along with various pieces of equipment, until at last, just the dimmest of blinking lights remained flashing over my daughter. The doctors all stood outside her room talking amongst themselves, heads nodding in agreement with each other. Occasionally they wrote notes on a clipboard or looked my way. Another specialist in the group called Portia away. They, too, stood in the hallway discussing Rae, their heads so close together that it looked like a halo of light coming from the nurses' station was glowing around them.

Had the situation itself not been so serious, it actually looked and felt peaceful to me. Portia was nodding in response to another doctor who was tapping his pen on the clipboard, looking as if he were making a point. Portia would occasionally look over at me, a flicker of a smile would appear on her face as if trying to reassure me.

A small, bright red Christmas ball wiggled in the stream of air coming from the air conditioner. The little ball looked lonely and tired, bobbing around up there on its own. I tried to stay focused on that little bobbing ball to stop me overthinking. As Portia approached, my muscles suddenly tensed with the fear I knew what she was going to say. My heart stopped, my head buzzed, I needed to lie down; I was on the verge of fainting.

'Tara, Rae is borderline, she needs our full attention. If we can't monitor and stop the seizures, we may have to induce her into a coma. For now, I need you to say goodnight to her. You need to go home and sleep, or at least try to, and please don't come in tomorrow. If there is any change, we will contact you immediately. Rae needs complete and uninterrupted rest. Her heart is strong, but her body is fragile after what it has been through.'

The word *fragile* rang in my ears and it felt selfish, as in that moment the thought 'so am I' popped into my head; but I nodded in agreement and made my way home.

It felt eerie to return to a dark house in the wee hours of the morning, with only me in it. Once more, I sat in the fernery looking at the fading night sky, praying from a deep part inside of me.

'If there is a God out there, please if you need to hurt this family anymore, please take me instead. Let Rae live a healthy, normal life with Jess by her side,' I prayed out loud, my sobs shuddering through my body.

CHAPTER 8

It was Gordi who woke me the next morning. The aromas of freshly made coffee and spicy aftershave combined, drifting around the room and into my nostrils. It smelt like Christmas all over again. How I woke up in my bed, I have no idea.

'The hospital called me, Tara. They told me about Rae. I thought you might need me to be here with you and Jess.'

My arms went around his neck as my body shook with sadness all over again. I sobbed openly. Gordi lay me back down with hushing noises, but I could not let go of him. I needed to hold on to another adult. He lay down beside me, stroking my back to quiet me.

'Let it all out; let go, Tara,' he whispered 'It's ok. I'm here.'

I did as he said, letting the grief of loss, shock, anger, despair, and loneliness take over. Our bodies spooned together as I let it all go. It was Gordi who led me to the shower and turned on the taps, holding on to me as the warm water soothed me. We both stood under the spray and I rested my head on his chest, his arms around me as we both became drenched. For some reason I saw us as others would see us; two people crammed into a small shoe box sized shower. The door would not shut properly, there was water all over the bathroom floor. We stood there soaking wet in our t-shirts and shorts, hair plastered to our faces as the hot water relaxed my tight head and neck muscles. I could feel the giggles building up inside me. I could not help it as my mind created a picture of what we must look like. It broke out of me in a spluttering, gurgling laughter, Gordi joining in.

They say crying and laughing is almost the same thing, like an emotional outlet. Soon we were both doubled up in the tiny wet cubicle. Gordi held on to me as the laughter subsided and then we shared our first kiss; a soft, tender, caring, kiss. Once again, my body responded as part of my brain yelled,

'What's wrong with you?' My emotions were now flicking on and off like a faulty light bulb. I could hear my heart saying I needed someone to be strong for me for a while, I was feeling bruised by the months of having to be strong for everyone else. Guilt never even had a look in. I was letting go and there was no holding back.

Our bodies, now slick with water and soap, became a tender pool of passion as we fell deeper, deeper into each other. My body took and gave pleasure. It was a dance I'd never forgotten, but it was now with a different dance partner. No longer in urgent need, we took our time, my back arching to meet his slow, sinuous rhythms, his muscles rippling under my fingertips as he lowered his head, nipping and caressing my breasts. His gasping release to our lovemaking causing a chain reaction as the world became a fuzzy, golden orb of ecstasy.

When the mist of passion cleared, I stood there, ashamed, like a school kid, feeling as if I'd just been caught out by my parents. I turned the taps off, my face and neck stained with the red of embarrassment. What should I say? 'Thank you? That was lovely'? or, 'Go away, I'm embarrassed?'

It was true, my entire body was flaming with embarrassment. Gordi stood behind me, his arms around my waist.

'What's the hurry, Tara?' he asked, feeling me pull away.

I must have looked so confused.

'This. Us. It's wrong!' I cried out as all the pre-shower tension returned, whirling through my muscles. Once again, I felt the old Tara emerging. I had to be in control.

'Stop now,' Gordi ordered.

For some reason, I obeyed.

'I have wanted to hold you like this for a long time. Was it really that bad to make love to me?'

I shook my head. 'This can't be happening, Gordi. I'm in my sixties, I have responsibilities, a family. Now I'm a mother to Jess, and a nurse to Rae. I don't have the time or the energy.'

'I know Tara, I know, you're in charge.'

He started towelling me dry. I tried to grab the towel. He whipped it away. I still glowed pink with embarrassment and pleasure. I just wanted to hide my face in shame. Then what I'd been trying to tell him dawned on his face.

'You're embarrassed to be in your sixties and still horny?'

He was right. I'd thought that at this age I should no longer want or enjoy sex. In fact, the opposite was true. It horrified me that my body responded so well.

Gordi was beside himself with laughter, then he gasped in a huge lungful of air.

'What's so bloody funny?' I asked, suddenly feeling annoyed. He answered by grabbing me and pulling me down onto the floor with him, he put his arm around me.

'Tara, we need to sort this out and now,' Gordi stated, matter-of-factly.

'Yes, we do,' I agreed. 'Do you mind if I get dressed while we have this talk?' My sarcasm did not work on him at all.

'No, you don't, you're not escaping this conversation.'

Swooping me up into his arms, Gordi was not afraid of nudity or what age did to nudity, though for me it was all a bit too much. He plopped me down on the couch. I arranged the cushions around my body. It delighted Gordi that I was a prude. He stood there, completely nude, baring his tanned, muscular body, uninhibited about his body or his sex. Then he strode off into the kitchen to make a pot of coffee. 'Gordi,' I scolded, giving him a look. 'I have neighbours,' which was my way of saying to 'please cover up.'

The belly laugh that came from him amazed me.

'What? You want me to invite them over? A little key party, you reckon?'

He smirked. Again, I had a mental picture of me in the nude on my couch with cushions covering bits I don't display for anyone. And Gordi answering the door in all his glory, my lovely neighbours standing there with a shocked look on their faces. I decided Gordi was another nut and I should get dressed as gracefully as possible and ask him to leave.

Leaving was not on Gordi's agenda at all. Instead, he produced hot frothy coffees laced with Christmas brandy, and cheese and crackers smothered with my homemade pickle.

As we chatted, Gordi informed me that Portia from Rockingham hospital had rung him. His name was on Rae's files as her carer. She'd also informed him of my situation, that she was concerned for me, and he'd taken the first night flight available from New Zealand to Perth. He'd caught a cab to Rockingham and let himself into the house at six am this morning. It made sense to give him keys to the house, but now I wondered if I'd given him too much licence.

'Now hurry up and eat Tara, we are going out.'

My first instinct was to say, 'No I'm not.' My second instinct, and the overriding one, was to admit that I was actually enjoying myself. I was about to say, 'Where to?' when Gordi put his forefinger to my lips.

'Eat, drink, and no more questions.'

His blue eyes dared me to disobey, so I did as I was asked. We drank our brandy-laced coffee, then Gordi suggested I dress casually. I'll be the first to admit there is nothing like intrigue to pique my curiosity. Was I being too suspicious? While I was dressing, Gordi rang the hospital.

'Tara, the doctors just informed me that Rae is comfortable, and her nervous system has calmed down. Tonight, would be a good time to visit her.'

Gordi's concern was genuine. He looked back at me expectantly.

'So, we have all afternoon. Shall we?'

Gordi asked for the keys to my car. I don't trust easily, especially with my car, but decided this time I would let it go. Our first stop was Rockingham Beach. We walked along the shore, leaving deep wet footprints in the white sand, the soles of my feet being caressed by small waves, and I did my favourite thing: watching families, kids, dogs, mums, dads, grandparents. But this time I was watching with envy, the happiness, the smiling faces, thinking this should be my family.

We ate ice creams. Gordi did most of the talking, sharing his reason for choosing this career. He talked about his parents and siblings and told me about his life until dusk fell around us.

When it was time to visit Rae, Gordi offered to drive me to the hospital and wait for me, and I accepted with gratitude.

The streetlight outside Rae's window cast a green tinge on her skin. Her chest rose and fell in time to the machine that pushed air into her lungs, and I could barely take my eyes away from her. My wonderful, pretty, funny girl, my baby, was struggling. I just had to be patient, which admittedly had never been my forte. Tears coursed down my cheeks.

Gordi drove me home in silence. I desperately needed to be on my own for a while, but it was not to be. As we pulled up outside, I heard people talking in the house. Jess was home.

Gordi had rung Jo to bring Jess back to me.

CHAPTER 9

As we entered the living room, there was Jess sitting silently, his eyes like two moons in a pinched, grey face. I held out my arms to hug him and Jess did the one thing then that took my breath away. Expecting him to turn and hug me, instead he shook his head, turning away from me.

'Jess?'

I went into shock when he screamed. 'It's your fault my mum is sick, and my sister is dead! It's your fault Granddad is dead too!'

I could not believe what I was hearing.

'You think you're so great with all your charity, giving us a home, we would have been fine without you. You interfered and played games with Mum and John. Mum told me all about it and I don't want to be with you. I hate you!'

With that, my grandson stormed outside onto the patio, his face a closed book.

Jo and Gordi made a grab for me as I felt the floor give way under my feet. It would take weeks before I was to regain some focus. A heavy fog settled over my brain. I lost all concept of time, even though I knew where I was. All I could hear was Jess blaming me, his words, *I hate you!* echoed in my head.

Why? What had I done? My mind wanted to work, but my body just said no. Gordi, who'd been hired to look after Rae, now became my nurse..

My diagnosis was stress, too much and too often. I could see this in the unfamiliar face that greeted me in the mirror. I looked haggard and my body ached. My weight dropped till my clothes hung off me and I suffered bouts of dizzy spells as a constant foggy headache settled behind my sore eyes. In hindsight, I should have heeded the warning signs. Instead of swallowing copious pain killers just so I could be present for everyone else, I should have slowed down. My self blame said Perhaps if I had, none of this would have happened.

Hindsight became my friend. Gordi reminded me that my job now was to deal with the basics of getting myself well, because then and only then, could I deal with my family and their needs. Jess went to live with Jo, and Gordi took it upon himself to update me daily on Rae's condition, but other than this, I became useless. The problem was that in the back of my mind I was slowly realising I was tired of the drama. Tired of denying I needed more than a squabbling, dysfunctional family whose basic instinct seemed to be greed, not need. The old 'She'll be right, Mum can do it or pay for it' had come to an end. The bags under my eye had grown so heavy I just wanted to go to sleep and never wake up. Every night as the house became quiet, lights and TV were turned off, the last words I heard as I tried to settle were Jess's 'I hate you.'

Gordi naturally became part of the arsenal of my healing. He encouraged me to write, paint, and exercise, stretching muscles that went unused during the weeks I couldn't even sit up properly. Diet became especially important too. Gone were the sugary homemade biscuits, (my favourite pick-me-up the afternoon). Sugar fixes were now banned. Instead, Gordi made real fruit juices blended with vegetables from my garden. Meat was discouraged until my system was used to eating solids again. Once I'd gained more energy, he allowed me to sit outside in the fernery, to do a little tidying up around the house. It was during this time, Gordi became my friend.

Doctors prescribed antidepressants to see me through the worst of it, but I felt so drugged with them. I opted instead for natural therapies, and who best to administer them than my live-in herbalist? My body bounced back. Within two months I was glowing with renewed health. I'd added weight to my bones, my cheeks looked as they should, not sunken, and the grey-blue tinge around my eyes had finally disappeared. My green eyes had returned to their clear sparkle, and Tara was almost well. It was the emotional hurt in my chest that would not leave. I could not forget Jess's accusations.

Gordi allowed one visit from Jess while I was unwell. Jess had sat on the couch, sullen and sulky, so unusual for my grandson. I wanted to leap up and grab him, shake him, hug him, and tell him he was my treasured grandson. Gordi saw my defeat and tiredness return. Jo took Jess home.

'Maybe in a couple of weeks we will visit again?'

I watched with sorrow as Jess stomped out. This was his home. I watched as Gordi insisted Jo take the bundle of money for my grandson's keep while he stayed with her and her family. I lifted my hand in farewell, Jo's blue eyes full of sadness as they left.

I hadn't seen Rae for more than a month ,and I missed her terribly. Gordi assured me that her hospital reports were all showing signs of improvement. I missed Jess too, but he was doing well under my friend's supervision. In fact, he'd become close to their neighbour, Kane, a young man in the navy whom I'd occasionally met at their home. Kane had kindly taken Jess under his wing and they got on well. Kane was even taking Jess to the hospital now to see his mum; he was quickly becoming the centre of my grandson's world. Jo trusted Kane and quietly advised me to do the same. Jess was searching for his place in the world, and it seemed like Kane was helping him to find it.

It was Gordi who took the phone call from the hospital saying Rae was had responded to the new medications. Gordi beamed with pleasure as he offered to drive me to see her, but only if I took it slowly. I agreed. I was still a little shaky when I overdid things, and in all honesty, I felt silly as Gordi held my elbow when I walked on the beach or in the park. The old Tara would have dismissed the last two months of stress entirely, wanting to take over from everyone and always be in control. The new Tara was slowly learning she needed help so she could recover, and hopefully the old Tara could re-emerge.

I'd dreamt of my recovery like I was in a cocoon, waiting for the butterfly to emerge and stretch its tenuous wings in all directions. I was not there yet, but one day the new Tara would emerge, the Tara who treasured herself, who saw herself as a gift, as we all do when we are truly aligned with our purpose. Maybe, just maybe, this was a learning curve for us all, Rae, Jess, and myself, with Gordi there to assist, gently reminding me that I was not here to check on Rae. Her medical chart was out of my hands, and I knew Rae was in the best place. There was nothing I could do.

Rae looked so peaceful as she lay there, her monitoring machines quietly beeping in the background. Then something happened. Miraculously, we both saw her hand flicker. Gordi quickly rang the bell for the nurse.

From that moment on, as Rae improved, so did I. Every day I felt the gentle touch of improving emotional health, which encouraged me to do a little more. One day I was up juicing my own breakfast and joining Gordi on the yoga mats, then I could shower. I even called Jess to talk to him, but the conversation was stilted on both sides. I was still finding it hard to forget what he'd said.

We bumbled our way through our phone calls, but a mutually unwanted conversation with a fourteen-year-old teenager was not for me. To be honest, I was tired of being the peacekeeper, the moneylender, the all-around martyr of all martyrs and I could sense that, deep down, big changes were happening. It was time for me to let go, knowing Rae and Jess were both safe. That was how I finally knew it was my time. To think this way was huge for me, but it was honest, and it felt so damn good to finally say to myself, 'No! I come first!'

Gordi became the catalyst to my thinking. We would often listen to Zig Ziglar, a famous motivational speaker. I'd been given books by Hay House. Enclosed were several DVDs spoken by Louise Hay, her words of spiritual encouragement slowly working their way into my psyche. In the lazy, warm, sunshine-filled afternoons we watched movies of all kinds. There were no more 'bang, crash, beat-them-up' war games that filled the house with violence and that Jess loved to watch. Gordi and I agreed it was more important to watch shows that either lifted us up or made us cry with laughter. I mended, knowing I'd an untapped strength, coming from a deep inner knowledge I was loved. And I loved me more than anyone or anything on this planet; for, if I did not love me first, then how could I love anyone else?

Ever so slowly, I healed. Everything physical was great, too. I realised I'd never felt better, but it takes time to recognise one's new pattern in life. I was now on a different life path, and, for the first time in a long time I felt excited about my future. And I recognised Gordi had come into our lives to help me on my way too. Not just for what I'd hired him to do, nor for our brief foray into intimacy, which in hindsight had been just that, a brief and wonderful memory. Now, we'd become the closest of friends.

CHAPTER 10

Gordi's decision to go back to the South Island of New Zealand to visit his family for a month came as a hard blow. I realised how much I was going to miss him, but he knew the healing of my mind, body, and soul was well and truly underway.

'Now I can say you are a powerful woman blessed with wisdom, love and understanding.'

'Thank you, Gordi,' I responded warmly. 'It is a mantle I'm happy to wear.'

A week after Gordi left, Rae was finally allowed to come home. Every day she was getting better and better, going from strength to strength. She was now up and about, slowly relearning to do things for herself. Her medication stabilising her, I was incredibly grateful to the Rockingham medical team. It surprised me to learn that Jess asked to come back home to live with us. His attitude towards me was not nice. It was an unhappy truce, but I tried to make the best of it. Then one day Jess introduced Kane to Rae. Jess virtually ignored me as I stood at the bedroom door smiling, to welcome Kane into our home. Finally, I offered my hand and introduced myself.

'Hi Kane, I'm Tara, Rae's Mum and Jess's grandmother.' Kane's hand was large and warm; it was a safe hand.

Kane became the ultimate healing kit that Rae needed. He popped in every day, often bringing her blood-red roses from his garden, and she blossomed in response. Jess also blossomed under Kane's care. His trust in Kane showed in his eagerness to be with him. Kane referred to Rae's neurological illness as 'wonky wiring.' 'We'll soon have you up and dancing,' he would say every time he visited her.

It was Kane who held Rae close as I broke the news about the death of baby Rose. As I sent the photo of Rose to her phone, it was Kane's arms she buried her head into as she sobbed out her grief. I left them alone, sensing my role as cheerleader and homemaker was no longer required. To my surprise, to be footloose and free again felt lonely and cold.

Jess's moods had not improved much. At least now he understood how destructive it was to all of us, so he would shut himself up in his room. But his attitude towards me had not changed. He still considered me to be the catalyst for all the problems at home. Jess wanted and needed a father figure. He wanted a male's attitude, a hero in his life, an invested dad. I could not fulfil his needs, and as his mum was not up to parenting yet, this left a huge gap in Jess's family life. I wanted Jess's future to be shaped by his choices, not by his circumstances. And I also wanted him to face his responsibilities, not to disappear into his room when it all became too hard for him.

While Jess's problems simmered, I continued my new regime, rebuilding my health and motivation. I was getting trim and flexible, the headaches were easing off, and my skin looked healthy. My thoughts of failure changed, and when Kane was with Rae, I took the chance to meditate, to allow positive thoughts about how much I'd already given, and now it was my turn to receive. A half hour meditation followed by working in my garden became a pure joy and was full of healing powers. I enjoyed every breath, feeling my rib cage rise and fall with every healthy sigh. I'd learnt I was not responsible for the bad decisions of others and at last I felt at ease with myself.

I'd come to the monumental decision that I was here to help Rae and Jess as much as possible, and then I was going to go on another tour. The universe, I would soon learn, apparently agreed with me as luck would have it. Even bigger news was that Jess had entered and won a bursary for one year at his college, which was also a boarding school. The school had rung him for an interview. Jess could see I was eager to be a part of it, but he kept his eyes away from mine, asking Kane to go with him. So be it. I felt awful I'd forgotten all about the application, what with Rae's problems and losing baby Rose, then my collapse, or should I say rebirth. But I was happy for him.

Life without the Jess I once knew and loved had become as sad as it was awkward. He no longer laughed with his mouth full of food or made cheeky jokes as the smiling, joyful, naughty, and loving grandson I once knew him to be. It was a big thing to get used to. There were times now where I would simply stand still, no matter what I was doing, and hug precious memories close to my chest. In my mind's eye, I could still see him teasing me playfully just because he loved me.

The new Jess could only treat me with dislike, and nothing I did or said could change his attitude. One night at the dinner table upon his saying something disrespectful towards me, I held my hands up in surrender.

'OK, Jess, you win. You don't like me, and I'm not too sure whether I like you anymore, either so, let's work on coexisting until you leave for boarding school.'

Jess nodded politely and excused himself from the table. 'I just want to be with Mum,' he muttered.

He threw me a parting look that was so nasty it would have made the fresh flowers shrivel up.

One night on the phone, I finally plucked up the courage to tell Gordi my plans for travel. It was the first time I'd spoken them out loud.

'If it's meant to be, it will be,' he said.

'Ok, Universe. I'm trusting!' I said. After confiding to Gordi, I was now on a mission to find a travel home I was happy with.

'Good for you, girl,' he cheered. 'No time like now to start looking. About time you had faith in yourself. Lose the fear, and just do it.'

'Phew! Easier said than done, Gordi, but I'm willing to give it a go. The way things are here at home right now, one of us must move aside and let whatever is going to happen, happen.'

I knew I had to break the news of my intentions to Rae, Jess and Kane. I waited for two days, consolidating my thoughts. When I knew they were altogether, I gathered up my courage, mentally wrapped it around me like big imaginary amour and knocked on Rae's door. Jess opened it; disapproval written all over his face.

'What?' he demanded. 'Mum's busy.'

I felt my courage falter for a microsecond. Then I sailed into what had once been the room my husband and I shared with its sweeping views of the gardens. I cleared my throat.

'Hello, all,' I chirped cheerfully. 'How are all the exercises going?' I asked to break the ice. Kane admonished Jess.

'Show respect, young man.'

Kane pushed a chair out for me. I sat down next to the bed reaching for Rae's hand, her other hand rested in Kane's. I immediately recognised the affection between them, felt it present in the room, all except for Jess, who glowered at me as though I'd suddenly become an intruder in their new-found threesome.

Thank you, Universe! Rae's nervous system was now on the mend, her improvement noticeable. In fact, Rae was taking large healthy steps back to mobility, just as I was taking large healthy steps towards my freedom. It was time to inform my family of my plans; not to seek their approval (although I knew Jess would be silently cheering), but to tell them that in approximately eight weeks I intended to be back on the road again. Rae's eyes widened, awash with tears. Kane's arm went around her shoulders to comfort, and Jess just looked down at the floor. Was that triumph I saw just flash across his eyes? My announcement meant they could now have the house to themselves. All I asked was that the room I was in be set aside for me to store my personal belongings. As for the rest of the house, they were welcome to live there.

The future, if any, between Kane and Rae was their responsibility; and how they involved Jess was also their responsibility. To my amazement, Rae completely understood why I needed to hit the road again. Kane and she'd both discussed the way Jess had been behaving but had left it between him and I to sort out.

'Mum, you know I love you, right? You know how grateful I am that you have been here for us all, don't you?' Rae asked with pleading eyes.

I did, but I also knew deep down that if I did not leave, I would be making it difficult for them all to become what they wanted to be, a family, together.

I'd begun searching Gumtree sales online for caravans. I combed the local newspaper, searching all the caravan yards. With my friends in my corner, plus the change in my personal attitude, I felt more motivated to get up in the morning and do my household duties. The grocery shopping that I once disliked was now a pleasure. I ate the best of produce, making soups and mainly vegetarian meals, cutting back on the bread and biscuits.

CHAPTER 11

I was spending my afternoons scouring the internet for caravans for sale. Often one or two of my friends joined in, sitting around the kitchen table giggling at the adverts. Some of the adverts seemed to imply the mobile home came with the male owner and the family pet! At times, a glass of cold white wine and healthy nibbles was part of our research. It made it exciting. I felt that there was a big wave of water heading towards me, ready to lift me up high, and away I would go.

I was still in regular contact with my friends in New Zealand saying, 'Go Tara,' cheering me on in my travel plans. It was after reading an email from Petra and Ronan, two of my wonderful Kiwi buddies, that I could let go of any niggles of self-doubt. Their message was loud and clear.

'Let your gut lead you, Tara. It's called intuition, and you have so much of it. Just let go and let the universe guide you.'

It felt right. It was time for me again, time to be who I wanted to be, a traveller, back on the road again.

There is nothing like comradeship. I considered myself blessed to have such friends. My relationship with Gordi was growing nicely too; his phone calls every week warm, kind, encouraging.

The day arrived to look at three possible mobile homes. One was a twelve-foot camper van, which meant it was a small space for one person only. It had little room to sit inside and watch telly, no bathroom, and personally I was against it from the start. Jo thought we should take a peep at it. One peep was all I needed. Nope! Not for me.

'Nowhere for him to hang his hat?' commented Jo.

She got a look from me for being cheeky.

'What?' she snorted. 'You're in your sixties, pet, you're not dead.'

Next was a fifteen-foot caravan. It had all the home comforts, including spiders, slaters, snails, and grass growing through the wooden floorboards. The owner grappled with the door that had almost rusted closed, while insisting he'd been away in it himself only months before. He was asking for six thousand dollars. Jo asked him whether the price included the wildlife and fresh greenery inside, and we were abruptly told to leave if we were not happy with it.

'Happy to,' was my answer. What would I do without my friend?

The last caravan was a twenty-foot pop-top. It had all I wanted and more. It was gorgeous, but the price tag of over twenty grand was a heart stopper. I asked if he would consider a drop in price?

'No'! Came his abrupt answer.

It was another sad, 'Ok, well no thank you,' from me.

We bought fish and chips at Point Peron that night, with my friend Millie and Jo's families joining us. What a happy, noisy crowd it was! Their grandkids all asked where Jess was. I told them he was home watching a movie with his mum as she was not well yet. It stung to watch them all playing cricket in the soft night air, all having family time, happy, laughing and teasing each other over who caught the ball and who was out. We packed up at dusk and shook out the sandy blankets. The young ones washed themselves off in the salty tide, while the older kids dared to go for one last splash. I said my goodbyes to my friends and their families' kids of all ages, calling out 'Bye, Auntie,' with both Jo and Millie giving me extra big hugs, 'to ward off the lonelies.' I promised I would call them the next day, and I know I looked as alone as I felt when returning to my car.

The answering machine was flashing red as I walked in the front door, and I noticed a soft light shone from under Rae's bedroom door, the tiny hum of her TV still on. Other than this, the house rested in grey twilight. It felt peaceful. I'd cut roses that morning, putting them in a vase on the kitchen bench, and their perfume wafted through the air. I could feel my body relax. It was good to sit down in my own home and breathe in the quietness.

I was not surprised to see Kane come out of Rae's bedroom.

'See you tomorrow, sweet thing,' I heard him whisper.

He did not see me in the darkening shadows. Kane was almost out the front door when he saw my car in the driveway. He took a step backwards, eyes scanning, then pinpointing where I sat.

'You should make some noise when you come in, Tara,' he said accusingly.

'Why?' I asked. 'This is still my home.' I looked directly at him. Thankfully, in that moment I could see he at least had the grace to be embarrassed. However, to be fair to them and their budding relationship, it was none of my business.

'Just be kind to them both, please,' was all I had to say.

My bed had never felt as good as it did that night. My heart ached for Kane and Rae and what might be their future. There are times when you have so much advice to give, but you know it will be rubbished. So you just have to walk away and keep saying to yourself 'it's their journey, their lessons, not yours.'

Scruff the kookaburra had sat outside my window every morning over the summer. He always looked a little dishevelled, slightly tipsy. That's why I christened him Scruff. His song always started off as a soft, breathless giggle, then it would take off. He cackled as though his life depended on it. Whenever he took a breath, his family of four or more took over for him. What a racket they made! The pure joy of their song rained in through my bedroom window and I smiled. Imagine if the whole world laughed like this when it woke up. What peace that would generate for mankind! No sooner did they finished their song of welcome to the rising sun then the noisy tribe flew off in a flurry of wings to alight two houses down. As the rays splashed the sky with pink and mauve streaks, they woke more inhabitants with an encore of their raucous laughter. I would miss them, especially as I had watched Scruff grow from a chick to an adult Kookaburra

Wandering out into the kitchen for a cup of ginger tea, I once again spied the red blinking light on the home phone. I'd forgotten about it. I pressed the playback button. A male voice spoke, calling himself Gary. He was answering my advertisement for a mobile home and/or caravan. I jotted down the phone number. The disappointments of yesterday's search had put a dampener on what could have otherwise been an exciting buying opportunity. I went back to bed as five in the morning was too early, even for me, a self-confessed early bird.

By nine o'clock everything had settled down. Rae was up and showered. She was slowly managing that by herself. And I'd made her a smoothie of protein powder and fresh mango. She was sipping on it while watching telly in her room, expecting Kane's arrival.

I made myself a muesli and yoghurt breakfast, adding fresh mango and banana. It was delicious. I'd already done my Yoga exercises and a little morning meditation. I was feeling so particularly good within myself when I settled down with a hot coffee and dialled Gary's number.

'She's a small fourteen-foot mobile home. It was my mother's but I'm selling it for her as she has been moved into a rest home. It's too small for me and my family, but it's in good, if not great condition. It's a little tired inside,' he warned, 'but the motor is excellent. It might need a tune up before long trips, but it is a dream to drive.'

Gary's description of its interior made me laugh. He'd called it 'frilly knickers ladies' stuff.' Gary had come across as a genuine seller and he was asking twelve grand in 'as is' condition. It was still a high price, but I jumped at the opportunity.

'When can I see it?' I asked.

'Well, I'll drive it over and you can take a good look at it. It needs a good run, anyway. I'll see you about twelve?'

I quickly agreed.

The timing was perfect for me. Lunchtime arrived and so did the motorhome. Gary had not been creative in his description of the interior. It was exactly as he described it: a lady's home on wheels. I loved it; it felt so cosy and warm. Yes, it needed a good clean and tidy up, but was this the one for the new nomadic lifestyle I was after? I felt a stirring in the bottom of my stomach where my intuition sat. A slow excitement burned. Had I found my new home after just two weeks of searching?

Inside was a small double bed that looked more like a large single. There was a small side table and slim wardrobe, a tiny bathroom, a minimalist kitchen with a gas stove and a small fridge. In one corner was a twelve-inch box TV bolted to one wall.

It was definitely aged and shabby, but, for some reason, my heart said, 'This is it.' My brain argued, 'No it's too old.' Gary offered to let me take it for a drive.

I got behind the wheel with Gary in the passenger seat, letting out the clutch and shifting her into first gear. Clearly, I was not used to a manual transmission. We bunny-hopped down the cul-de-sac, but I soon found my rhythm and we were off down the main artery of Thomas Road, taking the turnoff at Kwinana before heading back to Rockingham.

Gary was right, she drove like a dream. In the half hour it took to drive there and back, I knew it was mine. I offered fifteen hundred less than what he'd asked. Gary walked down to my letterbox and rang his wife. All I could hear was a hum of conversation. The look on his face conflicted with my feelings entirely. Oh no! They were not going to settle for my offer.

Gary reached the door of the motorhome. I was still in the driver's seat. He pulled open the door, held out his hand and said 'Deal.'

Bloody hell! He accepted. The excitement grew as I arranged with the bank for a transfer from my superannuation account to their bank account. It would take a day for such a large amount to go through. Gary handed me the signed the ownership papers. The motorhome was mine! I wanted to jig, shout, be sick and cry all at the same time.

Gary's wife drove over to collect him, and off they went, leaving me with the keys dangling in my hand. I stared at the key ring, a small plastic disc with *No Time Like Now* printed in faded black ink. It hit me. Serendipity? I'd never bought anything this big in my life without asking another's advice. Doubts as big as flying cows came crashing into my head as every *'what if?'* in the world suddenly hit me.

It was time for a strong coffee. I called my friends to come over, my heart in my mouth. For the first time, I'd bought something intuitively. Taking a break from my own inward celebration, I popped my head around Rae's bedroom door.

'Cuppa, honey?' I asked. Rae nodded, gesturing for me to come closer. I held her bony body in my arms. She smelled of Johnson's Baby Power.

'Mum, you don't have to take off, you know that don't you? Jess will get over his beef with you. I don't want you to feel you're leaving because of us.'

Obviously, Rae had been worrying. I knelt beside her and looked into her eyes.

'Sweetheart, I'm doing this because I want to. I miss the freedom of being on the road, and yes, Jess has a little to do with it, I admit. As for you, Rae, one day soon you're going to be my strong, scrappy daughter again. The one who makes me laugh one minute and simmer with anger the next. This is for me, honey, and me alone. It's what I feel I am being led to do.'

I could not hide the happiness from dancing in my eyes.

'Mum, you've bought it, haven't you? Oh my God Mum, you have, you bought it!' Rae started chuckling. 'Oh Mum, you're going to have such fun. I can feel it. I'm so jealous. I want to hitch a ride and come with you. Okay, help me up,' Rae suddenly demanded. 'I want to go and see your new home.'

In that moment, it was what we both needed as mother and daughter, even though it was only a short excursion to the front yard. We needed to explore my new home together before anyone else was invited. In the warm, sunny afternoon Rae and I stood discussing the merits of a mobile home. It had been too long, I realised, since we'd spent some quality time together that had nothing to do with illness. Nothing to do with anything, but just being together, laughing like two silly kids. In that moment, I could hear Rae's old laugh returning, too. It was the one that would make me smile for no other reason except for knowing that my daughter was happy. I struggled to get her over the high doorstep into the motorhome. Gingerly, she eased herself inside. Then we stood there together holding hands, just as we used to when she was little.

'Mum, it's so you!' Rae exclaimed.

'What is?' I asked.

'It's sort of kitschy chic, Mum. I can just see you in it.'

CHAPTER 12

I saw the motorhome through Rae's eyes. She fingered the cloth of the curtains, patted the two-seater couch. It obviously needed a good clean, but I could see it working. The table in front was scarred and stained; the double bed sagged in the middle, showing where the previous owner had slept. We figured the small bathroom had definitely been an add-on at some stage, its basin and toilet were stained and chipped. Rae was diplomatic, advising me where she could, in between outbursts of 'Mum, I can't believe you've bought this!'

Jess arrived home, scowling at me as he took in the motor home, his anger towards me showing in his eyes. Rae opened her arms to greet him.

'Hi Jess, how about making your mum and nana a cup of tea?' Rae suggested, gently taking him by the arm to steady her as together they wandered back inside, Jess talking about his day at school.

It was almost dark by the time I looked up again. I'd busied myself by chucking out the things in the motorhome I did not want. Jo and Millie had both agreed to come over the next day, to help me clean and decide what I needed to replace. I'd felt a little on the outer as the cup of tea never appeared, yet it was always expected I drop whatever I was doing to cook dinner for everyone. I felt hurt and allowed my cheeks to burn in anger before shame flooded me. Rae was still weak, and I should not think such childish thoughts. Maybe I would feel better in the morning. I called it a day and headed off to my room to shower and have an early night.

As I passed Rae's room on the way to mine, I could hear Kane had arrived. He and Jess were laughing about something Jess said. They were really becoming a close-knit unit. It was also obvious Kane had bought takeaway for dinner. I spied three food containers left on the bench. My plastic container of food was in the fridge. I was grateful Kane had at least bought enough food to include me, but I felt put out that they'd not bothered to call me to dine with them. I went to bed feeling very alone. .

No one, including the family that lived here now, was going to take away my feelings of excitement about today. I began happily drawing up lists of what I would need and who I would contact tomorrow. No one had permission to ruin today for me. I hugged myself. I'd bought a motorhome!

Early the next morning, I awoke to a glorious deep blue sky. A tinge of warmth in the wind tickled my bones and I was full of energy. Meditation and yoga were forgotten; even the family and Scruff took a back seat. All I could think of was the motorhome parked outside. I crept out of the house, not wanting to wake everyone, quietly manoeuvring a dustbin to the door of my new home. I unlocked the door and stood inside, inhaling the stale, musty air. First, I cleaned out the cupboards, pulling out the old drawers from the beside the cabinet, dragging the old mattress outside, binning the old blankets and torn lace curtains.

Jammed way back behind the top drawer, I found an incredibly old diary with a frayed rubber band clamping it together. Photos poked out untidily from yellowed pages. It became an instant magnet. I just had to open it. I carefully peeled off the sticky rubber band as the first pages fell out, giving me insight into a complete stranger's life. With the warm rays of the sun on my back, I sat and studied sepia photos of a group of people camping. Some stood with arms crossed, smiling into the camera, others were waving to the cameraman, all of them frozen in time. There were other photographs. This time of a wedding, circa 1900s, by the look of it. I suddenly had a feeling the previous owner of this tired little home on wheels was gazing back at me from a time long gone, the story of her youth in my hands. As interested as I was in the diary at that moment, I decided it was not mine to pull apart and read.

I rang Gary. I had a gift for him from his mother. He arrived looking puzzled as I relayed my discovery of the diary. He held the small leather diary in his hand, looking down at the fragile wedding photo.

'That was my folks' wedding day. There's me! Where did you find this?' A huge smile spread across his face.

'It must have fallen down behind the dresser drawer,' I explained.

Gary put his arms around me. 'Thank you for giving me this, Tara. Mum has slight dementia. I know this will mean the world to her; it may well be all she has from her wedding day.'

I pointed to a little boy holding the bride's hand. 'Was that you?' I asked, curiously. Gary nodded.

'Long story, Tara.'

I knew the conversation was closed. It was none of my business.

'Tara, thank you from my heart. You have given my family more than money could buy, thank you.'

My two friends soon arrived. They'd carpooled in Jo's car, which was full of buckets, disinfectant, polish. Millie sported bright pink, elbow-length, fur-topped rubber gloves. This woman could make me smile at any time of the day or night with her zany dress style. We were about to clean my new-old little home, ready to zap it into a modern-day motor home when we realised there wasn't enough room for three grown females to inhabit the tiny space. Millie and I worked on the inside while Jo worked up front, pulling the cab's interior apart.

Every so often we could hear Jo exclaiming 'Ew' and 'Yuck' as she peeled off seat covers, exposing a mouldy cheese-like texture. We took measurements for new curtains and cushion covers, ordered a new mattress and seat covers. All of which Jo insisted I buy if I was going to outfit her properly. My new home, I could see, was taking shape. At one in the afternoon, a good day's work had been done. It was time for lunch, and to check Rae had eaten the soft egg sandwich I'd left beside her bed for her.

The three of us were soon off to Spotlight–a local store that sells just about everything a girl desires. Wandering between the long aisles of material, finally I found a deep green material with fawn swirls through it. Jo suggested buying enough to cover the cushions as well, and Kieran found a deep green doona cover that almost matched the curtains.

Within a week, I'd revamped the ageing little motorhome and turned it into a place I could be proud of. It looked clean and smelled lovely. I'd a new memory foam mattress, new curtains, and pillows I'd sewn myself. Already she was looking much brighter for what had been a relatively inexpensive fix. I'd booked a carpet layer to put lay new grey carpet, indicating it had to be tough and enduring. The same company made car seat covers, so I asked him to take measurements and give me a quote. I booked my mechanic to give it the once over, asking him to please fix anything that looked dodgy, and ordering new tyres.

In the words of the mechanic, she was, 'an oldie but a goodie.' The adventure began calling me. I sighed with relief it was all happening smoothly.

Within two weeks I was ready to go, yet I still got goose bumps whenever I thought about myself being on the road. It was not excitement so much as fear, but why? The motor home was willing and able. I was willing and able. Rae was almost walking unassisted, so, was it just Jess?

Sadly, nothing had changed between us. Jess was still not talking, although I was pleased at least now he was making a real effort to help his mum. Kane had become his new best friend too, and my intuition was saying it was time, so why was I hesitating? It was Sunday night when I finally made time with myself to ask what was now holding me back? Why could I not jump in and go?

After making a light meal for everyone, I waited until Rae and Jess were asleep, then I sat and meditated. I let the sensation of warm air float across my shoulders, allowed the peace of the night to settle over me. First, I took a big breath, feeling the weight of hard work of the past weeks lifting itself from my muscles. I replayed scenes of the past week in my mind like a flip calendar, noting everything I'd done to my little house on wheels, then let it float away. Calm settled in the pit of my stomach, and then my questions were answered. Time to sort your book out, Tara. Of course! That was it. It was the green light I'd needed. I could not to go trekking until I knew I'd sorted everything.

The next morning, I called the infamous Mike on his mobile. He greeted me with such bonhomie I was lost for words, and I listened as he told me about the movies he'd been making in Asia. His next words astounded me.

'Your eBook has been published, Tara. It came out last week.'

'Why was I not notified?'

Mike's reply was short and offensive. 'I work for my living, Tara. I don't have time for melodramatics. Go online and see for yourself,' and he abruptly hung up.

I felt confusion again. What had happened in between the flattering comments like, 'I love your work; you're a great writer,' to the sudden cold departure of, 'It's online, see for yourself?'

What was I missing?

CHAPTER 13

My hands shook as I typed in the publisher's name. His website popped up and sure enough, there was my book. Not the hard copy on demand, just the eBook. Now I had to buy my own book? Well, so be it. Tears of embarrassment fell as I read my book online.

What a disaster it was! Things were misconstrued, misspelt; chapter five was where chapter eight was supposed to be. They hadn't edited it. I was horrified. All the hours I'd spent deleting and improving and they'd touched nothing! Awful did not even begin to describe this disaster. Not even the cover made sense. I'd agreed on one, knowing nothing about the existence of a second cover. The photo of me that Mike insisted on taking for the back of the book was disgusting. I looked like a duck. It was a complete disaster; the book was a disjointed, massive cock-up.

My deflating ego fell to the ground. How could this have happened? I'd done everything Mike had asked of me. It had been nearly eighteen months since I'd signed up, happy and confident, thinking I'd written a good novel. And this evil little twerp had ruined it. Callously inconsiderate of another's reputation, he'd taken my success and thrown it away. I'd known when Mike started ducking and weaving my questions that he was a dicey personality, but this was something different. This was my story, which anyone could buy and read with my name splashed all over it. My embarrassment turned to anger. How dare this idiot even call himself a publisher? I rang him four hours after he'd hung up on me. I got his voicemail, so I vented, my language abusive and abrupt. Either he took this book off the market and call me with an explanation within the next twelve hours, or I would see him in court.

Friends who'd reserved a hard copy to be sent to them were now calling me with complaints: 'I paid for a hard copy, not an eBook.' There were requests from people to get their money back. I gave them Mike's mobile phone number, but again it was no surprise to learn that he was, conveniently, out of the country.

Four of my friends who bought the eBook rang to ask, 'What's gone wrong, Tara? It's an awful mishmash.'

Sadly, I had to agree. One acquaintance, an artist, rang to say she wanted a refund immediately, was not going to call the publisher's phone number, claimed I would have made money from it, and demanded to be paid immediately. Her tirade continued. She would never bother wasting her money on such badly written junk, even if my name was on it.

Finally, Mike called me back. I have never wanted to attack another human so much in my life; I could picture myself with a baseball bat aiming for his knees. He of course blamed me, saying I had been unresponsive to his plea to pay an experienced editor to help me put the book in order. I was gob smacked by his accusations in that heated exchange.

'It's your fault, Tara. You should have paid the higher fee to have an excellent product. If you're too lazy to follow my advice, I can't help you. I've done as you demanded for months now, it's online.'

'Take my book off the website and every social media site you are advertising it on Mike; stop ALL marketing. I'm giving the contract to my lawyer. This is dishonest. I won't accept it,' I said, the sudden nausea in my throat warning me of an oncoming migraine.

CHAPTER 14

There was a pregnant pause, then Mike asked to meet up the following week, leaving me with only seven days to pull myself together and fix my writing reputation, if possible. I felt gutted; I'd trusted him and his 'publishing firm' with my manuscript. Mike ripped my trust apart. Should I say goodbye to four thousand dollars, get in my mobile home and take off? Or should I stay and fight for this mess to be cleaned up?

I chose to stay and fight. My decision made, I would meet Mike and I would clean up his mess. I knew I'd written a good book, and I knew folk would enjoy it; it was time to reclaim my reputation as a writer. Rae was sympathetic, Kane a little surprised as I spilled out my sad story regarding the bad book deal. Kane commented, 'You strike me as a person who would not stand for any nonsense, Tara, so why now?'

If only he knew. And I guess from where they sat in their own happy bubble, I might as well have been announcing I'd grown horns. Rae was the most concerned for me, and knowing she was still not one hundred percent, no stress was needed. I made light of my situation. Deep down, I was happy for them; it was time for them to have a home, build on their love and happiness, and I was happy enough to leave them to it. A firm friendship had budded between Jess and Kane, while Rae glowed with a deep joy for her son and the new man in her life. She'd fought hard for her health, and she was finally winning.

This insight put me on track to make a firm decision about when to leave. For now, at least, it would have to be after the meeting with Mike, if he ever turned up. It felt as though I were sitting on a powder keg that was about to blow. I knew Jess wanted me gone; and Kane had commented about my motor home taking up most of the driveway. Yes, this was my home. Russ and I'd bought it together as a safe home for our family, but I was not welcome here. That was the simple truth. I could have been difficult and put my foot down, I could have created such an angry emotional storm, but the new Tara knew better. This house was not mine any longer. No matter how we think it should turn out, life has a funny way of giving you what you need. It may not be in the pretty bow-topped gift box. Sometimes it is in a big knobbly sack you must sort out before your dream comes true. Mine was in the driveway.

Suddenly it clicked. I did not have to stay here. I could drive off, book into one of the three local campgrounds, and use that as my base while I sorted things out.

I was more than ready to take off. The following morning, I grabbed the keys to my new home, boldly marched out of my bedroom and announced to the three faces looking back at me from the breakfast bar that I was leaving. All I needed was for the two boys to help me move some heavy boxes into my room. Kane and Jess rose to the occasion, commenting all the while about the mess I was leaving behind. By lunchtime we were finished and my life as 'Tara the Homemaker, Wife, Mother, and Grandmother' was all neatly packed up and stored in one small room. I turned the key in the lock I'd organised to be installed when I'd asked to use this room, why? I did not trust Jess with my treasures.

I gave Rae the longest cuddle, lightly rocking her from side to side. Who knew when I would see my daughter again? She reminded Jess of the need to show respect and he offered a half-hearted, quick hug. It was better than nothing. I accepted his hug with joy, whispering, 'I love you.'

I shook Kane's hand, saying, 'Please look after them,' and walked out of my home, not knowing when or if I would ever return. Rae looked distressed, Jess and Kane both looked rather smug. My one secret wish was that Kane did not prove to be another user like Rae's first husband John. Still, there was not much I could do. These were their lives, and I have long since realised we all must be responsible for our own mistakes. I climbed into the driver's seat of the motor home and set off.

Driving away was the easy bit; sobbing till I wanted to be sick was the not-so-easy bit. At least this little motor home had a bathroom. It drove like a dream, and as I pulled her out onto the highway, I shouted to no one in particular, 'Mandurah motor camp, here I come!'

Mandurah was only an hour from Rockingham, but it was far enough away for me to get a feel for the road once again. Through tears and sobs and dry-retching, I cruised along the highway until I made it safely to my allotted parking space. For the next four days the deli beside the camp provided my nightly meals, while dark sunglasses provided a cover for my red swollen eyes. Under dark and starry skies, I'd found privacy at last, and this was what my soul craved. Some time for me to be alone. And here it was, in bucket loads. The sense of peace I felt was amazing and sleep came easily, a deep, restful, and soul-repairing sleep. How wonderful! I lay back on my bed, leaving the tiny wind-up hatch above me open. A cool wind stroked my face; it was my silent lullaby into sleep.

When my phone buzzed me awake one morning, it startled me out of my reverie.

'Tara! I'm back in Rockingham!' Gordi announced gleefully.

It was a bonus, especially to hear his voice, and the news brought a smile to my face. I explained to him where I was now living and told him I would say more when I saw him. I think I'd barely asked Gordi when he would arrive before there he was, tapping on my door.

Shock, joy, and disbelief raced through me as I threw my arms around this friend who I'd missed so much. Unbeknownst to me, Gordi had called Rae, planning to surprise me. She'd informed him of my whereabouts. Gordi, ever full of surprises, popped up once again into my life. Here he was at my door, producing two bacon and egg rolls for breakfast. I made us both a pot of tea while trying to get dressed in my tiny motorhome. We sat outside in the sun together with our brekkie, happy to be reunited.

With our tummies full of hot food and drink, we let our stories unfold. By midday, Gordi was determined to accompany me to see Mike. His anger at the situation Mike left me in was almost as fierce as mine. Gordi went so far as to call Mike a bucket of pus, plus other expletives. I had to laugh.

Gordi was the medicine I'd been searching for. Laughter, which he was full of, is absolutely the cure-all to everything. I believe by dinnertime, all the excitement and plans I'd shared with Gordi about my travels were laid out. Maps and routes were marked down in my diary.

Gordi's face changed, and his expression turned more serious. 'Would you consider me travelling with you, Tara?'

I stopped dead in my tracks. I'd never contemplated having another person with me. One after another, the excuses I tried to find for not taking him with me evaporated into thin air. Still, by midnight I still could not bring myself to agree to his suggestion. I felt I owed him an answer.

'Think about it, Tara. It could be fun.'

My tummy was now in knots, my motorhome was much too small for two.

'Gordi, come back tomorrow, we will go into Rockingham together and settle things with Mike. Then I will decide what I want to do.'

I was grateful Gordi offered to come and see Mike with me, but a travel buddy? This was serious stuff. There was only room for one person in my motorhome, and until now, I'd made all my plans with just me in mind. I felt my heart creak with sadness for Gordi as he walked off. It was not my aim to hurt him. I slept well, the morning sun waking me as the colours of orange and yellow crept around the edges of the curtains. I stretched my body, taking up all the double bed, big enough for one. Then I answered nature's call to my bathroom, also only just big enough for one, made a hot cup of coffee and crawled back into my comfy bed again.

As I lay there, memories of Gordi flickered through my mind. He was a good looking, decent, nice person. I'd fun with him. I could laugh with him, and we could talk about anything; yet to live with him? I argued with my reasoning. Why was I having trouble deciding whether I could see him inside my little home with me? I was confused, even though I knew I wanted to see more of Gordi. It was time to call a friend.

Jo answered my call. She teased me, throwing in a pinch of sarcasm for good measure, when I told her about Mike.

'Good Lord girl, you certainly know how to pick 'em!'

The conversation went from 'Why not, Tara?' to 'Is there enough space?' or, 'Will he cramp your style?' 'Will Gordi put the brakes on what you want to do?' 'Could he be the ball and chain you don't need right now?' 'Do you want a relationship?' Finally came the dreaded 'What about sex?' question.

Although Jo knew nothing about my recent experience, I certainly had no complaints in that department. Jo's advice was to sit on it till after we'd met with Mike. She was right, the decision about Gordi was not my immediate concern. I needed to steer my attentions first to my meeting with Mike and sorting out all the rubbish surrounding the book, getting it settled so I could get on my way. I was not going to let Gordi become a problem. Instead, I focused on setting up the motorhome; putting everything in place and making sure nothing would unbolt, untie, or slip out. I then checked the tyres, oil, and water. Everything was okay. I fussed around my new little home, completing my checklist, and writing a list of much needed grocery supplies: veggies, fruit, milk, butter, a big carton of water, batteries for torches, things for the medicine cabinet, mosquito repellent, band aids, painkillers, sunscreen lotion, cleaning gear and so on. The list was getting quite long. Camping or caravanning is not for the fainthearted. It never entered my head there would be height restrictions, or other people's road rage to deal with.

It amazes me how rude some people are to others. I had gone shopping, putting bags of food into my motorhome. I had one sliding side door open, plus a door to the cab. Placing bags of groceries into the van was no mean feat in an underground parking lot. A young mum with her four unrestrained kiddies in the back seat of her four-wheel drive screamed at me, 'Move, you manky old crow!'

CHAPTER 15

By the time I'd finished loading and found my way back to the campground, I was over it all. I wanted to rip someone's head off. That, combined with the prospect of meeting Mike, was rattling me more than I thought. Instead, I tried to stay determined and focused on my goal, telling myself that in two days' time I would finally be off, wandering under the wide blue yonder. However, when Gordi arrived, his smile firmly in place, my anger had not simply melted away, and the poor man's unlucky timing meant copping my frustration. All I wanted to do was confront Mike, then bugger off.

Driving into Rockingham this time, parking was easy. Rockingham Beach once again put on its beautiful display of deep turquoise-blue sea and pure white sand. The galahs screamed out their displeasure as we parked under their roosting tree.

I had made a booking for Mike to meet me at the Steel Tree on the beachfront; an easy going, street-side café offering hearty brekkies and outdoor seating that I frequented. Upon remembering my last encounter with Mike, I knew this time around he wouldn't get a free meal out of me. The staff obliged me by adding another table setting and chair for Gordi. I looked across at Gordi and my heart skipped a beat. Gordi looked grim. Finally, I saw Mike arriving. He looked so cavalier and cocksure of himself, and the attitude in his stride seemed to announce that all was well in his world. That was until he noticed Gordi sitting alongside me. Before I could open my mouth, Gordi stood and offered Mike his hand, introducing himself as my legal advisor.

'I thought this was between the two of us, Tara,' Mike exclaimed, looking surprised. He then jumped straight into accusations, and denying responsibility for my book's shoddy publication, becoming derogatory instead about my writing.

'Your book, your responsibility, your problem, Tara,' he told me straight up. 'And your constant badgering of me to publish your novel has resulted in bad editing and proofreading. In the end, we simply published it.'

I took a big breath to stop myself from stabbing this rude idiot with the fork that gleamed at me beside my plate. Gordi placed the contract on the table. The ad I'd answered was stapled to the top of it.

'Mike, here is the advertisement in the paper that I replied to.' I'd underlined the words. 'Full professional editing and proof reading applied to all work accepted and published,' taking great pleasure in pointing out this not so small detail.

At each word I uttered, I tapped my forefinger on the table, launching words at him. This time, Mike paled. I continued to point out I'd fulfilled my side of the contract. I'd produced, and paid for in full, a manuscript that the publishing company had eagerly accepted. It seemed the company was at fault here, as no editing or proofreading had been done from any professional I could see. I also questioned the fact Mike had recently told me he was the accountant now, no longer the head salesperson. if this was the case why were we not meeting with this head salesperson? Or, better yet, why weren't we getting all this nonsense cleared up by the acting owner/manager in the publisher's office, instead of at a local coffee bar?

Mike sat listening, then casually interrupting. 'Tara, we don't refund. What I can offer you, however, is a fresh contract to republish your first novel plus one other book.'

He went on to say the company would publish this at their own expense, but this time the editing and proofreading of said new book would be my own responsibility. The hurt burned deep within my chest. Why could this man simply not apologise to me, admit his wrongdoing? Not once did Mike's eyes meet mine. When he spoke, he looked over my shoulder and around the room. Gordi then spoke.

'How can you offer that to Tara, when you are no longer a sales consultant but only a bookkeeper? You need to put something clear and concise on paper and have it signed by the publishers or I will take this further young man!' Gordi's voice growled menacingly.

Where had the fun, happy Gordi gone? Sitting next to me was a businessman who meant every word he said. I simply stared. Gordi gave me a stern look of warning, not to interfere. Silence engulfed all three of us. Mike knew he was caught out; he'd nowhere to run.

Gordi then cleared his throat; 'I believe we should discuss this offer with the correct authority?' of this publishing place,

Mike's face burned. Gordi then turned to me.

'The choice is actually yours, Tara. We can take this so-called publishing business to court and maybe wait a year for the outcome. Or you could demand your novel is taken off all social media platforms and the manuscript it is returned within twenty-four hours. Plus your percentage of the sales made and a refund in full for the stress the publishing house has caused you, paid within twenty-four hours. Personally, I would not trust this so-called publishing person. In my professional opinion, I'm willing to start the procedure to sue immediately.'

Gordi then got up and left the table to order tea and freshly made scones. No sooner was Gordi out of range, then Mike leaned across the table, hissing out of the corner of his mouth.

'This is entirely your fault. If you had not pushed so much!'

His eye widened as he saw my fist clench around the lovely bright silver fork. He paled as I whispered back.

'You have only one option Mike, do as my legal representative has suggested, pay up with in the twenty-four hours, or we will see you in court.'

Mike's mouth snapped shut just as Gordi returned. 'Well, any decisions made?' Gordi asked.

I nodded. 'I feel I should take the offer suggested by you Gordi, twenty-four hours to deliver my manuscript and monies owed including a refund in total, plus all contracts cancelled.'

Mike glowered; he was beaten, and he knew it. Almost meekly he said, 'I will see to it once I'm back at the office.'

With sadness, I remembered the excitement and pride I'd felt signing my first contract to write a novel.

The waitress then arrived with Gordi's order; two large brown crusty scones with cream and jam and a large pot of tea, two teacups nestled beside them on the tray. She placed the tray carefully on the table and then turned to Mike.

'Would you care to order, Sir?'

Mike blushed; it was an obvious insult by Gordi.

Mike was scrambling to leave his seat when Gordi stopped him. 'You have twenty-four hours, Mike, to honour your word, or your company will hear from me, make no mistake.'

It amazed me that Mike swallowed the whole thing. Gordi had no proof of who he was. He could have been the local candlestick maker, yet fear and guilt worked. Mike knew he was in the wrong.

'You have my word; it will be dealt with in twenty-four hours.'

He hurried out of the café, phone up to his ear with his bravado destroyed, Mike looked small and shrunken. Hopefully, it would turn out to be okay. I'd done nothing dishonest, simply asked for a total refund and my manuscript returned and social media. It was now a waiting game.

Gordi's eyes now settled on my face.

'Ok, Tara. We have cleared that hurdle. Now, can we discuss the reason why you do not want my company on your trip?'

I had to admit I was now leaning towards the idea. Given that I enjoyed his company most of the time, I was struggling to find a reason not to have him along on the journey. Gordi took charge of matters, immediately relaxing the situation between us.

'Is it my new age stuff that upsets you?'

He asked innocently, his eyes smiling into mine.

'What are you talking about, Gordi?' I asked, puzzled. Then it clicked. 'Oh, you mean all the health and fitness regimes you set yourself? No, I love that way of life, however I like to do it my way.'

As I uttered those words, though, I suddenly knew he'd stumbled onto the truth. I wanted freedom, not a regime of five a.m. yoga sessions in the desert, plus constant cocktails of avocado and mango juice, plus the rest of my life planned out for me. I truly craved complete and utter freedom and with control over my life. We'd moved from the hot café to a park bench under the shade of a eucalyptus tree. The sea breeze had begun–the Freemantle Doctor, as we Perth people call it.

How do you tell a good friend, one whom you feel slightly attracted to, that what you seek is freedom from the details of everyday life? If I wanted to sit on my bum and admire the sunrise in the middle of the desert, I'd do it. All while eating a greasy sausage roll and slurping on a hot chocolate or sip a cold beer as I welcomed fellow campers. Or go skinny dipping in clear, shimmering cold waters in some creek I encountered in my travels.

Or drive all night, watching shooting stars streak across the night sky and sleeping through the heat of the day, this was what I wanted to do. But how was I to explain all this to Gordi?

I realised the best way, the only way to say it, was to say it outright, so I let the words spill out, as did the tears. I felt small-minded, selfish, and unworthy of Gordi's friendship as I suddenly blurted all my desires. And now I felt especially bad, given how much he'd helped with Rae and protected me from shonky dealers like Mike.

Gordi reached out; his strong hands covered mine.

'Tara, you Aussies are always saying, 'Give it a go,' so let's do just that. Give it a go. If we are unhappy in any way with each other, well, we are adults, and we can go our separate ways respectfully, always having love for one another.'

'What about my motorhome? It's too small for the two of us.' I uttered, immediately sensing that this, too, was too feeble an excuse. What on earth was wrong with me? Deep down I knew this was about to be the start of a wonderful adventure, made even more special by having someone to share it with. If times got tough, like Gordi said well, then I would just have to talk it over with him.

CHAPTER 16

'OK,' I said. 'When do we leave?' I asked. Just like that. It was so simple. Excitement welled up inside of me and Gordi wrapped me up in a big bear hug.

'You won't be sorry, Tara. Together, we are going to have a blast.'

There was no time to waste. Once back at the motorhome, we started preparations. 'Where is all your gear?' I asked. 'You will have to sort all that out before we leave, you know.'

Gordi nudged at a large backpack he'd put in the cab.

'Is that it?' I asked, incredulous.

Gordi looked back rather sheepishly. 'I was just hoping like hell that you would invite me along.'

He wrapped his arms around me again, holding me close. I could smell his maleness.

'God you feel good, Tara,' he sighed. 'I have missed you so much.'

His body snuggled into mine, his hands moved inside the back of my t-shirt.

'Friends,' he asked?

It was a good hour before I drove the motorhome from Rockingham beach. I was glad I'd parked beach side and not directly in front of the café.

It was finally time to go. The sun was shining and there was nothing more to stop us. I called Rae one last time, telling her we were heading out. I told her about my meeting with Mike. Rae was full of concern for my safety. Kane wished me a safe journey. I promised to keep in touch, and they promised to look on my blog site for photos and news of the day's happenings. I didn't add to our conversation that Gordi was joining me. Finally, I made one quick phone call to Jo and Millie, saying my goodbyes, once again omitting the fact I'd a passenger on board. Gordi picked up on my hesitancy about telling my family and friends, but this was now my decision, my time, my life.

Merriden was to be our first overnight stop, a free camp just outside the town of Northam. At last, I could feel the wind of the open highway as it came rushing into the cabin. Our first stop along the way was at New Norsia. We needed fuel, plus we wanted to stop for the olive oil and fresh baked bread made by the Friar Monks who live there. Their monastery always seemed such a lonely place to me, but Gordi loved it. As I bought that night's dinner, Gordi wandered into the monastery's chapel, his camera's flashes eerie as they ricocheted around the stone walls of this sacred space. Then we set out again, our destination, 'Merriden, here we come.'

Dusk is such a dangerous time to drive. Here in Australia, every bit of wildlife seems to roam the highway from feral camels to kangaroos, blue tongue lizards, emus, even the odd snake. Luckily for us, it was not quite dusk when we finally pulled up into the overnight free camp.

Our first day of travel done; now it was time to stop and boil the jug, pull out a camp chair, and relax. Time to watch that glorious ball of red sun sink into an orange and mauve sunset. It was time to breathe. Well, that was the intention until Gordi pulled out his yoga mat. He lay it down onto the red sand, not giving a second thought to the fact we were in the bush now where the insects have no mercy. Within a minute he'd leapt off the mat, his antics some sort of crazy slap dance as he fought the insects off. Gordi had me laughing so hard my face hurt. His bonhomie now squashed, I handed Gordi a cup of tea without sugar and some advice about our bush lore. Not that I am any great shakes at it myself, but I'd learned some things on my previous travels, one being never to lay down near any termite hills. They don't like it and will bite or sting you. Gordi had no other choice but to agree with me as he frantically continued to slap them off his body.

The night out here is so dark, and the Milky Way and planets so clear, it seems you only have to reach up to touch them. Gordi puttered around inside the motorhome, finding some space under the bed for his backpack, and putting his shave gear in the tiny shower space, commenting, 'Not much room is there.'

I immediately felt defensive but swallowed my reply. Gordi cooked dinner, curried eggs on toast with homemade dill butter. It was just what I felt like. The next day would be an early start as we'd planned to reach the turnoff at Coolgardie that would set us onto the Nullarbor desert road. Now it was time for a good night's sleep. Suddenly we found ourselves trying to figure out weird little things, like who goes to the bathroom first, and who gets which side of the bed? I smiled at this because nothing ever really changes, does it? People are creatures of habit. Gordi allowed me to be first in the bathroom and take the right side of the bed. We both settled in beautifully that first night, Gordi's breathing telling me he was already fast asleep. It took me a little while before I could join him in dreamland as I mentally started checking off all the things I wanted to do before departure time. Before long though, sleep eventually claimed me as well.

It was cosy waking up the next morning to an overcast and foggy sky, the paperbark trees looked forlorn. Drizzling rain is dangerous out here as huge trucks carrying goods country wide leave an oily residue on the roads, so I took the driving slow. I was in no hurry, with a hot cup of tea from the thermos and a muesli bar at my side, I was happy. Stopping off at the turning point to the Nullarbor, Gordi put in a disc by the New Zealand singer Bic Runga, her voice hypnotic as we drove along. Gordi was now at the wheel. I checked everything as we drove, writing down mileage etc., when I noticed there was a red light blinking on the dashboard. It was the E for empty gas light flickering, which snapped me out of my comfort zone. How could I have been so stupid not to fill up with gas and have extra gas on board as every good traveller should have. I felt the engine give a shudder or two, then we were coasting along. No engine, nothing. Gordi spied a sign saying Kambalda West. Thank God the exit ramp had a slight declination to it. We picked up a little speed and coasted further down the road. The petrol station was such a relief as it appeared and wonders of wonders; we coasted right on in and up to the pump. Gordi and I both let out sighs of relief, which then turned to laughter. We were safe. We just sat there for a moment with such wide, smug smiles on our faces.

As I looked around me then, I knew something was wrong again. The place was deserted. We'd coasted into a deserted petrol station. Now I felt really silly. Gordi went out on the main road, ready to flag down a car. Within minutes, a man stopped and told us the petrol station was closed. 'Thanks,' I said. I think Gordi and I'd figured that one out already. The man then said there was a new station about ten kilometres up the road that would be open. By now, it was pouring down rain. Gordi was soaked through, and I wasn't a happy camper, either. So, the kind young man offered Gordi a lift to the petrol station. Within a half hour, he was back with a container full of petrol, enough to get us to the next gas station and fill up. I got behind the wheel and turned the key. We were back on the road again. I turned to thank Gordi for his efforts when suddenly he flared up, snarling.

'Why did you not fill up at the last petrol station? Don't you check your petrol and water all the time? That was a silly move!' he said brusquely, eyes blazing with uncharacteristic anger.

So much for all that yoga and meditation.

The turnoff to the Nullarbor was up ahead so I pulled over as I'd promised myself I would do to take photos and have a celebratory cuppa with or without Mr. Grumpy-bum. But Mr. Grumpy-bum continued to whine and grumble about my stupidity, so as soon as we stopped, I turned to him, advising him either to zip it or move on. 'I am not interested in your comments if all you are going to do is shout and whine over a mistake.'

Gordi got out of the cab and walked around to the driver's window. 'Tara, are we having our first domestic?'

Big red signs warning went off. *Domestic?*

'We are travelling buddies Gordi nothing else. Nothing domesticated about it.'

In fact, that word seemed offensive to me.

CHAPTER 17

We both stood there for a minute each waiting for the other to give an inch, to offer a hug. At that moment, I felt like I wanted to carry on, on my own; his anger really bothered me. It seems Gordi was an anxious traveller, so I got back in the cab and moved off to a lay-by area just to be safe from oncoming traffic, then I turned the key off. It became so still, peace, how wonderful. Opening my little motorhome, I put the jug on the gas hob, and pulled out the shortbread biscuits, which Gordi claimed were full of Trans fats but I ate anyway. I found my camera and took some photos while waiting for the jug to boil. I then made myself a cuppa while Gordi sulked somewhere around the back of the vehicle.

Having cleaned up and checked that all was safe to carry on; I got back into the cab. 'Coming or not,' I shouted and revved the engine with my foot to the pedal. Gordi's face appeared at my window.

'I think it's my turn to drive this bus,' was all he said.

That was his apology. I said nothing and off we drove onto the Eyre highway, which is more commonly known as the Nullarbor. Gordi drove, and I relaxed, the hum of the motor lulling me into a restful snooze. I knew I trusted Gordi behind the wheel, but did I trust him with my heart? Should I be more giving? Or should I ask him to leave once we reached Eucla, at the border between Western Australia and South Australia?

We'd two more nights of free camping to see how I felt about this man whom I knew I liked, but now seriously doubted as travel companion material. Or was I the problem? Was I too old and stubborn to change my attitude? Only time would tell. I knew if it was to be goodbye at Eucla, then it was going to be unpleasant; but I was not prepared to bicker and fight my way around Australia, no matter how much I liked him.

That afternoon we decided to spend the night in a lay-by in the middle of the Nullarbor. Another couple had already made this their camp spot for the night as well, their blue camper van covered in weird and wonderful graffiti. They were cooking their meal on an open fire, which instantly horrified Gordi. He muttered something about bushfires and insisted on cooking a macaroni dish with bottled sauce on the small gas stove inside. I made a salad with both of us inside our cramped quarters, squeezing around each other as we reached for various items. It did not work all that well, but somehow, we managed. We ate outside, our plates on our knees. I washed the dishes while Gordi made us both a coffee. We sat in our camp chairs to watch the last remnants of the sunset as the stars came out, making their shining appearance felt in the night sky.

The other couple wandered over to our campsite, their tin mugs steaming in the now-changing, cooler air.

'Mind if we join you guys for a natter?' they asked, introducing themselves.

Eric and Dolly were a delightful couple in their thirties, and I welcomed them eagerly into our campsite. Before too long, we were all swapping stories. Eric and Dolly described themselves as eternal travellers.

'Always have been living the life, aye, Doll?' Eric winked as he put a huge, muscled arm around his wife.

He was a tall blond man, and she was a chubby dark-haired and pretty woman. The name Dolly suited her. She looked like a doll. She looked up at Eric with huge, adoring eyes.

'Amen to that, we are all living the dream,' I replied as we raised our mugs in salute to the night sky.

I sensed that our new fireside companions felt as I did; it was wondrous to watch the night sky, all of us lucky enough to travel through the Outback of Oz. We all stared up at the universal night show on display, watched a falling star leave a faint trail of light as it disappeared into the deep black. Dolly and Eric left us soon after, wishing us both a peaceful night. It was about two a.m. when Gordi's insistent elbow nudged me awake.

'Tara, listen.'

My first instinct was danger, and to think it was a camel or emu on the rampage beyond our little walls. My ears strained to hear angry animal noises, which I finally did. Only to realise what I was hearing were the noises of the two-legged animal variety, that I shouldn't be hearing, as our companions entered the throes of passion. Oh, to be young and uninhibited! When we woke at dawn, Eric and Dolly had left the campsite. I was relieved. I could think of nothing more embarrassing than to have to face the noisy love makers the morning after.

At breakfast, Gordi continued with the charade, squeaking as I served the Weet-bix.

'Oh please, yes, yes!' he cried, mimicking the sounds of the night before.

I found him silly. I took out the road maps, marking the next place I wanted to stop at. 'The Pink Crystal Lakes: check it out. It's another turn off on the Nullarbor, but I think it's well worth it.'

It took us about three hours to reach the turnoff from the asphalt road. Then it was miles of firm, white sandy tracks with nothing but pale green scrub on either side, and the odd bit of saltbush. I spied a few emus on their early forage before noon and dozens of small hawks circling lazily in the warm air. I spotted a lone kangaroo, and I knew that where there was one, there would be many more in the night. The white sandy track went on for miles, or so it seemed, Gordi taking all the tight corners and sandy bumps and hollows with care. Pink Crystal Lakes finally came into view. From where I sat, it looked like a peaceful lake with tiny white-capped waves tinged pink from some sort of algae. Along the side of the lake, there were large camp sites where visitors could park overnight, and long-drop toilets and cold-water showers. Each campsite had a fire pit too. Perfect!

Gordi could not complain about this campsite, surely.

I watched as he backed the motorhome in. Once the motor was off, I popped in some wheel chocks around the back tyres. Dinner was chicken fried rice, which was ready in no time at all. Gordi set up the small table and chairs outside and we ate as dusk settled over the pink lakes, turning their colour to a deep moonstone pink.

There is always that special hour when, as dusk or dawn approaches, there is no sound at all. It pervades everything with quietness; it is that space between night and day. I love it. As the busyness of the day recedes, it is that one special place where you can catch your breath. And there was no one at all out here except the two of us, just sitting, breathing deeply, and inhaling the pure clean air. Even the overly busy internal chatter of the brain becomes quiet. It was so quiet I could feel my blood singing, my face muscles relaxing, my body blending in with the peacefulness of this beautiful place.

Gordi felt the same. His eyes closed, his features relaxed, no longer stressed from the day's driving. It was hard to go inside and retire for the night; we both just wanted to stay out there under the night sky, enjoying the sounds of night and the cool air. Tomorrow, we knew, would be another day of driving in the heat, so we agreed upon an early night. Once inside, we got out the maps to see where our next free camp was, and I circled Ceduna.

As we lay in the cosy bed, I heard the unmistakable telltale thump of a kangaroo coming our way. First it was a continuous thump; then it slowed down to nothing. I sensed it was sussing out my motorhome. Gordi heard it too but had no idea what it was. He looked as though he was on the verge of being sick, he was so pale. I whispered I thought it was a kangaroo. Slowly, I opened the door, and there she stood, not three feet from us, a beautiful adult grey kangaroo. As my torchlight found her face, she stood to attention, looking back at me with her big, bright brown eyes. She was sussing us out, too. Were we harmful? Did we pose a threat? She bounded off, but not before I saw a tiny face poking out of her pouch. This, I quickly realised, was a mum and bub team. I felt as though I'd been given a gift to see this large adult in her natural home with her baby. Gordi had a stunned look on his face.

'Did you just see that?' he gasped. 'Man! She was huge!'

I guess for someone who has not lived in Australia, she was beautiful, proud, and healthy, a great omen for our bush life.

The birdlife at the Pink Crystal Lakes is amazing, and the dawn chorus is loud. I love it, because every bird within cooee lets you know it's alive and happily signals the morning's arrival. I nudged Gordi. It was time for us both to get up and move on. Gordi made the tea and poured muesli into the bowls. I had a quick sluice under the shower, dressed in fresh shorts and singlet, slicked on moisturiser, and stepped outside to take advantage of a few photo opportunities. I heard Gordi shower and when I stepped back inside the motorhome, I noticed he'd made the bed, and the dishes washed, dried, and put away.

I could get used to this.

As we drove back out onto the Nullarbor, the thrill of another day on the road was in my blood. We aimed to get to Eucla for our next break, then cross the border into South Australia. Just over the other side of the border lay a quiet little seaside town called Ceduna, and this was where I thought we would stop in at a campground. It would be a long day's driving on the flat Nullarbor plains, but if not experienced, it can prove boring as there wouldn't be a lot of scenery out there.

We made it to Eucla and topped up with gas, when Gordi spotted the temperature gauge was a little on the high side. I topped up the water as well, noticing it certainly needed it. The price of food, gas, and water across the Nullarbor are horrendous; but being in the middle of the desert the shop owners have prerogative and there is not much one can do. The prices shocked Gordi too; bemoaning the fact it cost him over a hundred dollars, but that was our agreement—we would share all the costs.

As we left, Gordi moaned that it was definitely, 'highway robbery.'

The conversation that had been all sparkly earlier in the morning had grown into long silences. I drove along deep in thought about the 'us' we were becoming on this journey. Gordi could not seem to settle back and enjoy the ride at all, note taking, fidgeting, a selection of music on and off, long sighs.

CHAPTER 18

Up in the distance, a black-grey thunderstorm was brewing over the desert. I could see lightning bolts hit the ground as huge flashes of red and greenish yellow crackled its way through the dark, gloomy sky. Vast fingers of blue-green light flashed from one point to another, scattering into myriad sparks. Gordi's moaning and complaints stopped as he became mesmerised by the light show.

Thunder boomed all around us. Fat plops of raindrops hit the window screen as the air temperature dropped. Then we found ourselves right smack in the middle of a storm. Rain pelted down hard. It hammered the motorhome. Trails of muddy red grit ran down all the windows. I wanted to laugh out loud; it was so exhilarating. Ten minutes later the storm had passed us by, sweeping clean the land before us. Even the trees and bushes looked taller and cleaner, their thirst now having been slaked. I hadn't noticed Gordi's silence. I hadn't noticed his eyes were as big as saucers until he let out the biggest sigh.

'God that was scary!'

Then I laughed. I laughed so hard I had tears in my eyes. It hadn't occurred to me Gordi had never seen anything like that before. It must have terrified him, while it exhilarated me.

The border was still about an hour away, so I pulled over and enquired whether Gordi would like to drive us across the border into South Australia. He reacted like a child with a new toy and ran around to the driver's side. As we drove back onto the highway, Gordi once again mentioned the temperature gauge looked a little on the high side. He was right. I'd noticed it creeping up, so we thought it best to get it checked out once we got to Ceduna. I was not in a hurry though, because I was having too much fun being a passenger instead and taking in the sights. I soon found out that Gordi was a 'point-and-drive-on' kinda guy, though, and all my pleas to stop for a photograph fell on deaf ears.

I love the border of South Australia. It has a huge plastic whale and kangaroo as its markers, and a tourist shop that sells everything from tiny plastic wombats to genuine didgeridoos. We had to stop and declare whether we were transporting plants, vegetables, or any other material that could be considered dangerous to the South Australia farming district. The inspectors were polite but thorough. They looked through all we had, including anything that might be in the shower, under the bed, inside the fridge or freezer, etc., and they asked questions about where we'd been travelling. I could see Gordi getting ready to argue with them as they removed the lettuce and tomatoes he'd bought.

I took Gordi aside and explained that here in Australia we do things differently; that this was the law, not some charade to confuse tourists. But he continued to huff and puff about it, and I was finding his attitude trying. Once again, the question of 'us' came back to me. Was this what I really wanted? My conscience kept telling me to give the man a fair go, so I would. By the time we reached Adelaide we will have been on the road for nearly a week. Surely, I would have discovered by then whether I wanted to continue to tour with Gordi?

We were on our way once again, Gordi driving us towards Ceduna Camping Grounds. I'd booked us a camp spot for two nights until we got the overheating problem fixed. As we drove into the camping grounds, the temperature gauge was high, the motor smelled sizzling hot. Thank God we got there when we did; the motorhome came to a sputtering stop at our allotted parking bay. Gordi was in his element. He contacted a mechanic, and soon we had found garage that thought they could help. We would soon learn that the town of Ceduna had a major aboriginal settlement. In no time at all, two young aboriginal men drove out in a bright orange tow truck, wearing bright orange overalls, introducing themselves as the owners and mechanics of their shop. They were professional, offering us advice that it would be too dangerous to start the motor again, and best to tow it to their workshop. They were proud of their TAFE certificates and diplomas, which took pride of place on the office wall. The workshop itself was spotless.

Gordi and one of the young men tinkered around under the bonnet for a few minutes. The young man who attended to me called me, 'The Missus,' while addressing Gordi as, 'The Boss.' This was a bloke's world. Best to say nothing. Mentally I began that old mantra, 'don't sweat the small stuff, Tara.' So, I sat back and enjoyed my hot coffee and chocolate biscuits while the men tinkered, 'ummed' and 'aahed' about the radiator hose, discussing belts, pulleys, tubes, all things connected to the radiator. That one hour passed slowly, and I entertained the idea of finding a movie theatre to while away my day. I was just about to enact my thoughts when a smiling Gordi walked over to me, his hands stained with grime from the motor.

'We have discovered the problem,' he announced before going into detail.

All I could hear were the dollars falling out of my wallet. My motorhome, my problem, so I paid for the work. A new radiator, hose and clips were fitted. It was all professional, and to be honest, we knew we could go no further without a good radiator. As I drove back to the campgrounds, Gordi shouted something.

'Look at this! They charged you for the coffee and biscuits. What a bloody rip off! I'm going to ring and complain.'

Right then and there, I knew there was going to have to be a deep and meaningful conversation between us. Everything seemed to set him off. And now, my head was thumping. I decided it was time for a lie down and two painkillers. I must have slept for an hour or so, because when I woke up, Gordi had found one of my frozen dinners for one. All he had to do was heat it up. A hearty serving of curried rice with veggies and lamb meatballs awaited us, and it smelled divine. We ate our dinner watching the sun setting into a blazing yellow ocean. I had to comment on how beautiful it all was. The sun seemed to hang there for a good half hour. The whole scene of a golden orb reflected off our water on an azure blue ocean. Who on this earth could ask for anything better right now than this fantasia light show?

'To us,' Gordi said as he clinked his glass against mine.

Gordi was so happy he wore a huge smile on his face. The sun reflecting off his sunglasses made me wince. My headache was still there, and although our dinner was delicious, I could only bring myself to nibble at it. I was about to take some more painkillers and head off into the darkness of the motorhome when Gordi realised I was not enjoying the food or the light show.

'Why not try this remedy?' Gordi suggested. 'Try putting your feet in cold water, then sip straight lemon juice with a little ginger powder mixed with it and put an ice pack on the back of your neck. It works for my aunt all the time. Instead of swallowing those toxic painkillers you seem to love, why not try something natural?'

I let the insult fly by. It would keep. Gordi was not the one with a pounding headache and nausea. I could feel the sight in my left eye going. This was a bad migraine, and I did not want to go rattling around in pain with cold feet, lemon juice and icepacks. I mumbled a decline, preferring to stumble back into the comfort of bed. Gordi helped me onto the bed; put a cold flannel over my left eye and massaged my feet. His hands expertly circled my ankle, working his way down to my toes; then, using his thumbnail, he dug into the top of my big toe. It was quite painful for about five minutes, then I could feel myself enter a state of pure bliss as the headache and nausea moved away. Gordi continued to work on my hands and elbows, digging into the space between my thumb and forefinger that also ached, then I felt it. All my muscles loosened and relaxed along the length of my arms and up around my neck.

Next, he asked me to roll over, and he massaged my upper back. It bought such relief to my neck and shoulders. By the time Gordi finished, I was slick all over with oil. The headache? What headache? As I stretched myself out on the bed, feeling light as a feather, Gordi's massage continued to other parts of my anatomy and I was happy to oblige, my body responding to his touch. My response was all the green light he needed. Now that is a migraine cure, no toxic pills needed. I was grateful.

CHAPTER 19

Gordi was a good healer, and so is sleep. When I woke, it was six in the morning. The seagulls hit high notes of glee as they dive bombed a shoal of fish swimming in a swirling frenzy not twenty feet from the motorhome. The sun was already beating down hot, and I felt positively marvellous and full of energy, the nagging ache behind my eyes completely gone. I'd planned on hot peppermint and green tea, followed by bacon and egg rolls for breakfast. Between that and the sea air, the stresses of should I or shouldn't I continue with my travel companion, I put that question to the side for a while. I was itching to get back on the road to Port Lincoln. I had a third cousin on my mother's side living there and we'd always promised to meet up if ever we found ourselves near each other's patch of universe.

'I feel really old,' Gordi groaned as he climbed out of bed.

I watched as he continued to groan with every step he took. Gordi moaned about the bed being lumpy, about the space being too small. How I hogged the bed, and he'd no room in the shower to stretch. It was a long list of unhappy comments. I now knew if Gordi was not happy, then it was expected the world would suffer with him. Gordi did not complain, he grizzled or tapped something loudly, until you paid attention to him, said your name over and over. These were irritating, that's for sure, but I wasn't comfortable with the snarling, rude mood swings. Where had the Gordi I knew, who'd nursed Rae and me with such care and consideration, gone?

I wondered if he needed some sort of counselling. The mood swings were so full on, and he seemed to oscillate from sad to glad in minutes. It certainly put a damper on the morning, though I now knew he would snap out of it by noon, then act as though nothing had been wrong. Once again, doubts plagued my mind about his accompanying me around Australia. I truly liked this man. I liked his gentleness, his generosity, and his willingness to help, no matter what. The mood swings I liked not so much, and I certainly did not want to mother him in any way.

After the last year or so of mothering Russ, Jess, and Rae, I was completely done. Anyone who has ever looked after others and given selflessly knows exactly what I mean here. There just comes a day when you say, 'Enough is enough, I'm done.'

I walked up to the camp office and paid the bill. While there, I spied a small aboriginal painting; it was of two kangaroos bouncing across a burnt red desert. I thought it was pretty, so I bought it to tuck away in the motorhome for the day I returned to Perth. Gordi instantly clucked his disapproval as he saw me pop it into a drawer under the bed.

'Waste of money, honey,' he commented, rolling his eyes.

I had to stop and check myself. It was none of his business what I did with my money. The returning look I gave quickly settled the score and definitively closed off any debate he was heading for.

Once we were on the road again, I hummed happily along with David Bowie's pop song 'Let's Dance.' Travel made me happy. Travel was in my blood. Gordi lay back in his seat, his dark glasses jammed tight onto his unshaven face. 'Are you unwell?' I asked.

'I'm fine, thank you,' he snapped back. 'Don't worry about me.'

The thought occurred to me that I might have another temperamental Jess in my midst. We were on the main Eyre Highway bound for Port Lincoln, and I turned up the volume that Tina Turner was belting out, and I joined in-*Nutbush City Limits*. The day was going to be a good one despite Gordi's mood swings. I was determined that I only needed to make myself happy, and I would be.

In just two hours I would be drinking tea at my cousin Mavis's home. I was quite excited about meeting this woman, who, although she was widowed and twenty years my senior, was now the closest thing to family I had. When we spoke on the phone, her lilting voice had been light, musical, and happy. I sensed that, like me, she now only wanted to live her life to the fullest.

I once again rejoiced in the great job those boys and Gordi had done with the radiator, trying to keep things between us light and happy. I teased him about his lemon and ginger migraine cure. There was not even a hint of a smile coming from him. So be it. I would soon be visiting with my cousin and Gordi could go off and amuse himself somehow. I would part company with this unpredictable man. I'd been miserable living with Jess and his moods, but Gordi was not a teenager. As I drove, I decided this partner/friendship was not for me.

Port Lincoln has a reputation for being a rough, dirty, seaman's port where pubs and booze are rife; but what I saw was nothing like that. The Port Lincoln I saw was bright and clean with friendly people doing their own thing. Its suburbia was like every other suburbia too, except every now and again, you would drive past homes that no one seemed to care for. Couches and old cars strewn, littering the front lawns, little kids running around with snotty noses and huge smiles. Just like every other township I'd ever been in. We all live life differently.

Mavis lived in a suburb called Green Patch. After carefully sorting the map out, I found her address. It was exactly as she'd described it to me. Her house sat on a quiet, sunlit street. Bright scarlet bougainvillea climbing over the trellis by her front door, while white climbing roses in large terracotta pots stood guard in front of the open windows. Lavender hedges bordered the path to her front door, and a white concrete bird bath graced the centre of the front yard. Inside the gabled doorway stood Mavis wearing an ear-to-ear smile of welcome as she held out her arms to enfold me. Her smile and embrace instantly wiped out any niggling fear I had of meeting her. I could see the family resemblances instantly. As I looked into her hazel/green eyes, I recognised my mother and myself.

'Welcome to my home Tara. At last, we meet.'

Gordi had fallen asleep, slumped in the passenger seat; I did not wake him with introductions. I was too intent to meet Mavis. We launched into our shared history of, 'Did you know such-and-such,' or 'Did you ever meet what's-his-name?' And 'Did you ever find out what happened to?'

It was wonderful to discuss my family with another member who could fill in the details of things I'd wondered about for years. Mavis invited me into her kitchen. On the table was a lovely spread of fruit bread, scones with whipped cream and blackberry jam. Covered with a bright red knitted tea-cosy was a large pot of tea. A small blue milk jug sat between the flower embossed cups. The whole scene reminded me of my mother's table in days gone by when she would have her lady friends over for morning tea.

Nostalgia gripped my throat, and tears stung my eyes as I suddenly felt the pain of missing my mum, who I still missed so much, even though she'd passed when I was young.

Does it ever go away?

CHAPTER 20

I was about to take a bite of Mavis's yummy morning tea when there came a knock on her front door.

'Hello! Anyone in there?' Gordi shouted.

Mavis rose to answer the door with a rather noticeable and pronounced limp.

Another link to my mother.

On her feet were old slippers, huge bunions poking out of the holes that had been cut out of the sides to accommodate them.

'I believe there is someone to see you,' Mavis remarked, raising an eyebrow in my direction. Gordi looked hot and frazzled; his eyes had the look of a possum caught in the headlights.

'What's wrong?' I asked him, taking in his hot and bothered state.

'You locked me in the motorhome and left me there without any windows open. I could have dehydrated!' he declared angrily.

I wanted to laugh. What a ridiculous accusation. Mavis stood there, her arms crossed against her ample bosom.

'Who is this person and what in the devil is he is he ranting about?'

Embarrassment flooded my face. This was not what I intended to happen in my first meeting with my cousin, and certainly not what I expected from Gordi. He was acting like a three-year-old that missed his mummy.

Excusing myself from Mavis's company, I sat with Gordi on the front doorstep to calm him down. The crimson bougainvillea that grew overhead made for a lovely shady spot to rest and talk. Mavis, I noted, did not offer Gordi anything beyond a glass of cold water. I tipped a little onto my hanky and put it on the back of his neck, then left him to sip the water in peace. I moved back inside with one eye on Gordi and trying to continue our conversation about family. But I found the warmth between us momentarily quenched. What I'd felt with Mavis was now gone as her arms remained crossed over her chest, her face like stone.

'I am sorry for the intrusion, Mavis. Gordi is a close friend whom I invited to travel with me. He seems to be having trouble with me or the travelling.'

'Men! Don't like 'em, don't need 'em,' her only hardened retort.

'Ditto,' I answered, having nothing else to add as we raised our teacups in mutual salute. The jug was boiled once again, both of us in deep conversation.

I could hear Gordi stirring outside. Mavis and I now had the family photos out and we were deep into playing the who, what, where of our family tree, when I heard the distinct sound of the motorhome starting up. I rushed outside to see Gordi driving the motorhome, backing into my cousin's driveway. He was destroying her property, low-hanging branches that shaded her plants now broken off.

'Look here, if I'm going to be stuck here for a while, I'm at least making myself comfy,' he shouted.

I wanted to hit him. Mavis hadn't invited me to park in her driveway. She hadn't invited me for anything other than a cup of tea, not to stay over. I saw red. Speaking through gritted teeth, I snarled, 'Out, now, get out. Go away. Now!'

'Keep it together,' he muttered.

'Just bugger off somewhere. I don't care where, just go far away,' I told him. 'I will call you when I have finished visiting my cousin.'

Anger was not a strong enough word I could use in that moment. I was positively boiling. Mavis had a look of disgust on her face as I returned and tried to regain what I'd been enjoying, a walk down memory lane. We both watched as Gordi walked away, his back ramrod straight as he marched off down the road.

'Men,' she spat out again with disgust. 'Don't trust the buggers. Never have and never will.'

'But you were once happily married, weren't you? Or at least that was the impression I was under,' I replied, curious. Mavis filled a jug with water and ice cubes and plunked it down on the table with some force.

'Impressions, my dear Tara, are just that. The truth is, we got along just fine as long as he kept his distance, and I, mine. He lived in the lean-to out the back and I lived in here. Pregnancy was why we got married. A silly one-night fling was all it was. We did not love each other. He gave me nothing, not even a child, as I eventually miscarried. Money was his enemy. No matter how much he had, somehow, he would find a way of spending it foolishly, and the bills and debts climbed sky high. I lost two homes because of his spendthrift ways. This house, my home, was my parents' last gift to me.'

I must have looked puzzled, because whenever I'd thought of Mavis, I'd thought of her as a content older woman, secure and safe. Mavis then told me her story.

'I was married at fifteen, from a dirt-poor family so more or less barefoot and pregnant.'

The early 1940s belief in 'keeping them pregnant and chained to the kitchen bench' had been her husband's preferred mantra. They'd been chucked out of their rental homes, time after time. When Mavis turned to her elderly parents for help, none was given. She turned to her in-laws to ask for help, she was again turned away. Her only way out was to work. At sixteen, Mavis was a slim, attractive albeit unskilled girl. She soon caught the eye of the local gang's boss, her fortunes turned, her husband now under tight control by the new man in her life. Mavis sold grog and managed the brothel for him, becoming the boss's woman. Her husband enlisted in World War Two; she never saw him again. Once she'd cottoned on to the power of sex, she charged the boss twenty quid.

'He was a kinky little bugger. He liked others to watch while we did the roly-poly if you get my drift, and his other so-called friends, they loved to watch. Oh, it was all tasteful. He supplied knot holes in the bedroom walls for men and women so they could peep at our actions in the bedroom.'

Adding, by the time she was twenty she was wise beyond my years in men's tastes and quite wealthy in those times. She charged ten quid a week to run the bar and two quid for one hour at the peepshow in the brothel boudoir. It was a small fortune in those days. I don't think my mouth closed once as she retold her story, and I admired the woman for her strength, turning a depraved situation at the hands of her husband into a success story.

I looked at the time on my phone, noticing there were three missed messages from Gordi.

Two of the messages were, 'Where are you? Call me!'

The last message he left on my voicemail.

'Come on, Tara, answer your friggin' phone!'

That last message? How dare he?

I winked at Mavis and once again said 'Men.' I was not here to jump to Gordi's call. I turned back to Mavis, asking whether it was all right to stay in the driveway as I wanted to stay and chat with her longer.

'Of course, my dear; you are most welcome. Stay inside tonight, please,' she said, her eyes glinting with laughter. 'Let's have a glass of sherry, and I'll order a small pizza for dinner.'

I readily agreed. 'Why not, I'm in no hurry.' I walked out to the motorhome and locked it up securely. Back inside, I switched off my phone. I was thoroughly enjoying myself. Why should I stop? This was Gordi's problem. There were so many ways he could have shown he was a grown man, but no, it all came down to drama. Enough, I was doing what I had wanted to do for a long time.

Mavis and I spent the rest of the evening together, chatting about her life, which in all truth, still left me a little shocked. We discussed my being married to Russ and having Rae and Jess in my life. Next, we wandered out to her backyard where Granny Smith apples hung in abundance. We picked some for her freezer and she gave me a few for my journey. By six o'clock we relaxed with a promised sherry together. Mavis smacked her lips together.

'Got used to this stuff when I was just a youngster. Back then, they couldn't even give it away!'

This woman mesmerised me. Then she produced a tobacco pipe, amazing me again.

'No way, you're pulling my leg!' I said, aghast.

Mavis waggled her thick grey eyebrows at me.

'See? Assumptions, my dear Tara, that's all they are.'

She puffed out big clouds of fragrant pipe smoke that billowed about the room. My dad had smoked a pipe. Vivid memories of my childhood flashed before me as I snuggled up on my daddy's knee, safe and protected from the world, his big arm resting around my small waist as we discussed our days. That same feeling of safety enveloped me here now. I felt safe here with Mavis.

The hot, cheesy pizza was delivered, and we downed two more sherries to toast our family and our connection. Gordi was the last thing on my mind as

I slipped into my single bed for the night, a little worse for drinking sherry.

The spare room, I could see, was no bigger than my motorhome. The last thing I remember was chuckling at visions of Mavis smoking a pipe while entertaining customers for the Shady Ladies saloon.

Daybreak was well and truly on its way when I heard my name being whispered. Mavis stood beside me holding a huge torch like a giant hammer and shining its pale beam into my eyes.

'Tara,' she whispered. 'That God awful man is outside your motorhome. He's trying to break in.'

CHAPTER 21

I was still foggy from sleep.

'What awful man?' *Oh, no, it must be Gordi.*

I heaved myself out of the soft bed, a slight hangover thumping in the back of my head. Opening the door, I called out, 'I'm here, Gordi, hang on, I'll get the keys for you.'

As I rummaged around in my bag, Mavis stood over me muttering her disapproval of that man. I could not blame her at all given her past experiences, but I'd no reason to distrust Gordi. Yes, he was bad tempered, and he pulled strange mood swings; but, so far, he'd proved himself trustworthy.

Gordi looked uncomfortable as I unlocked the motorhome. Once inside the cosy cabin, I'd some questions for him like why he'd sent that rude text message to my phone? I felt the need to scold him as he sat down beside me, but I didn't get the chance, because he took it upon himself to launch into all manner of accusations.

'You did, you said,' Gordi began in earnest, and 'I'm the innocent party in all of this!'

Calmly, I breathed in deeply. 'Gordi, my stopping at my cousin's was no secret to you. This was something I'd planned from the start. I have not misled you in any way. You were aware that Port Lincoln was my first stop, and I told you how excited I was about finally meeting Mavis, so why are you being so rude?'

His answer was 'Because we are together, we are sharing this adventure together, it's not just you Tara. You have led me to believe this was about us, and you disappear into that old lady's home without even a goodbye!'

There comes a time in some relationships when you know you can do no more to help another. There comes a time when your body, mind, and soul all agree that it's over. You're tired of being made to feel sad or upset because of the other person's continuous disagreeable behaviour. This, this was my time.

'Gordi,' I said, looking at him point blank, 'I don't intend to live my life defending myself. I think we should finish this before we are both in too deep. I will drop you off in Adelaide. There is an international airport there, and you can travel to wherever you like, but you will not be travelling with me.'

Gordi's eyes bulged open wide. 'You can't kick me out, Tara. We agreed,' he said, obviously angling for another argument.

'Yes, I can, and I will. And Gordi, if you're not in a more agreeable mood in one hour then I will simply drive off without you.'

I left him to sit with that decision and returned indoors to say goodbye to Mavis.

Mavis had made hot pancakes and coffee for two. It was rude to have to go when I did not want to. However, I must have looked guilty about Gordi's unwanted presence in the motorhome as I ate, because she leaned over and patted my arm.

'Don't you worry, love. You stay as long as you like. I will make sure he doesn't bother you.'

The difference between us as women was enormous. In her younger life, Mavis had worked extremely hard to get what she wanted, often bargaining with her body, and always because of men demanding she do so. I could see it had caused her immeasurable grief and left her with a strong dislike and disrespect for men in general.

While I considered myself similar to Mavis in that I'd worked hard on being who I wanted to be, I'd had an easy life. Russ, my deceased husband, and I'd had a respectful, honest, and healthy partnership. We had our differences as in any marriage, but they were not difficult. We'd agreed early in our relationship that if we discovered we were not happy together; we would not continue in our marriage. My theory had always been that if two people could not communicate and resolve their differences, then they shouldn't go on making each other miserable. Better just to say 'enough' and walk away.

But as for Gordi? If the mood swings were his way to vent, I was not interested. So far, he was proving to be hard work, and at my age I was simply not interested in the emotional roller coaster he wanted to take me on. If there was one thing I knew for sure, it was that life was too short to be a mother to an immature, angry man.

I showered in Mavis's home. It was so much stronger than the mobile home's little weak spray, and I relished in the powerful force of the water as it massaged my body. The hot strong jets of water felt good cascading over my sore scalp, relieving me of the remnants of a slight hangover. I changed into fresh clothes. It was time to say goodbye to Mavis. Giving my cousin a huge hug, I promised her I would be in contact.

I took three or four photos of us to remember our time together and gave her my blog address. I explained that if she went to her local library, they would help her log on so she could read my messages and follow my trip through my blog posts. Outside, the sun was shining bright and hot. Gordi sat motionless on the doorstep looking like a chastised child. I ignored him and got in my motorhome, starting up the motor. He knew I'd meant every word I'd uttered.

'Come on, Gordi, get in.'

Mavis waved goodbye as I drove down her driveway.

I drove back through the city past the suburbs and onto the highway, the GPS announced advising Adelaide airport: next exit, right. Gordi sat there, silent, his face a mix of emotions.

'This is for the best Gordi. I feel if we continue, we may turn out to be more enemies than friends,' I said, resting my hand on his knee. He shoved my hand away.

'Feel free to stop any time you feel you can no longer stand my company.'

Gordi's foul mood permeated the motorhome. By the time I pulled into the drop-off zone at the airport, Gordi had already stuffed his backpack full of gear.

'Bye, Gordi; take care, and thanks for coming this far with me,' I said sincerely.

I leaned over to kiss him goodbye. I wanted no hard feelings between us. Instead, his hand was in my face, pushing me away. He slammed the passenger door and stalked into the airport terminal.

CHAPTER 22

I drove away as feelings of relief coursed through my body, my fist punching the air with delight. Absolute peace flowed through me and my motorhome. It felt good to be in charge once again of what and where I travelled.

As I got back onto the highway, a desire to stay and explore this beautiful part of Australia settled on my shoulders, why not? Pulling off into a layby, I tapped into Google and before you knew it, I'd booked for one night. I decided: no more travel buddies. If I met anyone it would be, 'Hello, nice to meet you, and goodbye.'

The Dixie Chicks, an American country and western trio, sang softly on the radio as we hummed along, my mind ticking over what I wanted to see and do in Adelaide. I'd read in the paper at Mavis's place that Cirque du Soleil was in town. *That could be exciting.* Mavis had also told me about the German food villages in the hills just on the outskirts of Adelaide. She'd given me the address of a couple of her favourite places, which I'd written on post-it notes and stuck on the dashboard. More things to see and do.

It was afternoon when I pulled into the campground site. It had power and water supplied, all I needed to do was plug in. The huge elm trees surrounding me were leafy green, and I craved the newfound silence of this haven. Apart from a smattering of birds high above in the branches, there was nothing but silence. *Thank you, Lord!* Thoughts of my cousin and her dislike for men made me chuckle. God forbid if I ever turned out to be the same, though it appeared I could be heading in that direction. Or was it the fact I could not be bothered with the drama? With no one to please but me, I did exactly that and drifted off into dreamland, my last thoughts before sleep being that Gordi was not yet out of my life.

The fly buzzing its way around my head was relentless and would not let me sleep. It carried on and on. I even tried swatting at the air a couple of times in my sleep induced state, until I realised the buzzing was in fact my mobile phone. Still half asleep, I peeled back an eyelid to see who it was.

Rae's face popped up on the screen, I was instantly awake.

'Sorry, Mum. Did I wake you?' she asked, sounding concerned.

'Sort of, what's up, honey?'

Rae chuckled. 'Mum, what have you done to Gordi? He has just phoned us, and he is so upset with you and your treatment of him, after all he has done for you.'

Rae's chuckles continued as she relayed to me her conversation with 'poor old Gordi.'

I wanted to feel angry upon learning that Gordi had called my family to 'tell on me,' involving them in our private matters. Apparently, I was a vicious bitch with a disgusting mouth. Rae's laughter was too infectious. God, it was good to hear her laughing again! The more she told me about their conversation, the more we giggled together. I did not need to remind Rae that this was his version, not mine. Rae knew this was not who I was, or what I would do. I felt no need to add or deny anything, as what he'd said was mostly true.

Gordi had coloured it in with his drama. The conversation then became more family orientated as I told Rae about Cousin Mavis, about Port Augusta, and what my plans were going forward. To see the circus, visit the cafés and delicatessens in the German village in the hills. Then it would be decision time again, contemplating my next route and whether the road would take me to Melbourne and a four-week journey onwards to Tasmania. Or whether the road would take me further north into the country, to the towns of Mildura, Hay, Wagga Wagga and Goulburn. I'd end up in Sydney. I told Rae I would just have to sleep on it, see where the wind took me.

My hand was turning numb by the end of our hour-long phone call, so I told Rae I was going to have to hang up.

'Love you, Mum; always have, always will.'

That had always been our goodnight to each other, ever since Rae was a small child. Suddenly, all I wanted to do was hold her close, the distance between us too great.

'You too, honey; always and forever.'

Rae had come out of her stressful illness so strong and full of wisdom, and as a mother, I felt my heart swell with pride. I made myself get up. The bed was too comfortable and cosy inside my motorhome. My body felt tired, so I decided a long walk around the campgrounds amongst the Elm trees would give me some energy.

By the time I got back to my home on wheels, it was dark, my breath coming out in long white wisps. It was going to be a cold night here by the feel of it. By now it was late May, and the nights were still chilly in Adelaide, while in Perth it was just warming up and Rae said they'd predicted a hot summer. I must admit the frosty night air felt energising.

Time to make some dinner. A chilled white wine was also in order, along with the celebration that from now on, I would travel on my own. I'd planned steamed baby potatoes, a green salad, and some of my homemade fish cakes I'd stored in the freezer, my mouth watering at the thought. Dinner was a simple affair, and the self-promised glass of crisp chilled wine went down easily and mellowed me as I cooked. After dinner, I would turn my attentions to the laptop and work on correcting my novel. It was time I did something about this mess.

First, the banking to be checked and sorted out. I stared at the screen thinking this was a mistake. The publishing company had paid me out in full. He'd paid back everything including the sales commission. I checked my messages. Yes, an email from Mike. I noticed not under the publisher's name. He requested a receipt for monies and acknowledgement I'd received my cancelled contract. There it was on screen, big red letters right across my contract: Cancelled. I was incredibly grateful. I was nearly $5000.00 better off than two days ago. I grabbed my phone to ring Gordi to thank him. It rang out. I left a message, thanking him for his part in this.

Now to edit the book myself or try to, it was two in the morning when I finally put the light out. My mother's voice in my ear said, 'Never leave to others what you can do yourself.'

A small portion of my novel was finally done, and a quiet sense of accomplishment enveloped me.

Once my novel was correctly printed and published, I knew there was no way in hell I would ever have anything more to do with a publishing firm, unless they proved reputable. My sleep was my healing, and I woke the next morning to magpies calling my name, my clock saying it was quarter to ten. I stretched starfish style and smiled at the day. There were no demands to answer to, no quarrels to resolve—it was just me in my little home, safe and sound. How blessed was I! This, now *this* was the life.

CHAPTER 23

After a warm shower and a small breakfast of porridge with honey and yoghurt, I sipped on hot coffee. I booked my tickets for the circus, which I hoped wasn't sold out plus my planned trip to the German village in the Adelaide hills. I intended to stock up on some groceries, then drive into the city and park near the circus if I could find a spot. My phone beeped. On screen was my confirmation ticket for my circus seat. I was booked for the six p.m. show. The excitement whirled in my tum and I felt like I was five again, off to the circus with my folks.

Just as I packed up and drove out of the camp, the heavens opened, and it poured down. I swear it was the heaviest rain I'd seen. It came down in torrents, silver sheets of water washing over the mobile home and thundering across the window screen, hitting the road so hard it drummed. Cars began pulling over as they were skidding on the wet road. I thought it a wise idea to pull over, but finding a park large enough for the mobile home was the problem. There was no choice. I had to pull over into the only space that could accommodate me, a bus stop. I waited for the storm to pass over. Thankfully, no buses beeped their horns for me to move out of their way.

Finally, the bruise-coloured skies cleared, and I drove up into the beautiful green hills of Adelaide. Artisans of every description had their billboards out, and I wanted to stop at every single one of them. Realistically though, I knew I could stop at a few, and get back in time for the circus. The sign to the Handoff German Village sailed past my window and a burst of excitement ran through me. Soon pulling into a park bay, big enough for my mobile home, it once again began to rain.

My first steps, or should I say, nose lead me into an authentic German bakery that sold handmade pickles, relishes and jams with bread and cakes, yum. I sampled a few from the little tasting dishes they had on display, soon finding my all-time favourite, the Shiraz berry jelly. Wow! My taste buds hummed with the flavours of champaign and berry wine.

I purchased all the things I liked in pickles, cheeses, spreads and jellies, rich buttery shortbreads, and a large piece of black forest gateau. And for tonight's supper, soft bread rolls along with some bitter black chocolate flavoured with chilli salt. Yum, it was heaven. Finally, the rain stopped long enough for me to go exploring further. I locked my food parcels in the motorhome and set out to discover more of the village. Finding a small community garden in the middle of the grounds, and a quaint wooden Gazebo, its white wooden beams laden in bright purple wisteria. The rain brought out the fresh and heady scent of its perfume, while nearby rosebuds opened, releasing their sweet smell of the many varieties of roses circling the lush green lawn. This was a picture postcard of a German village, if ever I saw one. I took many photographs like the snap happy tourist I was, conscious time was not on my side. I wandered into a cheese shop and a pickle maker's shop, each one offering workshops I would love, but no, not today.

Walking down the opposite side of the street to where my motor home was parked, I noticed a beading shop. So many gorgeous glass beads, and beside this shop, a beautiful lace making shop, again tuition offered. I needed at least two weeks to do all this at least. Time was ticking away, and I sprinted back to the motorhome, realising I'd less than thirty minutes to get to the circus. I was on my way to see a wonderful show I'd been longing to see again; years before I'd taken Jess to see their first show in Perth. So many memories flooded me then, of happier days when Jess was younger, and I was still his much-loved Nana.

I sat in my seat and enjoyed two hours of mind-blowing acrobats, tightrope walkers, clowns and trapeze artists flying up and around the tent as the circus master made ribald but funny comments. When the clowns ventured into the audience, being silly, playing practical jokes on a few, I felt like a child again. Everything felt so magical, it filled my heart with wonder. It was hard to come back down to earth once the show closed and I realised I hadn't worried about Rae, Jess, or Gordi even once. Nothing had distracted me but for the event unfolding before my eyes. Maybe I'd missed my calling. I should have run away to join the circus once Russ had passed over.

Now it was time to get back to the campground and make plans for my next stop. When you don't have a time limit anymore, you realise that nobody cares, except yourself? And, without the urgency of having to do any of the real-world stuff anymore, it dawned on me that there was also nothing to stress about. I had time, because in a strange way I'd run away. I had money, thanks to Mike the publisher, and only myself to keep happy. So, I decided not to worry about it, to stop picking at an imaginary spot. Isn't it funny how fate steps in and decides for you?

There I was in the abolition block with another woman my age, my aim to have a hot shower. We got chatting as people do, especially when camping. The woman informed me they were heading north from where I'd just come. So, as good travellers do, I passed on the information I had about the roads, the overnight camp spots and especially about the Pink Crystal Lakes. The woman then listened to my dilemma about taking different roads and overnight lay-bys.

She suggested, 'Why not flip a coin, sweetie? Both roads are good.'

It made my decision sound easy. I wished her happy travels, returned to my motorhome and sitting down, pulled out a twenty-cent coin. Then I took one large gulp of my hot frothy milo and flipped.

It landed, rolled off the bedside table and across the floor, spinning lazily as if it could not decide, then it settled and fell to one side, heads winking up at me. There it was my fate was sealed; I would head off across the Mitchell Highway, then across to the Great Western Highway. Simple. All I needed now was a good night's sleep. I eyed the huge chunk of chocolate Gateau. 'Not tonight,' my tum said back.

The rain now gone, a warm wind billowed through my little hatch window and I mulled over whether to stay another day, perhaps a workshop or two? It was such a beautiful city, but my gut was saying, 'No! It's time to move on.' I needed to listen more to my instincts. Besides, the coin toss had already decided for me.

Just pay the bill, Tara, pack away your belongings, turn the key and drive off. How easy was that? I stopped to gas up and do my regular check of all the bits and bobs a vehicle owner must check oil, water, tyres. Then, with any luck, I would find a nice lay-by to stop at somewhere off the road and have a big brunch, which would do me well until dinner time.

Mildura, as I looked at it on the map, was a small township about a four-hour drive away. It looked good to me.

Once again, I was on the road, humming along to Fleetwood Mac, telling me that 'You Can Go your Own Way.' I sang at the top of my voice, maybe a little off key. I was happy. I'd researched Mildura on the internet and in Aboriginal, the town's name was Latje, or 'Red Earth.' All I could see were fields and fields of grapevines, so green and full of fruit. I guess that's why the region is also known as Victoria's food bowl. Citrus fruit, olives and asparagus crops are grown here in abundance, the local art is prolific too.

Finally, Mildura. I stopped just outside the township at a pretty lay-by. Pale green saltbush dotted the deep red sand, while in the distance, tall, pink ghost gum trees were shedding their bark, displaying their pink bare underbellies to the world. In Mildura you can park in most lay-bys overnight, and already I could see there was another camper tucked in.

A bright red bus, the name 'Bull' emblazoned across its front and rear. The smell of stew drifted in through my window, tantalising my taste buds.

If it had been Eric and Dolly, I think I would have turned tail and quickly left. Luckily, it was another couple, and given that it was about three in the afternoon, I was glad I could stop. The wind was warm, stirring up fine red dust which blew in tiny whirlwinds we call 'Willie-willies' around my feet. Three hours of nonstop driving had cramped my leg muscles. I leaned on the door for support and wait for some feeling to return to my legs. My wobbly exit from the cab must have been cause enough for concern as an older man approached me.

'All right, mate?' he asked.

His wife looked over my way and called out in a singsong voice.

'Join us for a cuppa, love!'

What a wonderful sound to my ears. A cuppa!

'Oh please,' I replied enthusiastically. The man pulled up another stool, and I wobbled over to them, my calves aching.

'Looks as if you're dehydrated, love. Here, this should fix you up,' she said.

She passed me a tin mug of hot black billy tea. As she stood up, I saw her upper body was in a sort of sling.

'Hold him for me, will you?' she said suddenly, gesturing towards the bundle.

I was taken aback. *What on earth?* I automatically held out my arms as she swung the heavy bundle over to me. Two large, brown furry feet poked out one side, then on the other side a black, wet nose appeared. *A puppy?*

I was so wrong! It was the cutest baby kangaroo that suddenly wriggled around in my arms to see who I was.

CHAPTER 24

'Doug's me name. This here is Joey,' he said, pointing to my moving bundle. 'And this here is my wife, Marion. Have a seat.'

I sat, cradling the beautiful baby bundle in my lap, its eyes half closed. The afternoon sky deepened; twilight was not far away. Marion handed me back my tea.

'Welcome to Mildura. We live in this bus permanently, and we have made it our job to save baby kangaroos from their dying mums, 'coz there's a fair amount of roadkill around here. Guess you could say we've taken on the unofficial job of being road rangers.' Doug chuckled.

'Yes,' he added, 'there's no such service in Australia, so we patrol the roads, stopping at any signs of fresh roadkill because sometimes, you know, there'll still be baby joeys inside of a mum's pouch. Can be a bit it of a bloody gory job, but someone's gotta do it, or the little ones would starve to death. Or other times they'd just stay in their mother's pouch 'coz they're too stunned and don't wanna move away from their mum's warm body. But if they stay out here, they won't last the night; bloody foxes will attack and kill them, or other carrion eaters. So, Joey here's found a new home with us, for the time being, that is,' Doug said, pushing his hat off his forehead.

I quietly nodded. Baby kangaroos spent many months still developing inside their mother's pouch after birth, but I could not get over this wonderful couple before me, doing what they did every day to save them. I felt privileged and humbled, but a little sad, too, as I had a sudden pang of regret knowing that Gordi was not here to share in this moment. Doug and Marion asked if I would like to have a meal with them; they were of course vegetarians, which I knew Gordi would have liked, too.

Joey and I became fast friends. He squirmed around till he found a comfy spot, his little brown face popping out of the sling from time to time, checking his new parents were still there. He was so cute with his little upright ears, long furry face, and big brown eyes. When I stroked his front paws or his ears, he would half close his eyes, almost purring with pleasure.

Marion took Joey for night walks. There was no leash required or need to tie him to them for fear of his running away, because he already knew these folks protected him. I was in awe at how Joey and Marion communicated, too. She would make clicking noises if he strayed too far, then his head would pop up, his beautiful bright eyes searching the landscape, until he bounded right back to her. It reminded me of the unbreakable tie between a small child and its mother; the child so full of energy and love for its mum it could never be severed, and I was so humbled by the experience. Doug and Marion told me they were soon delivering this little one to a kangaroo park close by.

'Joey is not our pet. We are merely the custodians, and our role is to make sure he is safe and secure. Once we deliver him, a vet will check him out. He will join twenty or so other little skippies, (another Aussie name for joeys) that have lost their mums to traffic on the highway.'

It surprised me the death rate was so high and told Marion so.

'It's the road trains, mostly,' Marion explained. 'Once they've got their speed up, they cannot suddenly stop, not as much as a car can. Although I have seen cars that have driven at such excessive speeds that after their collision with a kangaroo, both animal and driver come out badly injured. These are big solid animals, and the damage to car, driver and animal is usually immense. People can die from such unfortunate accidents, so why not drive a little slower?'

I nodded emphatically; Marion made perfect sense to me.

It was Doug's words that soon had me in my tiny shower, scrubbing myself with hot water and soap.

'Watch out for ticks and fleas, Tara. The little buggers are covered in them.'

I'd forgotten this rule of the bush, be aware of sheep ticks and sand fleas, fire ants, yuck. Must admit, though, the hot water released any lingering aches and pains I had. My neck muscles had taken a beating recently, so it felt good to stand there and let the hot water soothe me. It was only eight-thirty, and I felt exhausted. As I went to turn out the bedside light, I noticed a green light blinking on my phone: a text message. Do I answer or ignore it? I turned off my phone for the night. Sleep was a high priority for the next long day on the road.

I was awakened at five a.m. by a flock of crows cawing so bloody loudly it deafened me. Doug and Marion were already up next door and building a small fire to boil their billy. I love the smell of wood smoke, and the sound of Doug snapping twigs only added to the comforting feeling. I climbed out of bed, yawned, and stretched. It was time to get up, have a wash, and make myself some toast. The weather was already warm, and Doug said we were in for a scorcher.

I put the phone in my pocket and lathered my arms, face, and neck with sunscreen. Pulling back my hair into a short ponytail, dressing in yesterday's driving clothes my comfy shorts and singlet, and pulled on a pair of soft leather boots. Now I was ready for the day. I emerged from the motorhome feeling well and happy, and Marion beckoned me over for a cup of boiling hot tea.

What nice people these two were.

They asked me about my plans, where I was off to and whether there was anywhere special, I'd found in my travels.

I was about to inform them of my plans to get to Sydney in December when Marion cut me short with an unusual request. She wondered whether I would consider dropping the joey off for them, given that I was already headed towards Mildura? If they did it, Marion said, they would have to double back. I was about to say I did not think I could do it because there was nowhere to store a joey in my mobile home when my phone gave off a shrill ring.

Joey got such a fright at my phone ringing that he took off into the bush, knocking over the pot of billy tea as he did, which then splashed Doug, burning his leg. Marion threw her tin mug in the air and took off after Joey as Doug howled in pain and my phone kept trilling loudly. Doug was now cursing, while Marion was yelling after Joey, and I just stood there as if in a dream, watching the nightmare unfold.

'Turn your fuckin' phone off!' Doug screamed at me while holding onto his leg.

Marion and Joey, meanwhile, had disappeared into the bush beyond. The crows protested at all the noise and ruckus, and in one big screaming cloud, they took off, black across the sky. I pressed the green button.

'Hello. Tara speaking.' There was silence, then came Gordi's sorry voice. 'I'm sorry, Tara. Can we give it another go?' Who else but Gordi would be saying that?

'Where are you?' I asked, suddenly having the awful feeling he was going to walk out of the bush and say, 'Surprise!'

Gordi, I could tell, was determined to convince me we were meant for each other. I could at least give him points for that. He informed me that he'd stayed overnight in Canberra and could find his way to wherever I chose to meet up. I had to smile. *If only he could see me now*. I needed to be honest with the man.

'No, Gordi. I'm in the middle of the bush about to pick up a baby kangaroo and take him to a shelter in Mildura. That's many, many miles from where you are.' Again, there was silence.

Then, 'Can we *please* let the past go and try once more to travel together?'

I hated the thought that he was about to beg. I liked to think I was easy to get along with, but Gordi always seemed to get on the wrong side of me.

'I will call you tonight, Gordi, once I have delivered the young Joey to the vet.'

'So, where are you again?' Gordi asked.

'South of Mildura, about a day out of Adelaide,' I replied. I already knew what Gordi was going to say. I knew he was going to ask if we could meet in Mildura, but my gut replied for me. 'I've got to go and help catch a Joey, Gordi. Talk to you later. Bye.'

CHAPTER 25

Marion was now walking back towards the bus, the happy escapee tucked under her arm. I could hear her telling him off in a gentle voice.

'You silly boy,' she chided. 'You could have been lost to me forever.'

I looked over at Doug, who was by now examining his scalded leg; it looked red and sore. I knelt beside him to offer some assistance but his barked rebuff of 'Go away,' hurt, so I retreated into my little home and made a coffee, waiting until everything had settled down. Finally, Marion approached, and the laughter in her eyes told me all was not as bad as it looked.

'Men are such big babies,' she said, crinkling up her nose in a slight chuckle. 'Take no notice, Tara. They're both fine. I have one in his sling, locked inside the bathroom while the other is covered in ointment, from his elbow to asshole. They're going to be fine.'

Her comment made me laugh out loud. 'Yeah, but which one is locked in the bathroom?' I answered cheekily. I invited Marion into the motorhome and poured her a coffee. 'Sorry, it's instant.'

Marion once again broached the subject of my taking Joey to the Mildura vet for her. I liked this woman; she was straight up, no nonsense. I agreed to help her out, and we shook hands on our agreement.

'One day, Tara, you will think back on this and smile,' she said, and I laughed.

'I know I will.' Meanwhile, I could hear Doug tramping about outside. Marion saw the look of sorrow cross my face.

'He's fine, Tara; he's a male.'

If I'd known what this day would bring, I think I would have stayed in bed.

She handed me a lumpy moving bundle in a large cardboard box, advising me not to put Joey on my bed.

'He may still have ticks and fleas. Leave him in the bathroom or in a box on the passenger's seat,' Marion warned. 'Remember, too, he's more curious than scared right now.'

Joey's head popped out of the top of the box. He looked so funny. Doug handed over two baby bottles filled with milk for Joey's lunch and fondled his floppy long ears.

'Be a good boy, young man,' he advised.

He offered me his work-worn hand that felt more like a piece of wood in mine.

'Thanks, Tara. Sorry about all that,' Doug said, apologising and looking down at the ground.

'No worries, Doug. It was my fault the phone went off when it did.'

I drove off with my new driving companion, a baby Joey staring out the passenger window as I tooted and waved goodbye.

'Take care, both of you,' I yelled back, then turned onto the Stuart highway. 'Mildura, here we come,' I said to Joey, who stared at me with huge brown eyes and long eyelashes we ladies would kill for; what a cute little furry faced creature he was! Joey obviously felt safe with me as he pulled himself half out of the box and looked out the window as we drove. I had to laugh again. If only my family and friends could see me now, riding along the highway with a baby Roo riding shotgun. They would not believe me. Mildura was a little farther than I'd thought. By eleven a.m., I was thirsty and hungry, so I decided it was time for a drink and snack. I pulled over to the side of the road, Joey watching everything I did with sleepy interest.

I set everything out and did everything Marion did to call him, making the clicking noise with my fingers. The sling and box proved no hindrance to him as he popped up and out and came over to where I was sitting. I picked him up and held him as one would a baby. I wrapped a tea towel around his body. His little brown paws held onto that bottle in a vice-like grip. His tiny cheeks billowed in and out making big slurpy noises as he sucked back the milk bottle mix that Marion made for him. Then he fell asleep. No fuss, no bother, just curled his little head under my arm, and it was goodnight. I gently placed him back into the sling in his box. Now it was my turn to eat and drink, but what I really wanted was to have had a little snooze like Joey. But then I remembered the chocolate gateau. It was divine. I left the other half of it for another day.

By one-thirty, we were parked outside the vet's office. I took Joey inside where we were met by a smiling receptionist. The vet and staff thanked me profusely for helping to save Joey, then it was my turn to say goodbye to my furry little passenger. It was a sad moment, because in the five or six short hours of having him with me, this little Joey had bounced into my heart. I now understood what Marion meant about how hard it was to give up her bush babies. The vet took Joey away to befriend his new family while I got on my way to find a campground and decide about Gordi.

I asked the receptionist if she knew where a motor camp was, and she gave me a map and directions to follow. I found the motor camp, alright. It had a gorgeous pool, and, after paying for one night and nudging my little home into its parking space, I headed straight for the pool.

Mildura motor camp had wonderful amenities, and it also boasted about its restaurant. As I swam in the cool pool, the smell of fried onions wafted over to me. I glided through the water, swimming six laps freestyle, then another six in backstroke. I was puffed, but it felt good to use all my muscles. I was sitting in a sun chair when a smart young man strode up and offered me a menu. Why not! I thought and ordered a vegetarian egg and pineapple burger with a white wine spritz. Ah! It was pure heaven, my taste buds loving every single bite. When the waiter cleared my table, he asked if I would care for another drink. I'm not normally a big drinker, but tonight was different.

'Yes, please,' I replied, thinking back to all the chaos that had ensued earlier that day, and knowing too that deep down I was stalling about calling Gordi back.

I was in two minds. This was my future. If I once again agreed and asked Gordi to join me, then it would be unfair of me to keep asking him to leave every time his angry moods got too much for me. I needed to be sure this was what I wanted. By the time I'd returned home I was feeling mellow, deciding now was as good a time as any to call. I dialled his number; it only rang once before Gordi picked up, his voice full of anticipation and hope.

'Gordi, how are you?' I asked. I really wanted to know.

'Finally,' he said, sighing. 'Finally, you've decided to call me back.'

I don't know why, but his reply annoyed me. In accordance with his attitude, it appeared I was supposed to fall on my knees, beg his forgiveness and pretend everything had been wonderful.

'We have to talk, Gordi,' I warned him, speaking slowly, deliberately. 'We have to talk over the phone now, not tomorrow. I do not want what happened last time, ever to happen again. I hope you have sorted yourself out by now.'

Immediately he was defensive. 'I'm disappointed in you, Tara, after all I have done for you and your family. You keep egging me on and then dumping me. And you are blaming me for your inability to cope with stress. I think it's more serious than that. You need medical help. Not pain killers Tara, but maybe antidepressants and or counselling.'

It floored me. Nothing had changed. On top of his arrogance, angry, antagonistic, attitude he was now making a diagnosis?

'Gordi,' I said abruptly, 'your attitude is foul. Don't ever bother me again.'

I switched my phone off. In that moment I totally agreed with my cousin, Mavis, and Joey's adoptive mum, Marion.

'Bloody men!' I shouted to no one and the walls. 'Who needs them?'

Going to bed angry is not good for a sound sleep, so would it be a walk around the park, or another swim? The swim won, and since my swimsuit was still wet, I donned my old faithful two piece. There was no one about. The restaurant had closed, and the pool was softly lit, the water a clear, inviting green. I slipped into the cool pool, allowing the water to relax my body. I did about six laps treading water at the deep end, when a large black hairy head popped up beside me. A scream bubbled in my throat.

'Oh, sorry,' he said, 'I did not see you.'

I swam to the edge of the pool, ready to get out, when his voice stopped me. It was the young waiter who'd taken my order for a dinner.

'Don't go because of me. Stay and chat for a while. I'm Buddy, and I know your name is Tara.'

We shook hands. Buddy turned out to be a talker, and boy could he talk. It was as though he'd swallowed a lot of words and was now puking them out.

He told me all about his family, lifestyle, where they all lived, his loves and hates in life. Buddy was a country boy with dreams of farm-ownership, marriage, mortgage, kids, and a dog. He followed the simple philosophy that, if he did no harm to others, then no harm would befall him. I listened to him for over an hour until I was cold, and my skin had shrivelled up.

Begging tiredness, I made my way back home. I don't remember turning off the light or locking the door, I just fell on my bed into a deep sleep.

The next morning, my phone informed me it was going to be another scorcher, expecting to climb into the 40s by midday. I thought it felt like that now, and it was only eight in the morning. Mildura, I'd decided, was one hot town.

CHAPTER 26

I decided Hay was my next short stop, a small township about two hours away. There were so many small townships with so much to see and do; my problem was that I wanted to see and do it all. Plus, I'd the feeling that, since Gordi knew where I was, he would probably try to find me, so it was best that I keep moving. The feeling that Gordi was stalking my every move was proving stressful. I studied the maps, realising that if I could make Hay by ten a.m., I could find a quiet park or shady lay-by and add to my blog and finish of my journal. I wasn't ready to tackle my manuscript yet.

A small township called West Wyalong was my marked for next stop. It was about a five-hour drive. I figured I could do this. It would be quite a distance travelled, and a successful travel day, and I would be as far away as possible from any meeting with Gordi. It was settled. I'd go have one last dip in the pool, swim some laps, then get back on the road.

After my dip in the pool, Buddy caught up with me.

'Morning Tara, I've a been looking for you, I have had a man on the phone twice this morning wanting to know if you had booked in here.'

My heart skipped a beat. 'What did you tell him, Buddy?'

He must have seen the fear in my eyes as he reached out and touched my arm.

'Nothing really. I told him all clients were confidential.'

Now I really knew it was time I moved on. I did not want to meet up with Gordi at all, and I knew that once I was at Hay, I'd the perfect opportunity to either go to West Wyalong or across to Wagga Wagga. Buddy's hand was still on my arm.

'Tara, if you're going to West Wyalong, could you drop off a parcel to my parents' place for me? They live on a small farm just off the Western Highway in a place called Rankins Springs. I'm sure they would love to meet you; perhaps you might like to stay on the property for a couple of days.'

Decision made.

So, I agreed to deliver Buddy's parcel. *Why not?* I told him I'd call into the office for his parcel on my way out. I changed from swimsuit to shorts and top, made sure I'd stored everything away in my little home, and turned the key. Hay, here I come. First, though, as promised, I would pick up Buddy's parcel. As I walked into the office, Buddy was busy answering the phone and a large parcel sat on the countertop. I waved to him, saw he'd addressed it, picked it up and left. Buddy ran after me, his face a mix of emotions.

'Tara, that man who's been ringing around to find you. He's in town.'

How Buddy knew I did not know or care, I was instantly on the alert, my eyes darting everywhere. Why was Gordi hounding me?

Buddy closed my cab door, patted the side of the van as I drove off.

'Enjoy the farm, Tara. It's peaceful there, and my mum's a mean cook!' Buddy yelled.

I waved again and drove off. Why could Gordi not understand I couldn't cope with him, and why should I have to? We were not attached in any way or form.

'This is stupid,' I said out loud. I pulled over and took a deep breath. I refused to have my travels ruined by this mean-spirited person.

The flat grass plains were crisp brown, burnt from the harsh sun. They'd been harvested, and now the cattle and sheep roamed over them, fossicking for any tasty leftovers. The other fossickers were Emus. I'd never seen so many in one paddock. This mob was huge; from the tall and elegant adults to the tiny chicks, all well known for their scatty antics. I drove slowly, remembering my last, less than favourable encounter with the feathered beasts. Stopping occasionally to take a photo, I found that, if I got too close, the Male emu would walk towards me, his head held high, the huge wingspan puffing out wildly as if to say, 'Back off, lady, these are my babies.'

The landscape out here was dry, flat; there were no hills, no ranges, just brown stalks, brown dirt even the sheep were a dirty brown colour. The one saving grace were the gigantic trees. These mammoths that had survived fires and floods, weirdly shaped blackened stumps telling tales of fires past, their new canopies of green providing shady relief for all the animals. It had its own raw beauty out here in the Outback, every tree a staunch and stoic giant, protecting its flock.

Faded white farmhouses way off in the distance appeared, then civilisation; food stalls of fresh produce with honesty boxes sat in driveways, some sold eggs, some fruit, others sold veggies. I also found one that sold honey in the comb. Yum, my favourite. It had been a year or two since I'd last tasted this sort of honey, the memory of it on my tongue, thick and syrupy.

Bees buzzed about the garden, a calming, relaxing sound, and a sign pointed down the driveway to the front door. The scene reminded me of a chocolate box photograph and was not anything like the drought country I'd recently driven through. A cheerful young lady answered the door, cradling a child on her hip.

'Hi, there. You here for some honey or eggs?' she said.

'Both please,' I replied as I rummaged around in my pocket for some money.

'I'll have to go get the eggs.'

She opened the fly screen door, and, as if I were an old friend visiting, she held out her child to me.

'Hold Sophie for a minute. I'll collect the eggs' she said.

Sophie sat in my arms, happily sucking her thumb while her mum walked down a sandy track out of sight. I heard some noises, then in a few minutes she was back, her basket containing two large blue-green emu eggs.

'Sorry, lady. That's all I have today.'

The shock showed on my face. 'They're huge!'

She settled the basket at my feet, held her arms out to her child, and went to a refrigerator.

'I'll get the honey for you. Its inside in the fridge.'

I nodded, but I wondered how I was going to eat these things. They were massive. I'd eaten emu omelettes once before when Russ was alive. There was no way I could eat one of these eggs on my own, but I purchased one anyway, along with a jar of honeycomb. I nestled the egg between the pillows on my bed, put the jar of honey in the fridge, and drove off. She'd charged me ten dollars for both. I felt like this was 'Charge the Tourist Day.' As I left, the woman advised me if I didn't want to eat the egg, I could take egg-blowing and or decorating classes in town. I would have loved to, but I was on a mission.

Hay was another hour away with more of the same scenery. As I drove into the township, a new cluster of homes came into view. I manoeuvred the motorhome down small streets, trying to find a park, but every spot was taken. Unbeknownst to me, a country fair was on. Someone advised finding the community fields, where there was free camping for overnight stays, but this was not my goal. I wanted to eat, stretch, and drive on to Rankins Springs.

Driving out of town proved equally hazardous. There were four-wheel drives, Holden Utes, Fergie tractors, in fact so many big vehicles in this one small township. I was glad to be leaving. Overall, the din of traffic, farm dogs, sheep dogs and home dogs barking and growling at anything that looked strange to them, it did not feel welcoming. It was such a noisy town, too, and the noise was horrendous. Kids ran everywhere across streets, their parents yelling at them to watch out. All this, I decided, was noise I did not need.

Leaving the township of Hay and all its noise, I drove next to a stream. There were a couple of parks available on the riverbank, and this suited me more, as all the vehicles parked there seemed to be empty. I pulled up, shut off the engine and sat and listened to the water and the wind in the trees, a gentle peace settling over me. I climbed out and stretched under a tree, allowing the serenity of the place to envelop me and breathed deeply. My sense of calm was instant, and I closed my eyes and as I bent forward, felt my muscles stretch out.

I was about to move into another stretch position when a young voice asked, 'Watchya' doin' lady?'

I opened my eyes to see a young child, her bright blue eyes level with mine and her hair in a massive tangle of carrot-red curls. Green snot clogged up her nose, which she picked off and examine, sticking the offensive piece in her mouth and chewing it as though it were a lolly. One large cold sore sprouted on her top lip and she sported a large bruise on her chin. Her clothes were dirty and ripped in places, and I suddenly had the strongest urge to bathe this child.

'Hello there! Where did you come from?' I asked instead.

She pointed to an old broken-down caravan. Grass had grown up around the wheels and next to it, a rubbish tin overflowed with what looked like soiled nappies. The crows were having a ball, picking out bits of rubbish and scattering it all over the ground. Even the windows of the caravan, I'd noticed, were broken. As I was taking in the mess, another small bright red head popped up.

'Ma!' my new companion screeched, 'A lady's 'ere.'

'Ma' had to be no more than twenty. She looked tired, beaten down, lined and dirty. She stomped over to where we were standing. '

'You stupid little bitch! I've told you before, stay inside,' she cursed as she raised her hand to strike the child.

Automatically, my arm went in front of the little girl.

'Oi, hang on just a minute! She only told you I was here. What's the problem with that?' I challenged in defence of the child.

The woman stared at me now, her brown eyes full of distrust and dislike. This time she raised her hand again, as if to hit me instead.

'Calm down.' I raised my voice to say, 'Stop now!'

Our eyes locked, and though her hand remained raised, she looked as though she did not quite know what to do. She lowered her hand and grabbed the little girl, yanking her back along behind her.

'Get inside you little bitch, before I kick your ratty arse,' she barked, slamming the door.

I listened then, and my heart fell as I heard her continue to scream so much filth at the child that I cringed inside. No one should ever say things like that to their kids. What should I do? Do I interfere? My gut screamed yes, so I called the police. They took their time getting there, but finally a park ranger appeared. The screaming stopped, and so did the sounds of hard slaps and kids crying.

'Sorry, Ma'am. I'll see to this,' a male voice boomed behind me.

This park ranger was built like a brick outhouse; there was nothing soft about him. He marched up to the van and banged on the side, wrenching open the door. As I got back into my motorhome, tears coursed down my face at the cruelty I'd just witnessed and the conditions those kids lived in. No one should ever have to live like that, and she should never have put her kids at risk like that. However, it was none of my business and I did not wait to hear the story. I did not want to see the outcome. I did, however, leave the emu egg on the park ranger's car seat with a post-it note attached, which read 'For the kids.' The little redhead girl watched me back out my motorhome, her tiny hand waving goodbye. It broke my heart. I wanted to

THE CUPPA TREE

help but did not need to get caught up in another drama. But I did wonder if the young mum's life had been so awful she was now passing her unhappy heart to her kids. I'd enough of my own problems to sort out.

CHAPTER 27

It was time to find my next stop and deliver Buddy's parcel to his folks. It was about another two hours' drive on from where I was, and Buddy had written full instructions, including a phone number. I dialled the number, but there was no answer, so I left a short message saying I was a friend of their son's and was calling in to deliver a parcel from him.

The temperature outside was high, but with the air conditioner on, I was quite comfy. I'd bought myself some sandwiches before leaving Hay and found a cold bottle of soda water tucked away in the fridge, so I was all set. I turned onto the Western Highway, the motor humming along nicely, the disc I'd bought from Cirque du Soleil playing in the background.

I looked around at the flat barren landscape beyond my windshield and the hypnotic endless road of black tar that lay ahead, and my thoughts returned to that little red-haired child and it troubled me. I wondered if Jess knew just how lucky he was. Next to that little one, he was wealthy and richly loved. Soon, signposts appeared for Rankins Springs, promising me it was 'up ahead,' and I looked over at the clock on the dashboard and estimated I was about a half an hour away. Per Buddy's instructions, I was to look for a mailbox with the name of Wallow and Co. written in red and turn off into that driveway. Then I was to continue driving on for another good half hour until I arrived at the house.

I'd no need to look for the mailbox. I'd slowed down to read the numbers and there was Buddy's entire family, from the grandparents to the babe-in-arms standing right there under a large elm tree. The whole family had turned out to greet me. What a wonderful welcome.

The children, so well behaved, stood by their parents' side, while the grandparents, parents and all of Buddy's siblings waited patiently while I parked and got out of the cab. The man who greeted me was huge in height and breadth, his chin sporting a large bushy beard, his dark, weathered face smiling.

'Welcome to our farm,' he rumbled, his voice like the crack of a whip amongst the quiet chatter of the smaller children.

He then offered me his hand, and it was a true farmer's hand, hard, callused, and honest. It was also the biggest hand I'd ever seen; mine looked pale and childish tucked inside of his.

'Name's Ted and I guess yours is Tara, local shop gave us your phone message. Been waiting for a while in case you missed us. Follow us, there's a cuppa and cake waiting inside.'

That was my formal introduction to the Wallow family of Rankins Springs, and I would not have missed this opportunity for all the tea in China. I must admit, I was wary. The calmness and order of this large family was a little unsettling at first. A horse and dray waited under a tree for them, each one patiently waiting their turn to get in the back. Ted circled around the dray, checking that everyone was tucked in safely, then eased himself into the driver's seat.

By this time, I was back inside my mobile home, and I followed Buddy's family at a sedate pace down the dust bowl of a driveway, their home at least another twenty minutes from the main road. We drove over a small hill and, as we descended, I saw a magic sight. These folks had built their farm near a billabong. The greenery that met my eyes almost hurt; it was in such stark contrast to the miles and miles of dry, cracked, and parched earth I'd become accustomed to seeing. But this abundant oasis was amazing.

I now understood the longing I'd seen in Buddy's eyes when he told me about his family. His descriptions of home were true, while I'd simply put his longings down to a bout of homesickness. As we continued down the driveway, I saw a large gabled house with a huge vegetable garden on one side next to a large barn, plus what seemed to be another house being built. Around the far side was a white posted corral of sorts, the fields full of healthy cows and sheep.

In front of the house sat the billabong, its waters dark, the birdlife prolific, and the trees looking like willows, its long, sinewy branches spreading out into the shallows of the lake. This was a pure piece of real estate heaven.

The Wallow family stopped in front of the house, which wrapped itself in a large bull-nosed veranda that offered much protection from the hot

Australian sun.

With the help of Ted, the family quietly disembarked off the dray. Again, it was strange to see how orderly they could all be, their body language so calm, so subdued. They ushered me into a large living room, a huge wooden table with many chairs lined up neatly around it. Two long wooden couches with colourful quilts on the backs of them sat along the walls of a massive room. Displayed on the walls hung more colourful handmade quilts. The quietness was unnerving. One of the older women entered the room where they'd asked me to wait.

'Hello, Tara. My name is Ceri. Would you enjoy a refreshment?'

I was so full of questions they were bursting out of my chest. I accepted her offer, and we walked down the long hallway, the back and front door at each end open to a slight breeze that cooled the house down. She offered a small bathroom for me to wash and tidy up in. I washed my face and hands, tidied my hair. I noticed that, in this one small room, everything was homemade. From the pale wooden walls to the purple and green rag rugs, a faded purple facecloth hung on a carved wooden handrail, alongside a pretty mauve hand towel. Resting in the small soap dish, a lumpy hand-pressed lavender soap. It may have been a simple bathroom, but it was beautiful in its simplicity. I had a gut feeling these people were Quakers.

This was not a normal Australian family where the kids mainly ruled the house with noise, telly, or music. Nor was it a house of the typical Australian parents, who looked worn out under the pressures and demands of family, jobs, and mortgages. In a harsh land that often took away from those working on the it, it could devastate and maim, or bring out wisdom and strength, however these folks were different. Here, I could see that their quiet, elegant, and modest qualities were not so much a choice but their faith, a family history rich in religion that connected them with the land and God. I was longing to know more.

Their son Buddy was off having a year's break and going out into the world to find himself. Ted and Ceri stood at the head of the table together, their hands clasped in prayer as the family bowed their heads and words of thanks in a foreign language followed.

I stood awkwardly by listening to the foreign sounds; the most I understood was Gott (God) at the end of the prayer. Ceri held up one small work-worn hand to formally introduce me to the family, and what a large family it was. Six adults and ten small children, the family ranging in age from a tiny baby bound to its mother's chest to an elderly octogenarian.

They introduced me to the family as a guest. The adults lightly clapped, they and the children all wearing welcoming smiles, so healthy and wide it brightened the room. Ceri offered me a chair next to two of the female adults. They served the meal in an orderly manner. It was an enormous feast. They placed platters and more platters of home cooked food on the table, the two young women serving weaving between chairs back and forth to offer us food.

As Ted ate at the head of the table, he talked quietly with his sons, giving instructions what he wanted done next on the farm. With the details of farming being discussed in the background, Ceri made small talk with me about a quilting bee she'd entered and the next batch of soap she was making. Which was almost ready to pour into molds. The small children were fed and watched as other members of the family ate; then they all lined up to have their hands and mouths wiped by a young girl. No one ran, skipped, cried, or ate with his mouth open. No hair was out of place. They removed the bibs from the young ones, who were then taken into an adjoining room for an afternoon nap. That left the teens and adults, once again and in order. The teens finished their meal and asked to leave the table, all quietly returning to don their work boots they'd left by the door.

That left five adults, as one adult had taken the baby to bed. I sat quietly, sipping my lemon cordial as five pairs of deep blue eyes now stared at me.

Was this now when I was expected to talk? As I opened my mouth to speak, Ted held up his hand.

'We are an honest family of farmers,' he announced. 'We work with the land, and we praise Gott as we work. You are welcome to share our food while you are here, but you must earn your daily bread.'

I was being offered a chance to work and get to know these folks, and Buddy had warned me that this was a working farm. The offer made sense to me. Ceri, her two daughters, Ruth and Essie, and their three sons, Ruben, David and John looked at me expectantly, awaiting my reply.

'Thank you, Ted and Ceri. I would like to help you with your work here. I also would like to be able to stay for a week if that is possible.'

Ted looked at Ceri, nodded, and pushed his chair back from the table. 'Welcome to our home,' he proclaimed, his manner serious.

Ceri took my hands and held them tight. 'I am glad you are staying with us; you can tell me how my son is doing. Is he well? Is he happy?'

I gave her the package from Buddy. She placed it on a side table to be opened later was my guess.

This family, I was quickly learning, had no interest in the outside world. They all dealt solemnly with their farm goods, their home, their land, and family, all of which they praised God for. They used a two-way radio for emergencies if they needed either a vet or doctor. I had wondered how Buddy informed them about my passing by. So, it was with a small gasp of surprise from Ceri and her daughters when I produced my cell phone to show them a photo of Buddy. Ceri stared at the picture of her son for a minute, asking me to remove the phone from their home.

'It is part of your world,' she announced, 'It has no place here.'

I felt awful. I'd been here not even an hour and had already broken their sacred house rule of no worldly contact. Ted invited me to park my mobile home at the back of the homestead, away from overhanging trees as he said the falling seeds and nuts would keep me awake all night. I explained to Ted and Ceri I was a writer so I would often be up at night, anyway, writing on my laptop. My night-time activity was reluctantly accepted with a frown and a curt nod. They were clearly not happy with my chosen profession, but they allowed it, considering I was a guest. It was also an unspoken rule: I would not bring my laptop into the house or anywhere near the children.

CHAPTER 28

Dusk arrive earlier in the country or maybe it was the way everything settled down earlier, the morning's chores were over before the heat became too much. The large meal I'd joined in I learned was their regular midday meal, and as the day wound down, we all partook in a light and simple supper of delicious rice pudding, made with eggs and cream.

Ceri asked if I would like to join the quilter's club that night. I'd never learnt this craft properly, but I accepted the invitation, the women of the house and I gathering to hand-sew a small pattern onto a calico swatch. Once Ceri examined the swatch, she would take it over to one of the two treadle machines she and her eldest daughter operated for the swatches to be machine sewn in.

We talked quietly amongst us, most of the questions aimed at me as their curiosity grew about Buddy and the outside world. Kerosene lamps and candles lit the cosy room, the features of lined faces now softened in the mellow light.

Suddenly, Ceri put her scissors down on a bench, announcing it was time for all to be in bed. This surprised me because it was only eight p.m. The family packed away the quilts, the sewing machines were covered with spare calico, and everyone retired to their beds like obedient lambs.

I kept reminding myself that this was their journey, not mine. I was only a temporary guest. I finally found the front door, and there stood Ted, the friendly giant who'd been waiting for me. He offered to light my path to my home, cautiously taking hold of my elbow as we left the front porch. Ted quietly asked me not to bring the Englishman's world into his home.

'They are portals to a satanic system we would rather be without,' he explained firmly. He also asked for no photos to be taken or given, as these were considered graven images of themselves, and an abomination to The Almighty Gott.

That night I tossed and turned, listening to the wind in the trees, and the settling of insects and nocturnal animals. I realised that any contact I wanted to make with the world would have to be undertaken from the confines of my motorhome. If I was going to take this opportunity to stay for a week, then it would have to be on this family's terms. Although at the time I'd thought eight p.m. was far too early for bed, I found I'd two bars out here. I texted my family to tell them I was out of range for a week on a farm stay, then fell headlong into a deep sleep. By five in the morning, hunger was gnawing at my tummy. I got up to make myself a cup of tea, open the curtains and let the fresh air in, the sun barely peeping over the tips of the ranges beyond that I'd yet to explore.

What greeted me instead was the view of a household that had long been awake, everyone already up and bustling around sweeping porches, cleaning windows, beating rugs. These folks lived according to their faith, waking up with the dawn and returning to bed at dusk.

Ceri greeted me warmly, holding out a bundle of clothing; one was a long blue skirt, a cream calico blouse. I realised I was to wear them.

Ceri gently adding, 'While you stay with us?'

I was about to decline when she softly put her finger to her lips in a gesture of silence.

'We don't want to be a temptress, do we?'

Laughter bubbled up inside me against my better judgement. *Me? A temptress!* My mind silently spluttered at the absurdity of it. The other women who'd been busy tidying the porch now gathered around their much-loved mother as looks of welcome turned to looks of dislike.

'If you wish to live amongst us? Then the choice is up to you.'

I felt as though I were being chastised as a teen being caught with a smoke. I dislike long skirts or long-sleeved blouses that do up tight to the chin. What is the point? But rules are rules, and this family intrigued me. Ceri gave me a curt nod as I emerged from the bathroom fully dressed in their costume. A white cap was offered as well because they believed it uncouth for a woman to put her hair on display. The only good thing was I could still wear my comfy leather boots.

The next week flashed by. I became integrated in the Quaker daily life through performing household duties. What a difference it made to be working with a light heart as we worked laboriously in the garden, reaping all they'd sown and, believe me, the bounty of vegetables was enormous; not one thing was ever wasted. My second and favourite chore of the day was to accompany Ceri on the horse and dray to stock up at the roadside stall. Here, the women and young children would carefully load all the spare vegetables onto the dray, and Ceri would harness Ben, the horse, for us to make our return.

It was my job to make sure all foodstuffs were tied down securely, then off Ceri and I would go. Ben's hooves kicked up little puffs of sand as the soft clip clop and creak of the dray washed over us. The sun had just pinked the edge of the horizon as we swayed along the path for a half hour to load up at the veggie stall. Once we were there, Ben would have fun pushing either Ceri or myself around with his big black nose, puffing out sweet, scented breaths of hay.

Everything on this farm was big, including Ben, the dray horse with a sense of humour. It was up to me to care for him at the gate stall; so, with the help of a tin bucket to stand on, I climbed up and attach the feed bag to his harness. The first time Ben eyeballed me, I could read, 'city slicker' in them. Ben gently shook his head while I was attaching his nosebag, and I went flying. The tin bucket went in the other direction and I also got to wear the contents of the nosebag. Ceri tut tutted 'naughty boy,' so while her back was turned, I made this horse a deal, muttering close to his ear.

'Do that again, Ben and I'll ring the glue factory.' His ears twitched, but he stood still for me.

Every morning I would help Ceri finish loading the vegetables. Then it would be time to head back to the homestead, Ben's big black tail swishing at flies, his big bum swaying to and fro before us in the dray. Magpies called to each other, crows cawed, the feeling was of peace. Quakers, I have since learned, do not believe in chatting. Anything spoken was to be strictly about work, prayer, or their minimal social life. I thought about all the times I'd wished for silence, and for peace. Now I had it.

I'd found myself in antiquated, yet simple times, living and breathing in the Quaker lifestyle. Sunday mornings meant big, hearty egg and bacon breakfasts, which we would only sit down to at seven a.m. after having already completed a series of chores.

The women, I noticed, had been up for hours already, milking the cows and making homemade bread and porridge with cream from the milking. Housework was also attended to by all the women, such as bedmaking and cleaning. Washing was hand done in a tub and moved around with a sturdy stick. A fire was lit under a large iron tub, the clothes, and flakes of handmade soap, then added for the washing. Once they'd boiled it; they wrung the clothes through an old wringer. All the women had tasks to perform, and they all loved the work they did, no matter how big or small. I watched in admiration as their hands all worked in unison while singing soft songs of praise to Gott as they worked. Peace and happiness shone within these walls and I felt a sense of unity here I felt did not exist in the outside world.

By midday, there was always a large meal ready for the family at the communal dining table. Men were traditionally honoured as the head of the home, farmers and caregivers to the family, their seat at the head of the table, while the women were regarded as the skilled homemakers. Their contributions, however, were not cast aside as mere feminine what nots. These women were real artisans, this family treasured every skill a family member brought into their lives.

They taught the smaller children during the day in a small schoolroom on the property. I would wake to hear the men and women starting their day as they milked the cows and fed the animals Ben the horse being brushed and Butch the sheep dog being patted, and fed. Ducks and geese scratched, whistled, honked, and quacked all the while around the garden. I loved the sounds that came as the men folk harnessed Bertha the Ox to plough the fields. John, the eldest son, chopped wood for the family's use. In a large wooden washhouse outdoors sat a bathtub, and every night we took our turns, as I was an older woman, my turn came after Ceri's.

CHAPTER 29

One day, the heat was at its worst and not even the flies, who were usually a constant annoyance in the outback, were hanging around. On days like this, they allowed a swim in the lake once the day's work and dinner were over with. This particular day, Ceri and I made a basket of sandwiches to take down to the bank where the family was enjoying another moment together.

I felt Ceri could sense that I was dying to plunge into the cold water.

'We can swim when the men have gone inside, Tara,' she explained.

I raised my eyebrows in answer. She smiled and calmly continued to feed the young ones. After we'd all eaten and the men and young ones had had their swim, we women cleaned up, putting all the picnic makings carefully away. Ceri and her daughters led me to the other side of the lake that was heavily screened by rushes from the house. I wanted to cry out with sheer relief. The heat was awful! The woman taking off their long, dark blue skirts and matching long petticoats; folding them up, placing their work boots besides, leaving their underwear on. Only then did they calmly walk into the cold water, where they did not so much swim as dog paddle a little, then stop to relax by the side of the bank. By sharp contrast, I pulled off my sweat-soaked clothes and jumped in headfirst, determined to swim to the end of the lake and back. Upon my return, I trod water. They all looked at me as though I were an idiot. Had I broken another rule? Essie, one of the young girls, saw the confusion on my face and attempted to answer me.

'We work hard all day; so why work hard now when we can finally relax the mind and body?'

She was right. Why not simply relax? No talking, no swimming, just a half an hour lying back in the water. She was onto something. I secretly made a mental note.

While I stayed with this family, they taught me how to make tallow candles, slice up homemade soap; rug making, quilt making, clothes mending, bread-making the old-fashioned way and yoghurt, and a little food preparation was demonstrated in a whole new holistic light. Seven days was not long enough for me here. I loved the gentleness of this family, loving this whole new way of living. I also knew that, although Cerci's faith discouraged it, I, the English woman, and the Quaker were becoming close friends.

One Sunday she asked me to make a cake for afternoon tea following their church sing-along. Eagerly, I made my famous carrot cake. I knew Jess and Rae and my family in Perth loved it, so did all my friends. I normally used a tad of rum when soaking the mix overnight, but this time it had to be alcohol free in keeping Quaker traditions. Baking it in a wood-fired oven, was a surprise as it turned out delicious, Ceri asking me for the recipe. Their sing-along mesmerised me; the harmony this family had was beautiful. The quilting nights were often a time where the ladies practiced; in fact, they practiced whenever they were together. I would often hear Ceri start a new hymn, the others quickly joining in and following her rhythm. This woman was skilled at teaching her large family, and she guided them in the ways of pretty much everything.

There was one time, and one time only, when we all fell about laughing. They'd asked me to help them collect the honeycombs from the hives. I felt comfortable doing this since this was something I'd done as a child with my father. I donned the beekeeper's hat and gloves and found a hive smoker from the shelf; the day was ending, so I expected the bees to be quiet. Famous last words. Essie, who'd asked me to help, had a beekeeper's hat and gloves on too.

We walked between rows of sunflowers that stood a good four feet tall, the odd bee whizzing past on its last excursion of the day. There was no small talk; there was only an uneventful journey to the three hives. All was going well, Essie collecting honeycomb while I fed smoke into the hives, when a bee or two must have got into her hat. Essie screamed, and took off, her long skirts hampering her run, so she upped her skirts to her hips and ran for her life, screeching all the way.

She looked funny, and my sense of humour took over. I was laughing so hard, I had to sit down between the sunflowers. When I asked if she was okay, Ted answered.

'Our Essie had been stung on the neck. This is not a laughing matter.'

His whip crack voice silenced any more laughter, but I saw a twinkle in his eyes as he helped his daughter up and took her off to be attended to by Ceri.

CHAPTER 30

The following day, I felt it was time to carry on with my journey. I was about to inform Ceri on our morning ride to the roadside stall when she suddenly leaned over and held my hand.

'Tara, please don't think of us in a bad light, but Ted and I both feel it's time you moved on.' There was a small silence between us as we clip clopped our way down the dusty drive.

'May I ask why?' But I was not sure that I really wanted to know.

'It's not you, my dear one. It's how our children perceive you. They talk about you at night when they are tucked up in bed. They see you on your computer. And they are curious little ones. We don't want them contaminated with the world before we can ingrain our life and faith into them. Our children think you are exciting, mysterious, and worldly; it's dangerous for them. I don't apologise for what we believe in,' she said and shrugged.

The conversation had ended. They'd asked me to leave.

I'd no idea this had been going on. As far as I was concerned, I'd been in the privacy of my home, writing. Embarrassed, I brushed Ben the horse down as they'd asked me to do and led him to his stall. I knew my stay here was on the clock as I washed up and got ready for the breakfast I normally had with the family. Embarrassment flushed my face as I saw there was no place set for me. Ted stood up and held out his hands to me.

'I would like to thank Tara for being with us and thank Gott in Heaven for sending another pair of such capable hands; however, Tara is leaving us today.'

The dismissal in those words stung more than any bee sting ever could. This loving, close family presented me with bars of lavender soap, honeycomb, a packet of their best candles, a gorgeous handmade quilt, and herbal shampoo. My arms and heart were full. I'd been asked to leave in the nicest possible way, after gifts and a hug or two had been given. To leave with a fuss I knew would have been ungracious, insulting to us both.

I jammed the armful of gifts onto my bed, plugged my phone into my printer, and printed off a photo of their son, Buddy; I knew it was a sin to them; the graven images of one another took the glory off their Gott, and all that. But I also knew a mother's heart and a mother's love, for this kind of love has its own separate, universal language. Ceri, I knew, missed her son Buddy with all her heart as repeatedly on our many trips to the roadside stall, Ceri quietly asked me about her boy. The photo was grainy, but you could still make out his smiling face. On the back I wrote his work and mobile number, adding with a grateful heart and my mobile number, should Ceri or Ted ever wish to contact me.

Starting the motor and reversing out, I waved goodbye. The women stood on the porch, the men had gone to work. They waved as they sang a song of prayer to me in their farewell, asking their Gott to protect me, and keep me safe. Tears welled in my eyes. Who would not want to spend more time here surrounded by the peace and love these people practiced every minute of their day? Pulling over by the honesty box by the roadside stall, I dropped off the photo of Buddy, spent twenty dollars for some vegetables and drove away.

West Wyalong was not too far off, and judging by my map, it was about an hour's drive. I would stop there and fuel up, check out oil, water, tyres. It felt so darned good to be behind the wheel again. I'd really enjoyed my stopover in Rankins Springs and had learned so much in such a short time, but now it was just me and the road again, and I could taste my freedom. I would never forget the Wallow family, but I'd also learnt that the Quaker life was not for me.

West Wyalong was a small township and once again, the farmers were the lifeblood of the community. Finding a small petrol station on the main road going past meant I did not have to drive through the township itself. I popped the hood looking at the oil, water, brake fluid, the petrol meter ticking over. A young teenager came out to see if I wanted my windows washed.

'Twenty for the lot,' she offered.

These kids knew how to make a dollar, that's for sure. I agreed and handed her a twenty-dollar note.

As she washed and wiped the windows, we chatted. She asked whether I knew that there was a bushfire close by. I'd seen the darkness in the sky ahead but assumed it was rain clouds. I'd broken one of the first major laws of driving: check your weather forecasts every day. The simplest way is to just switch on the radio and listen. If there is a problem, they will announce the forecast every ten minutes or so, and if there is danger, it is all over the airwaves. In my ignorance, I'd done none of the above.

Chills ran up and down my spine when she showed me where the fire was headed: Rankins Springs. In fact, as we talked, we both got a faint whiff of wood smoke. She packed up her gear, I paid for my petrol, and fear rolled around in the air.

The shop owner asked, 'Which way are you headed, Ma'am? Rankins or Forbes?'

I wanted to race back and help the Wallow family. What if they needed help? And yet I'd no way of contacting them. The shop owner saw the indecision in my face.

'Family back there?' he asked again.

I shook my head as tears bottled up in my throat. 'Good friends,' I replied.

'Best go to Forbes, Ma'am. That's one less the fire brigade will have to worry over.'

I knew he was right, but my heart and head were arguing between friendship and common sense. To help make my decision, I called Buddy. He sounded puzzled to hear from me. I explained I'd left the homestead just this morning. I said I was concerned about a fire that was headed straight for Rankins Springs. Buddy assured me it was all right to go to Forbes.

'My family is well aware of fire. We are more than secure with all we have in place for our safety.'

Buddy seemed dismissive, and it wasn't long before the line clicked.

I was not one of them. I was a Westerner. An enemy of sorts. They lived a cloistered life, wrapped up in their worship, family, and land, and I was now being told to mind my own business. I was hurt, and he was rude, but in the end Buddy was right. It was none of my business. To race back there might prove detrimental to me. In that moment I could see I'd always cared too much for others, and not enough about myself. Forbes, here I come.

I did not expect the flood of tears that streamed down my face as I drove towards Forbes. I offered a prayer as I drove; praying that their Gott would protect them all, keep them all safe. I could hear Ceri's words now.

'Worrying cannot change it.'

'Thank you,' Ceri, I said out loud to the clouds in the sky. 'I hope one day we meet again, so I can thank you for your kindness and wisdom openly shared with me.'

Forbes had once been a gold rush town; now agriculture was its lifeblood. Roads once built for camel and bullock trains to turn in, remained their original size but were now tar-sealed and massive. Buildings from the late 1800s still stood tall and proud, and the town's clean lakes and well-maintained parks were made pretty by boxes of shaded flowers. The heat had taken its toll, but there were still green spots everywhere you looked, especially around the community parks and picnic spots. Their tourism shop was closed for the afternoon with a map of camping places and their phone numbers sticky taped to the window. The closest was Forbes River Caravan Park.

I called the number, hoping to book a spot. It was nearly October, and I knew nomads of all ages were now heading towards cooler climates as summer beckoned, which meant holiday parks were filling up fast. The answer to my query was, 'No, sorry, we are full.' Fingers crossed, I called the other three numbers, hoping to find a camp spot for the next night or two. The second answer was the same as the first. 'Was there something on? A festival of some sort?' I asked the campground manager.

'Oh yes, we have auditions for the show, *Madame Butterfly*.'

I knew from my previous travels that this would be a big production for the surrounding community; this was their night to shine.

I was running out of options; there was no place to stay. They pointed me to the local municipal park where I was told to contact the local ranger to see if there was a space for me. But finding the ranger was tricky, as he did not appear to be answering his phone. There was only one thing for me to do. I would drive to the municipal park myself. I wanted to stay in Forbes, the place looked interesting, plus it was getting dark, and I am not one for night driving. As fate would have it, my headlights shone on the ranger just as he was locking the gates, and I could not get out of the cab fast enough.

'Stop! Don't lock up yet! Do you have a small space for me to park overnight?' His name badge glowed in my headlights: Otto, Park Ranger. He straightened up and peered at me through thick glasses, unlocked the chain across the driveway and ushered me in.

'Park over by the toilets' he instructed. 'I will be back in the morning to sort a space for you and collect the fees.'

He flashed his torch to a small sign that read, 'Toilets.' I drove over the uneven ground, bumping my way to the sign, and pulled up on the side where he'd directed. The sky was now a blue-black, and bright stars cascaded everywhere like little diamonds. *What a stunning sight!* I got out of the cab, my back and bum aching from sitting so long. It was then the stench hit me. I gagged as it rolled down my nose into my throat, the smell of a long-drop toilet used by thousands of happy campers every year, and I was parked almost on top of it. My stomach gave up the struggle. I retched up my afternoon tea, and then I lost all hope of containing anything at all.

As I moved away, my feet made an awful sucking sound, and I realised I was standing in poop up to the tops of my sneakers. Mosquitoes screamed all around me, settling on my bare skin. Slapping the damned things away, I felt my foot slip, and suddenly there was nowhere to hang onto. My haven was parked a good two feet away, too far for a leap of faith. I knew if I moved, I would end up in big pile of poo. I was going down, and I knew it, my one possible exit to slide my feet across the stinking slime until I could hold on to my cab door. The stinking goop filled my right sneaker as I slid my foot across, it worked! I was safe. One small slide step to go. Yes, almost touching the door handle. Then both feet went from under me, down I went with a wail of disgust.

CHAPTER 31

I was covered head to toe in poop; it was in my hair, on my face, clothes, and legs. It stunk so bad I was now retching nonstop. It was even up my nose. There was only one thing to do. I had to strip off every piece of clothing I had on, bra, panties, and shoes. It all came off, each piece thrown onto the ground. I sat on my little doorstep now totally nude in the dark, sobbing. I continued to retch my guts up, wiping the muck hanging off me as best I could with my hands, poop now caked inside my fingernails and toenails. There was no way I could get rid of the foulness that clung to me.

My wails of despair had by then attracted a neighbour who'd wisely parked quite a few metres away from this puddle. Sensing I was in dire straits, I heard him as he called out to his wife to come see if I was all right. She now stood as far away as possible, flicking a torch over me in my sorry state, a rag over her nose and mouth.

'There's only one thing for it,' she said. 'Derek, find the fire hose, and bring it here,' to which Derek retrieved the hose, dragging it to where she stood.

She aimed the hose at me. I have never felt so frightened as freezing cold jets of water pounded my body. It hurt like hell as it pummelled my skin. I gratefully scrubbed the brown muck off as she aimed the hose at my face and hair.

'Right. I think you're done. Derek, turn it off now.' She walked back to their camper van. 'Might be better to heat some water up and have a proper wash with soap and hot water,' were her parting words as their caravan door banged shut and the lights went out.

I stood there, naked, and shook with embarrassment and anger, my thoughts turning towards my now greatest desire to have a hot shower and recover from the ordeal. The small hot shower stall had never felt so wonderful to me. I lathered up, using the shampoo and soap from the Quaker family, deciding this was the most beautiful smelling creation in the universe. The water eventually ran cold, then ran out altogether, though I could have stood there scrubbing myself all night long. I padded the top of the bed with towels and used an extra-large towel to cover me. Curling up into a ball, I fell asleep, my face wet with tears.

What woke me at five a.m. was a female voice that shrieked with full gusto into operatic song. I instantly recognised the tune. All I could make out was 'three little girls,' and then whatever she continued singing I decided was not in English. My eyes shot open as memories of the previous night's fiasco played over and over in my mind. It was truly awful, my eyes looking at the trail of wet crusty footprints across the floor, the stench making me heave once more.

To reach the Lye soap the Quakers had given me, I would have to get it from the glove box in the cab. I'd seen this in action, and it was lethal, but that meant I would have to get up, get dressed and walk around to get into the cab. I dressed in gumboots with a fly screen over my hat and rubber gloves up to the elbows. I donned a short-sleeved t-shirt, plus my old comfy cut-off shorts, and then I was ready to face the buzzing swamp outside.

Black clouds of blowflies erupted as I took my first step forward through the filthy muck I was parked in, my books sinking up to the ankles. Maggots writhed beneath my feet in the oozing black muck. Each sucking step I took, they rode up on my boots, fat squirming bodies all wriggling to get back where they belonged in their stench. Reaching the cab door, (and remembering my catastrophic slip from the night before) I took each step carefully, gingerly, deliberating upon my every move and swallowing to fight back the nausea building in my throat. All while my brain screamed out, 'Move, now, quick!'

I'd never been so glad to reach the driver's wheel. Kicking off my gumboots and leaving them outside in the puddle, I turned the motor over and inched my way out. We slid and slurped for maybe a minute or two, and then we moved forward and crawled out, driving straight to the kitchen block where hopefully the fire hose was located. I got out of the cab and spied the red coil. I pulled it out, opening that sucker up full bore and spraying water everywhere, over the wheels, the body of the motorhome, everywhere. Otto the park ranger suddenly arrived on the scene, pulling up with the screech of his brakes.

'You, hey, turn that hose off!' he yelled. 'You're breaking the law,' he screamed.

All five feet of this little man looked as though he were about to pop out of his park ranger boots and charge at me.

I don't know if I'd even thought about what I was going to say next, but it was all lost now in my action. I aimed the hose at him.

'Take that, you stupid bastard. How dare you put me in danger! You must have known the state of that toilet,' I screamed back at him.

I was now in competition with the soprano. Otto lunged to grab the hose from me, so I aimed it at his face, knocking his thick glasses off, and he scrambled around on the ground trying to pull himself up. I was not letting go of the hose or my anger for this short, bald, myopic, twerp who'd humiliated me publicly. He went down in the wet muck out from where I'd just dragged my home.

His screams of anger met the riding notes of the soprano as he slid even further away from me, small bundles of dirty poop paper plastered to his face. He did his best to roll over on the wet mucky grass, his short arms and legs madly circling in the air. I had to see the funny side of this disaster, because if it had not been so awful at the time it would have made for a great comedy skit.

Things weren't so funny, however, when Otto scrambled to his feet, handcuffing, and making a public arrest, then marching me off to his vehicle. By this time, I was laughing so hard that any struggle would have been futile. It all seemed so stupid. I was angry at Otto; he was the one who'd caused this. If only he'd looked after the camp as he was hired to do and had directed me to a place to safely spend the night, not over a broken-down outhouse. Well, that was my reasoning anyway.

The concrete grey cell at the local police station had a chair and a bed in it. The policewoman confiscated my phone, took the keys of my home away and was now informing me I would be there until the judge resumed court duties and was back in session after the weekend. And I don't think it helped matters when I kept giggling as I told my side of the story. I also don't think it helped that the person I was talking to was Mrs. Otto. The park ranger's wife was the police officer. Such was the nature of small-town social structure; everybody knew everybody, and I was the intruder. She arrested me for disturbance of the law, destruction of a public amenity, and use of foul language in a public place.

I'd watched so many cops and robbers movies with Jesse, so I asked for, and was allowed one phone call. Mrs. Otto glared at me but allowed it. I called home and tried to tell Rae what was going on, she fell apart in fits of giggles laughing at my tale of woe, which snowballed in my laughing my head off again.

Mrs. Otto slammed my dinner down in front of me, hurled two woolly blankets at my bunk and slammed the cell door shut, switching off the light. I sat in the dark and ate the cold fish and salad dinner I'd been given, but everything tasted like the park toilets, and I still stunk. I rinsed my mouth out with a disgusting bottle of warm water and lay down on the bunk, wrapping a blanket around me. I wanted to cry, but the image of Otto's face as he went down in the muck looped around in my mind on instant replay, and I could not stop the giggles that escaped me.

It appeared I'd been locked up for a while when the light in the cell flickered on and Mr. and Mrs. Otto stood together outside the cell door, their eyes squinting back at me in dislike. Keys jangled, and Mrs. Otto unlocked the cell door.

'You've been bailed out,' she mumbled coldly.

Who could my saviour be? I walked around the corner and there stood Gordi. Who else but Gordi? The smile on his face was huge.

'I believe you need saving,' he said and smiled as he stepped forward, wrapping me in the biggest warm hug. 'And definitely a shower, too.'

I was never so happy to see anyone in my life. Explanations why and how he was there remained unanswered till I'd showered. Gordi signed the bail papers and escorted me outside to his hire car.

CHAPTER 32

Once I'd showered at his motel room, Gordi placed a hot sweet tea in my hands, wrapping a large fluffy towel around me. He gently pulled a comb through my wet hair and massaged my shoulders. I let go a great big sigh, allowing all the tension escape my body. I just wanted to sleep. Gordi found my keys to the motorhome, gave them a good wash with soap and hot water, and tucked me up in the bed.

His parting words were, 'I'm just going to go check on the motorhome be back soon.'

When I woke up, Gordi was sitting in a chair beside the bed, reading a travel magazine. He saw my eyes open, already the question out of my mouth. Why he was here?

'Rae called me, Tara, and she asked me to help you. That's why I'm here, not for any other reason.'

What could I say? 'Thank you, Gordi. I appreciate it,' I said, sounding like a strangled chook as tears blocked my words.

Gordi just sat there and let me cry it out. Once my sobs quietened, he placed his hand on my back.

'Want to tell me what went wrong?'

Sitting up surrounded by clean, crisp white pillows, I told Gordi the story of Otto and my long-drop experience at the municipal grounds. By the time I'd finished, Gordi was lying in the chair, his body shaking with laughter.

'Tara, that's insane!' he sputtered in between breaths.

I had to agree. Nothing made any sense. My emotions fluctuated between my outrage at the pompous five-foot twerp and his arrogant wife, and the hilarity over an assortment of mental pictures. That included me hosing the overbearing twit down. I could not contain my laughter. Finally, I drew a big breath. Gordi sat up and held out his arms to me.

'Give me a hug, Tara. I have missed our friendship so much.'

I scooted over to where he sat, and his arms went around me. I felt safe again. Suddenly, I needed comfort, and grateful I had a friend, not a foe. We ordered pizza and Gordi went to collect it and buy some bits and pieces we needed. He kissed me on the forehead on his way out the door.

'Snooze, Tara. Watch some telly, relax.'

For once, I heeded Gordi's instructions. My body felt like a tight wire. I could hear Gordi on the phone to Rae as he left.

'Your Mum's fine, Rae, bit worse for wear, but all is okay now. She is safe with me.'

Gordi returned with hot cheesy pizza. It was delicious. As we drank hot tea, we read over the police report and bail papers. Specific to my terms of bail, I was not to leave the district of Forbes until my court hearing, scheduled in two days' time for my supposed crime. If I broke bail, the $500 bail money would be forfeited, and I would be apprehended and incarcerated again. Sleep did not come easily for me that night.

There was only one thing to do, hunker down for the weekend and see it through. Gordi asked if it was all right to stay in the mobile home until I was ready to get back on the road. I knew he had a hire car from Adelaide and his motel for three nights would prove taxing on his budget. I offered to pay for both plus refund the bail money, which he willingly accepted. And I also knew that my little home would need a professional clean out.

'Fine with me, Gordi, but let's find somewhere decent to camp until my trial is over.'

Gordi called around the three campgrounds, suggesting he give his name as by now my name was most likely mud on the town's hotline. He contacted a Big 4 camping ground.

'They squeezed us in, although they were chockas,' Gordi said, rolling his eyes in relief.

Chockas is Australian slang for 'full up.'

They have squeezed us in. The downside is that it's located between a shed and the main swimming pool. This meant it would be noisy with teens and kids in the day, but quiet at night-time. Power was provided, but we would have to use our own bathroom facilities. Gordi packed our few belongings, and I paid for our motel stay. The receptionist looked bored, but as I signed us out at the register, she piped up.

THE CUPPA TREE

'Oh! You're the one they're all agog about!'

I waited for her anger to show, but she smiled instead.

'Good for you. That man's a disgrace to our community.' I got out my credit card to pay.

She added, 'We have been on his back for a year now to clean the park up. He says it's the council's problem.'

I nodded in full agreement, but I was not going to be pulled into another argument with the locals. Gordi was outside waiting for me in the mobile home. I was to drive his hire car, he'd booked it for the week.

'It's much easier to tour in this car, than hauling your motor home everywhere, and if I'm not wanted, I won't have to walk to the airport.'

Bless him, always considerate with a bit of sarcasm for good measure. Nothing had changed in that department.

The Big 4 camping ground was huge, and when they said 'chockas,' they were not kidding. Cars, tents, caravans, mobile homes, swags, every sort of travel convenience were parked on site. The manager showed me to where my mobile home was to park for three days. I expected just what they described, a spot between a pool and a shed, but was surprised to find it was a beautiful site. It looked divine. I was parked on lush green grass, a semicircle of flowering agapanthus around me. The sparkling pool alongside had a water fountain, and I could hear the gentle sound of water splashing softly into the pool at night. I could have hugged the camp manager then, who apologised that my site sat behind his work shed.

'It's an emergency spot,' he called it.

I called it heaven. Gordi parked my mobile home and was as surprised as I was with the site.

All he could let out was a big 'Wow!' and 'What a score!'

Shrubs, flowers, grass, and a fountain surrounded us, and it was ours for three whole days. I could feel myself recovering from my ordeal. Gordi went up to the office with my card to pay for the three days. I unlocked my van and the smell of caked, dried poop hit my nostrils. I wanted to cry. My pretty little home was ruined. It positively stunk. The carpet was stained; the cupboard and the bed had handprints all over where I'd stumbled to get to the shower. And the towels I'd slept on that awful night were also stained. It wasn't until I felt Gordi's hand on my shoulder that I realised tears were flowing freely down my face.

'Come on, Tara; let's show 'em what we're made of. We are bigger than a bit of dried shit on the carpet. We don't need professional cleaners; we can do this.'

He was right, Gordi's humour had once again saved the day.

We both got stuck into the scrubbing, using bucket after bucket of hot soapy water with the Quakers' disinfectant soap. I filled up two of the laundry's washing machines with sheets and towels, pillow slips, soaking anything that looked slightly dirty; even the curtains were washed. Gordi took out the mattress and vacuumed and wiped it down with disinfectant. By mid-afternoon we'd almost finished, the washing turning bone dry on the line with the heat wave that had hit New South Wales. The curtains were rehung, the cushions had been in the hot sun now plumped up, the carpet still damp, but the place was clean and smelled of disinfectant. My shower and toilet had never looked so sparkling thanks to the herculean effort of Gordi. He'd even used an old toothbrush around the taps, just in case any disease was lingering there. I was so grateful for his help.

I treated Gordi to an early dinner of hot fish and chips by way of thanks. I smothered it in a bloodbath of red tomato sauce, just the way he liked it. We sat on the green grass in the mini park I was parked in, chased the greasy chips down with cold beer, and then sat back like two fat turkeys, content after our feast. I knew it was time we discussed sleeping arrangements. Though I cared deeply for Gordi, I was definitely not after a committed relationship; but I could sense that Gordi wanted this to be the start of something new.

How do you tell a person who has just spent money and time coming to help you, that you value their friendship, but without the ties of a relationship? I thought about what he'd done for Rae, nursing her as he'd done, and then nursing me as I fell apart when Rae was healing, and now this. It was hard to say it out loud, but had to be said, and after I'd finished blurting it all out and explaining how I felt, Gordi just sat there, silent.

I tried to enjoy the sounds of the beautiful night, the fresh air, the perfumed fragrance of flowers around us. Waiting for Gordi to erupt as he normally would, push my feelings aside, his opinion being all that mattered; I waited for the righteous anger. But he said nothing. Finally, he spoke with a calmness that astonished me.

'It's OK, Tara; I've had some time to think. I want what you want. Let's do friendship only. Being in a relationship with you proved to me you're hard work. You know what you want; you have been married and you already have your family. I also want that, but I want my own, not someone else's. I want what you have already had. I'm not willing to settle for anything else.'

If I'd been an onlooker, I would have cheered for Gordi then. This was an adult's reaction, and a well thought out and rational decision. I was about to bring up sleeping arrangements, but Gordi read my mind.

'Oh, and before you ask, I've kitted myself out with a swag.'

Problem solved.

CHAPTER 33

There was still a small odour in my home on wheels. As for my friend sleeping outdoors, well, deep inside, I knew I liked Gordi's companionship, the way he was concerned for me. What I'd really disliked was his wanting ownership of me, but hoped that now, with our new arrangement, we could be travelling buddies, without the hang-ups of a relationship.

I was optimistic that it could work. This was a new day; tomorrow is always another day. Come to think of it, and with luck, this would be a quiet day after all the drama of the days before. Sundays were supposed to be relaxing and quiet. I woke early. Somehow, I'd settled all the frustration in my heart and head in my sleep and I felt pretty good. The pool outside looked inviting, the early morning sun winking over the deep blue ripples. Slipping on my swimsuit, being as quiet as I could be, I slid into the pool, enjoying the feeling of my body stretching out, loving the way my body responded to exercise. By the time the campground was awake and becoming active, I'd already towelled off and returned to the motorhome.

I made us both a big bowl of muesli, peaches, and yoghurt, plus a big pot of green tea with freshly sliced ginger and mint. Feeling ravenous, I tucked in immediately. Gordi emerged from his swag looking like a white owl, his skin pale, his huge blue eyes tired-looking, his ginger hair all bushy.

'I don't feel well,' he said before bolting for the men's toilet.

He staggered back to the site holding his tummy, then doubled back to where he'd come from, green in the face again. There was another gent on his way to the toilets, but Gordi got there first, flinging the bewildered man aside. It was the best rugby tackle I'd seen in a while. Twenty minutes later, Gordi emerged, looking dreadful, moaning, and still clutching at his abdomen. I was about to suggest he go to bed and drink some tepid boiled water as an antidote to possible food poisoning, but there was no need, Gordi was already in his swag, shivering with a fever. Do I call the doctor or take him to hospital? He refused all ideas I put to him, and I raised my arms in surrender. There was not a lot I could do when all help was refused. I warned him I thought he had food poisoning, and he just flagged me away, collapsing in a heap inside the swag.

I drank my green tea, finishing off my muesli and continued editing my manuscript till lunchtime, and adding to my blog site. I'd gained many followers from many different countries, which was great as far as my book went, a readymade audience. Then I had another swim.

By mid-afternoon, Gordi was sleeping peacefully. His groaning had stopped. I'd heard about the Japanese peace gardens in Cowra so did some research on that as I wanted to visit this tourist spot. Also advertised was a massage therapist that worked with hot stones which also proved interesting. Then I realised it was only a few weeks before Christmas. Where had October gone? Soon it was my birthday. Eek! Another year had gone so quickly, yet, in that year, so much had happened.

I called the Cowra camping grounds to make sure I could book a site. Yes, they had powered sites available and a pool, and yes, in this heat that was important to me. I booked for three days, and then wanted to connect with my family in Perth for a chat about my travels, Gordi, and life in general. I boiled the jug while I waited for the phone to be answered. Jess picked up. I expected him to be surly, but what I got instead was a warm greeting.

'Nana! Where are you? How are you?'

Jess's warm greeting was a pleasant surprise.

'I'm good, Jess, I'm in Forbes. How are you? How's school going?'

It was good to hear his voice so bubbly again. *Maybe it's true what they say about distance making the heart grow fonder.*

We chatted about school and where I'd been. It shocked Jess to hear when I admitted I'd been sent off to jail for a day, even chuckling when I said, 'that wasn't exactly in my itinerary.' That was the first time I'd felt close to Jess in a long time. Maybe he was growing up? Rae's healthy, strong voice then greeted me with love.

'Mum, how are you? God! You had us all worried. Sorry I had to involve Gordi, but we felt that was our best option to help you.'

There was such concern in her voice. I did my best to tell her all was fine when she interrupted me.

'Hang on, Mum. I'll put you on the speaker, that way we can all hear you.'

'Well, Gordi and I are getting on well, ironing out our problems,' I said, omitting the fact that Gordi was ill. Then I retold the story about Mr. and Mrs. Otto. I still got the giggles when envisioning Otto, the Park Ranger going down under the fire hose, and I loved hearing my daughter laugh as I told the story. I told them about the baby Skippy I'd nursed and taken to a shelter. I told them about my stay with the Quaker family and how I admired their hard, but honest lifestyle. At the end of our one-hour phone call, I said I would call again from Cowra.

'Stay in touch Mum, we want to speak to you on your birthday.'

Gordi emerged from his swag looking a little better, though still pale. He swallowed some boiled water and two Panadol, looking worse for wear.

'I think I'll go into the township and do a little touring.'

Gordi just shook his head. 'I'm going back to bed, but you go. Take my keys.' Gordi headed back to his little swag. 'Remember, it's Sunday, and nothing is open,' he mumbled.

After a shower in my tiny bathroom, adding a little makeup and swapping boots and shorts for a summer skirt and pretty sandals, I took off in the Getz, leaving Gordi with the keys to the motorhome.

Forbes, empty on a Sunday? Not this Sunday. It was jam-packed! The opera had opened, and someone had plastered flyers all over windows and lampposts announcing two sessions, Saturday, and Sunday. *Why not?* I found a park for the car, wandered over to the town hall and purchased a ticket for the midday show. I looked in shop windows, popping into the smaller ones still open that hoped to attract extra customers and take advantage of the weekend opera goers. I found a small café that sold fresh pastries and hot chocolate and left a message to tell Gordi where I was, and that I was going to the opera and to not wait up for me. I watched the world pass by as I sipped on a hot chocolate and devoured a fresh croissant.

The ticket-seller told me to arrive ten minutes before curtain call and I could just hear the orchestra tuning up. Goose bumps went up my arms and my skin tingled in anticipation. I adore theatre of any sort, but the circus and the theatre really do something special to my soul. A queue of people slowly made their way in and I was so glad I'd taken the extra time to tidy myself up; the Forbes community was dressed to the hilt. Every woman had adorned their body with the family's coveted bling. There were long and short evening gowns in a rainbow of colours, sequins and fabrics, and high heels glistened under sparkling foyer lights. It was quite a dramatic change from the everyday farm wear.

The men looked uncomfortable, wearing stifling tuxedos or dark evening suits, double chins bulging over starched collars, black and red bow ties looking like small propellers. The air sang with excitement and the musk of sweet perfume hovered around us. Slang greetings, once shouted as 'G'day mate' now become properly formalised articulations, dropping additional vowels in. 'Good evening, how nice to see you.' Gloved hands were offered up as a greeting.

I felt as if I'd stepped back in time to when life was slow, gentle, and appreciated. Forbes was on display this night, and what a beautiful sight it was to see.

The buzz of the town hall quieted as the single lonely figure of a violinist began to play. With everyone seated, the lights dimmed as a little bell went off and a hush crept over the audience when the deep violet stage curtain was raised to the orchestras opening tune of *Madame Butterfly*.

I was entranced as Chi Chi sang high operatic soprano notes next to Prince Yamadori's melodic tenor. It was a magical waterfall of emotions as their voices entwined in dances of jealousy, love, and hate. For two hours my heart rode a wave of emotions. As the music played, I thought about Gordi, and honestly did not think I could do any more jealousy or anger, or the stuff of 'you're mine, I'm yours.' The energy it took to keep Gordi on steady emotional ground had already proved too much, and the emotional rollercoaster was taxing for both of us. Already I felt a sense of relief in our newfound friendship, and I was willing to give it a go.

CHAPTER 34

I bought a DVD of the opera on my way out, my mind in the clouds. I was blown away by the whole evening. I got back into the car, eager to tell Gordi of my experience. Car brake lights flickered and faded into the night as I made my way home. I spotted a huge sign, knowing it was my turn off. 'Almost home,' I sighed to myself, ready for bed.

Two huge headlights blinded me when I turned into the camp driveway. I slammed my foot onto the brakes, skidding in a semicircle on the gravel. Then it was total blackness as the headlights turned off and a large four-wheel vehicle pulled up beside me. Mr. Otto leaned out of the driver's side, glaring at me, and put two fingers up in the V-sign, tapping his cheeks then pointing them at me. He was 'watching me,' his gesture implied. He looked like a right idiot. How dare he threaten me like that? I got out of the car and marched towards him, words of indignation already spilling out. He revved his engine, and a hungry roar filled the air as he spun his wheels, covering me in sharp, hard gravel as he took off.

'You dumb bastard!' I yelled after him.

I arrived back at the campsite with little trickles of blood seeping from my arms and legs. I was too furious to do anything but shake with anger. Gordi once again came to the rescue, who was feeling a lot as he swabbed the scratches. I'd one serious, deep cut on my chest, which worried him. We decided a police report would be of no use. I would only be telling Mrs. Otto, the town's police officer, that her husband was a psychopath.

'Let's get some sleep, I'll be right outside if anything happens,' Gordi said reassuringly.

He hugged me tight.

'It's okay, Tara, you'll be fine, hey, tomorrow's your big day.'

'Oh, thanks, Gordi.' I replied. 'I certainly feel my age tonight.'

He looked at me strangely. 'No Tara, not your birthday. I meant it's your day in court!'

I'd forgotten all about it. Despair filling me, I pulled the doona over my head.

'Goodnight, Gordi,' I murmured. 'Sleep tight.'

In the midst of my whirlwind gala night out, I'd completely forgotten all about it.

I wanted to be on my own. And I wanted to weep for the meanness of heart of some folk. I did not understand what this park ranger was all about. I accepted the fact I'd humiliated him, but he'd done the same thing to me. He'd known the condition of those toilets, but still he'd told me to park in that spot. I fell into a disturbed sleep, wondering what tomorrow would bring. When I woke, I could hear a lot of scuffling outside. It was Gordi packing up his swag, packing the Getz. He must have seen my head bob up inside the window.

'Come on, sleepyhead!' he called out. 'Time to get up,' he announced.

He pulled the doona cover off my face.

He was about to start singing, 'Good morning to you,' when he stopped, saying, 'Oh Shit! Tara! Your face, it's awful!'

He passed me my hand mirror. He was right. I looked awful, a sickly green sheen with deepening mauve and blue blotches covering my face, my arms and chest, everywhere. Amazing what sharp hard stones can do. My face puckered up to cry. It hurt like hell.

My day in court. Do I withdraw? Cringe? or whimper? Or do I simply say, 'Stuff it! Bring it on!' It was hard to decide, considering I could hardly open my right eye. I entered the courthouse; and who should sit before me on the Judge's chair, dressed in court robes, was the lady who'd hosed me off! The opera singer and the judge.

The Honourable Winifred Turnstone was the presiding judge for this district. I knew she knew the truth about my poop puddle debacle. I watched as the scene played out before my eyes; the judge looked from me to Mr. & Mrs. Otto, then she withdrew into her chambers, asking to speak with them both.

The awful pair scuttled off, almost crawling through her chamber door. Then, from behind the door, I could hear as the Honourable Winifred Turnstone's voice reached high notes, before one embarrassed Park Ranger scurried outside behind his red-faced wife.

The Bailiff returned to tell the court the case had been dismissed and informed me the Judge would like to speak with me. I sighed such a long sigh of relief, feeling my bones turning to jelly. What now?

The judge's chambers were no more than a broom closet; her robust figure now squeezed between a little table and the door frame. I almost had to stand outside the door so we could have a conversation, face to face.

Judge Turnstone began, first enquiring about the condition of my face. She nodded and jotting down notes as I informed her, then asked whether I wished to press charges. I knew this would only go in circles and end up nowhere, except for being a big waste of my time.

Judge Turnstone leaned forward and spoke softly. 'It's up to you, my dear.'

I stood there and thought about it. It almost choked me to have to decline her offer.

'Thank you, your Honour, for your kind offer of assistance, but I respectfully decline to pursue the matter,' I said, just wishing for it all to be over.

She beamed. 'Very well, dear. You're free to go now, but I would advise you to make haste and move on no loitering!'

Was this a veiled threat? Gordi who'd been standing nearby grabbed my hand, almost dragging me out of the courthouse and into the car.

'Tara, look over there right now,' Gordi said, nudging me in the ribs as we drove away.

Standing there, with their arms crossed against their chests and leaning against the local police car were Mr. and Mrs. Otto, their hate swirling across the road back at us. We decided leaving Forbes as quietly as possible was best.

Back at the campground, I suggested we take one more swim. It had been such a heavenly site, despite all that had happened. Gordi, however, did not have it in him to stay a minute longer. He reminded me that there were two vindictive people just waiting to cause trouble if we did not leave as soon as possible. How sad to have this hanging over our heads, when all we'd ever wanted to do was have some fun, meet like-minded people, and travel.

We packed everything away, and as we drove out of Forbes, we found ourselves quite literally at a crossroads. Should we take the Newell Highway north to Parkes, although driving to Sydney from there would take us weeks, or should we head to my preferred destination, Cowra, following the highway west? Australia was ours to explore, so why not take it one day at a time?

Gordi followed me in his hire car, which he'd to return in two days' time to the hire car company in Sydney. I drove along to the sounds of Eric Clapton playing guitar, happy to be in a convoy with Gordi again. It was one of those beautiful, cloudless days and I was finally free from the evil twins at Forbes, excited to arrive at our next destination. Cowra, move over and make room for two more!

Cowra was a pretty township, not so much known for its gold or farming as it was for its history. They detained Japanese prisoners here during the Second World War. The campground looked almost empty, and the temperature was in the high thirties by the time we arrived. I paid at the office for a week to stay on a powered site and the camp manager walked us over. Great! The site was positioned under a large, old, shady tree, which meant I could have all the van's windows wide open with all insect screens tightly secured. While Gordi set up his swag, I announced I was off to the pool for a cool down. Gordi surprised me, claiming tiredness.

'I'm going to head on up to the camp office to buy some maps, then take a nap.'

I let the pool cool my body down and would not have been surprised if the water around me sizzled, my body was so hot. My cuts and bruises healing not so my indignation. After a dip, I headed back, and the scene that greeted me took me by surprise; Gordi had bought me an ice cream cake from the camp office shop, and it was melting fast in the heat! The candles had already been lit and were going lopsided and sliding off in the humidity. Gordi sang Happy birthday to me. His efforts, I decided, deserved a quick kiss on the cheek. He scooped up big spoons full of melting ice cream cake for us both that was fast becoming liquid.

CHAPTER 35

I was almost positive the temperature had gone up five degrees while we ate, and it only continued to climb. Out of nowhere, Gordi produced a long white envelope.

'Ta da,' he warbled.

He waved it under my nose. Across the front in big red letters it read, 'From Your Family.

It was not a card; that I was sure of. I ripped it open with excitement. The contents made me chuckle, then cry. The family had obviously put their heads together to buy me the most wonderful gift they could think of. In my sticky ice creamy hands, I held a return plane ticket to Bali, plus a seven-day hotel booking.

'Happy birthday, Tara!' they all cried over a zoom link Gordi had opened on his phone.

I looked up and I blew kisses to my whole family, who were now watching me.

'Thank you, all of you, so much. I will enjoy every moment, I promise you.'

Gordi interrupted, 'You don't get off that easy, Tara; we are all going as well.'

I could not believe what I was hearing. I was going to meet my family in Bali in two weeks' time. Smiling, I wanted to shout with pure joy. I'd gone from grim to grin in one day. I was one lucky woman. It was not until later when Gordi's words finally registered with me he'd said, *'We are all going,'* not just, *'your family'*. Was Gordi going with us? It felt weird. Gordi was my friend now, not my partner, so why would he be included? Then my conscience kicked in.

'Don't be so mean, Tara,' it wailed. 'He has been really good to you and has come to your aid repeatedly when you needed it.'

Once again, I found myself stuck at a crossroads between emotion and logic as I battled uncomfortably with the conflict in my chest. Normally, I would have taken the bull by the horns and asked Gordi outright why he was coming with us. Instead, I tried to pose my question as one coming more in the form of a statement, so as not to offend him.

'So, you're coming to Bali, then' I said casually. Gordi looked at me blankly.

'Yes, I suggested it to Rae, and she loved the idea and arranged it herself.' Annoyance flickered across his face. 'For God's sake, Tara. Give it a rest, will you? You don't want me involved, I get it.'

His voice raised enough that our neighbour now looked out her window. I waved and smiled, my face flushed with embarrassment. The only way not to get into a full argument was for one of us to walk away. I'd at least learned that much in my relationship with this emotionally unpredictable man. I was grateful Gordi had come to my aid when I needed him most. I was so grateful, too, when his moods were not swinging like a pendulum, because he really was a nice bloke. But I still felt on some level that because he'd helped me; he expected I simply accept his behaviour. Well, guess what? The answer I arrived at was an emphatic 'No!' I was not prepared to compromise my emotional growth simply because I was grateful to him.

'Have it your bloody way,' he scowled and stomped off into the park, the darkening sky as moody as his face.

My proverbial birthday balloon had popped. I sat there in the cool night air listening to the birds settle in the trees. A cool wind had risen, and the heat of the day was fading away. Sipping a hot tea outside my little motorhome, this was my favourite time of day. I loved this reflective time when it started to feel like the day was nearly over. I could sit and listen to the rustle in the leaves, the peace in the trees as they told me old stories. A voice startled me.

'Pain in the arse, aren't they?' the voice said. 'Sorry. I didn't mean to frighten you. My name is Matilda, and you're Tara, am I correct?'

Where this old woman came from, I'd no idea. Matilda had the merriest brown eyes that sparkled out of her seamed and wrinkled face, her nose, and ears disproportionately large on such puckered features. A long faded green cloak surrounded her thin body. Her silver hair looked like a bird's nest. It sat on top of her head and wobbled precariously as she talked.

'Mind if I take a seat, love? My back's a bit crook these days.'

I pulled out a chair and did what we all do when camping; I offered her a cup of tea.

'I believe you're a collector of stories. Let me tell you mine.'

'By all means, but first I have a question. Where on earth did you come from and how do you know my name?'

'All in good time Tara all in good time.'

I was fascinated and in seventh heaven, a hot cuppa, and a story! Silence fell all around us as the birds, insects and all the animals quietened to listen in to this ancient one telling her story.

She began with, 'I was a Romany Gypsy by birth…'

She'd been a wealthy woman by marriage to a Jewish tobacconist, and a mother of two. She'd been jailed in Europe for being of the Jewish faith. After five years in a concentration camp, Australia had offered her and the two children a haven. She was offered work in service for a bakery in the 1940s, being married to a bakery owner, but, within two years, she'd become a widow. This led her to a life of making ends meet, her inherited knowledge of herbs and midwifery often saving her from the workhouse. Soon she became known for her skills. Most women preferring a midwife to a male doctor in the birthing room. To while away the time as the labour progressed, she would make herb teas and chat to the ladies in the room about hygiene. She demanded from the home she was visiting to boil sheets and cloths with her own homemade lye soap for a disinfectant. She'd delivered many healthy babies. Her popularity grew to be spread around the many districts, a home for her own children and horse and cart were procured.

'I was not rich, but we certainly made ends meet.' she added.

There was a silence in the air, I knew there was more. Matilda took a huge suck of her tea. I hadn't touched mine since she'd arrived. Once more her quiet voice began.

'Then one day I became aware of a white witch in the district. She, too, claimed to be a midwife. I wanted nothing but friendship, so I visited her one night as I rode back from a birthing. I saw nothing but beauty as she danced and spun on her toes as she called to the spirits. A white fox appeared. It sat beside her, its fur glowing in the firelight. I was entranced.

It was magical to watch as she cast spells into the fire pit. She noticed me standing there and invited me in to drink herb tea; it was one of friendship. I accepted, and I came under her spell. We ended up living as one, where I went, she went and vice versa. I accepted her offer to call my own spirit guide. A white owl came to my hand.'

Matilda smiled.

'For two years together we roamed this country, healing and casting out the spirits of illness and misfortune. I learnt so much from her and her from me. The two of us together were a team of herbs and magic. I loved her like no other. Our embraces filled us both with such love for each other. We heard the whispers and accusation of witches. We decided to move on, but before we'd the chance to do so they found us together one night, entwined one another's arms. They tarred and feathered our bodies, sealing the doors off, and then setting fire to my home.'

A movement to my side alerted me that Gordi had also joined in to listen. I was much too busy being enthralled by Matilda. When I looked down at my watch, I saw it was close to midnight; my glancing at my watch alerted Matilda it was time to go. We'd been sitting outside for hours.

As she rose from her chair, I thanked her for sharing her story with me. It was a lovely, albeit sad story, and if it were true, she would be over a hundred years old. But whatever had caused this old soul to share her fascinating story, there was no harm in it. I'd listened to much more extravagant tales in my travels, and I'm not here to judge. Gordi had not spoken a word to me all night, except to say, 'What a weird old bird. Did she really think we would be interested in such crap like that?'

I was a bit taken back. I did not like being judgemental?as who would believe my story about Mr. & Mrs. Otto?

A quick wash-up before I went to my bed. My body was sore. The cuts and scratches from Forbes were healing, but opened up whenever I bent or twisted in the wrong direction. Gordi was asleep in his swag.

Sleep came easily, but at one a.m., the words from Matilda ran through my head.

She'd said, 'I was.'

What did she mean by that? It did not make sense. Sleep claimed me once more. I was not disturbed again until at seven-thirty in the morning. Gordi was banging on the door.

'Come on, Tara, let me in!' he cried. 'I want to boil the jug!'

I stumbled out of bed feeling more woozy than sleepy. In fact, I felt light-headed, and a headache had crept its way into my neck; my head was in a vice of pain. I reached for two painkillers, wanting to return to bed to sleep it off. Gordi made some tea and toast.

'Try to eat something. I'm going to have a look around Cowra,' he announced, and off he went.

Once again, sleep was my friend. When I awoke later, my head had almost cleared, but I still felt drugged and I could swear that, somewhere in my dreams, Matilda had been beside me.

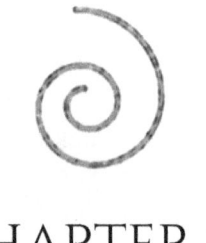

CHAPTER 36

When I told Gordi about my experience, he wondered aloud whether I'd been hallucinating, or was I suffering from heat stroke, dehydration, or had I taken too many painkillers? Such proposals sounded ridiculous to me. I knew I'd spent all last night talking to Matilda; she'd drunk two cups of tea with me! I just had this gut feeling Matilda was still around, somewhere, somehow. Gordi thought I might have had a nightmare, because let's face it; Matilda was an unusual person and a tad creepy, but she'd left such a strong impression on my mind that maybe Gordi was right after all. Maybe I'd been dreaming and dreamt she was beside me. I liked his logic and agreed that's what it was, just a dream. My gut disagreed.

I made dinner that night, hot, fat, spicy brown sausages together with a healthy salad and ice-cold lemon water. A normal night was what I needed right now. I enjoyed listening to Gordi's descriptions of Cowra; it sounded quaint. We decided we would go together the next day to see the Japanese gardens of Peace, and afterwards, the museum. By nine o'clock, I was so tired I barely made it onto my bed before falling into a deep, restful sleep. Gordi offered to massage my neck and back. I would have loved that, but I knew what it would lead to from my experience, so I declined.

We both had to laugh though, because we knew both his intentions and my weakness with massage were a recipe for disaster, but it gave me an idea. Tomorrow, after touring Cowra, I would go in search of a massage therapist, one with no hidden agenda. The morning was glorious. I showered in the ultra-clean camp bathrooms. Warm jets of hot spray on my neck eased the tension still there. Hot porridge and a cup of green ginger tea greeted me as I stepped into my motorhome, where a tiny bunch of yellow wildflowers in a china cup sat on the bench. There were the times I could hug this man, and there were times I could kick his bum really hard. Today, I thanked him. Gordi could see I was not myself, and I admitted to still being light-headed with a headache behind my eyes that would not go away. Gordi thought it might be too much driving and hot sun, and maybe he was right. We made new plans. The next day Gordi had to return the little hire car, even though I'd become quite fond of the Getz as it zapped us about quickly. As for the motorhome, it was a constant challenge trying to find a car park big enough to accommodate her. It was a delight to live in but cumbersome to park, and when we drove up hills, we held our breath as other trucks, cars and caravans all raced to get ahead of us.

We cleaned up the brekkie dishes, chatting about family and Bali. We were excited about our upcoming holiday, although I noted we'd never finished the conversation about why Gordi was coming with me in the first place. Still, we got going and made tracks to head to Cowra. It was everything Gordi had said. It was a small, quaint town, and the Japanese gardens were amazing. One could only enter the gardens via the café, then it opened out into a stunning park full of spiritual healing. Peace was everywhere.

When does one attain complete peace? It was here. I felt it gently settle around my shoulders. I knew this was what I needed, what I craved. Finding a flat grassy knoll, the warm sun on my face, I lay down on the green grass. Then I contemplated the enormous grey-white boulders before me, the waterfall spilling over rocks leading down into a stream that led to a large pond. I was in heaven. I could feel my whole body relax, the ache behind my eyes slowly disappeared.

Gordi picked up on my mood.

'Nice to have you back, Tara,' he said jokingly.

A massage was my next mission, but not with Gordi. Leaving this small piece of heaven in the middle of Cowra was hard, but one must finally move on and we'd been there for over two hours. The masseuse as advertised was a local physiotherapist and her gentle hands and hot rocks were divine. If the peace park did not quite relax me, then this lady and her magic hands did the trick. Wow! The energy raced back into my body and I felt wonderful, in control, my emotions stabilised at last. Thank heavens! Who would have ever thought that being shut up in jail would release the last year's vault full of stress and worries? We were still booked at the motor camp for another three days. I figured I'd time for another massage and booked one for the morning of our departure. Gordi looked at his watch as I walked out.

'Hey, smiling at last. Feel good? Feel like a drive?'

'Why not?' I replied. 'Where to?'

Gordi handed me a local map with a large red circle drawn on it. He suggested our first stop be Woodstock, as there were some vintage homes and an old pub there we'd both wanted to see. Then, we would head on to Orange, Canowindra, Forbes, Grenfell, Young, then back to Cowra for the night. If the roads were good, it would be a six hour round trip as there were many stops to be made for photographs and sightseeing. I was game if Gordi shared in the driving, changing over on our way back from Boorowa.

'Game on,' he shouted.

He gave me a high five as we left the physiotherapist's office. The receptionist smiled.

'Nice to see a happy couple.'

Gordi smirked. I felt my spine stiffen but did not have the energy to correct her.

We filled up with petrol before heading down the Olympic Highway to Young, buying two packs of ham salad sandwiches plus a chocolate ice cream each on the way.

'Think we are going to starve?' Gordi laughed.

I threw the sandwiches at him. 'Don't be such a smart arse; just say thank you and enjoy now drive.'

This was exciting stuff. We were touring, taking photographs, and meeting and talking to people, just as I'd imagined we would. As we munched and licked our melting ice creams, I spied an old railway bridge that was maybe half an hour out of Cowra. It was abandoned, falling apart, a photographer's dream. Gordi and I were spellbound as we wandered around in the field around it, both of us vying to get the best shot ever. Talk about competitive. The bridge was amazing. It had to be early 1900s and built with handmade bricks that climbed up into stacks at least thirty metres high.

On top sat massive wooden railway sleepers, with steel railway tracks placed on top of that, built across approximately a ten-acre valley to form a bridge the steam trains had once thundered over. You had to stop and think about how on earth they'd built all that? It brought back memories of my father and stories told of how he'd worked with his father building tunnels. Dad was only twelve years old at the time but worked full time for my grandfather running a bullock team, yet he always referred to it as the good old days! I stood there and wondered about the people who lived and died there, building railways across Australia, and the families, wives and children that came with the flow of railway workers. Most of them had been Irish/Italian immigrants. Where did they all go to from there? Did they all survive, and where were the families of those survivors now?

There was a sign that said 'beware of snakes' on the gate leading into the field. I guess as a traveller, one sees so many warning signs along the way that after a while they just become blasé until something happens.

A long brown snake slithered across Gordi's boot, resting on the top of his bootlaces, then casually carried across the top of the boot. I stopped talking, which alerted Gordi, who picked up on my cue and followed my gaze, looking downward.

'What?'

Then he froze too, and we stood as still as statues, watching it as it moved between us, the brown, sunburnt grass the perfect camouflage for its body. Gordi's eyes widened until he saw the tail end of the snake slither away from us. I'm not terrified of snakes, but I certainly have an extremely healthy respect for all Australian snakes; some of them named the deadliest snakes in the world.

Gordi was not calm, having a loud anxiety attack, and lifting his boots up and down on the spot like a German slap dance.

'Fucking snakes!' he roared at the other tourists, at the cars travelling by, and into my face. He was the most hysterical I'd ever seen him, white-faced, eyes bulging.

'Gordi stop, it's gone,' I yelled, trying to snap him out of it. He was so intent on roaring his fear to the world, I finally had to slap him. He stopped and looked at me with disbelief, his chin wobbling.

'You just hit me.'

'Sure did, Gordi. Now shut up and listen. The snake's gone, and so should we.'

I grabbed him by the hand and dragged him back to the car, stuffing him into the passenger's side. By the look of him, he was not even capable of turning the key. Young was a two-hour ride away, and Gordi's colourful imagination of his meeting with the snake only grew with his retelling of it; he'd me entertained the whole way from Cowra to Young. The experience for him had now become something of a ten-foot anaconda that spat fire. By the time we'd reached our destination, Gordi had become the equivalent of Australia's Steve Irwin. In fact, he'd become New Zealand's first snake whisperer.

CHAPTER 37

The history of New South Wales' smaller towns was once gold; now it's wineries and farming. Young has the history of being the first township to turn on electricity in New South Wales. Pulling over we found the museum, taking photographs of different interests, before climbing back in the cab.

Canowindra was another exceedingly small township that boasted an amazing glass window in St. Mary's Catholic Church. It was everything the brochures had said it was, beautiful. The way it caught the sun's afternoon light, teasing the blues and reds to come out and play on the quiet, carpeted aisles of the church, weaving a rainbow of colour. But it was late afternoon, and we did not want to miss the next small township turnoff, so we got back behind the wheel, chasing the dying sun back into Cowra.

The roads in the country are bare of heavy traffic. In fact, you're lucky if you pass another car every half an hour. The fields in the hot sun are burnt bare, though the one thing you can plainly see is where the last fire was. It leaves a sad trail of blackened stumps, trunks, and branches. The miracle is that beyond every recent wildfire there is evidence of new life bursting forth from empty husks in the form of green buds, leaves, creepers, grasses everywhere. It is Mother Nature at her best, busy repairing what fire has destroyed. With Gordi calmed down and now behind the wheel, I could focus on taking photos, though I was not that comfortable with this camera as it was fairly new to me. It was time to play with my limited knowledge of digital photography. It was time to have some fun.

The sunset was amazing. You know a bushfire is somewhere close when you see orange and crimson stains across the sky. That was the scene as we drove towards our last stop. Gordi stopped the car and we both got out and leaned across the bonnet in awe of what was unfolding before us. The setting sun glowed like a drop of crystal amber hung against a deepening blue sky. Clouds of deep orange and red surrounded it, staining the sky dark crimson as the night closed in. A golden line across the horizon gave off a sudden flare, then darkness took over, both of us mesmerised by the display of colour and light. There seemed to be a momentary hush, a silence, before the power of nightly force took over, inviting frogs, beetles, crickets, and insects to sing their nightly songs.

The only place that looked open on the road going back was the Ostrich farm. When we drove up the owner was already bringing in the signboards, but she unlocked the shop so I could have a look around. Gordi was not interested in tourist curios, so he sat in the car talking on his phone. I went inside, admiring the beautifully carved and hand-painted Ostrich eggs on display in hand-carved wooden cradles. They'd worked mosaic art into the eggshells, and the famous oil for arthritis sufferers came in tubes and tubs of all sizes.

The shop owner was extremely helpful; telling me in detail how the oil was extracted and how the small community all helped to support each with their arts and crafts to contribute towards the running of the shop. It reminded me of the Wallows, the Quaker family who understood the power of community and unity. A warm feeling came over me as I remembered my time with them.

Cowra was deserted when we drove back to the campgrounds; our site looked gloomy under a tree with no lights on.

'Time for a coffee?' Gordi enquired.

I made toast and smothered it in lemon butter with Gordi producing mugs of frothy cappuccinos, and we took them outside to enjoy in the night air before it was bedtime. Gordi had pulled the maps out again and was marking the road to Sydney.

'Anywhere you want to stop off on the way, Tara?'

Through a mouthful of toast, I garbled, 'Bathurst and Katoomba.'

'And what time does Madam choose to be on the road? When do you think you will be awake?'

Sometimes having a conversation with Gordi felt like I was going on a quiz show.

'Gordi, we have just come back from a five-hour trip. Can we please digest that first? Can we just have a quiet supper and get up early to plan the next stage of our trip?'

Gordi slammed down the map and flung the remains of his coffee on the ground.

'Fine! Have it your way.' And once again he stomped off into the campgrounds.

God give me strength. He was doing it again. This time, I got up, put my plate and mug inside on the bench and went to my bed, locking the door behind me and switching off all the lights, leaving him out there in the darkness.

Sunlight seeped through the curtains and the birds sang a morning chorus, then I was up and in the camp shower. I felt brilliant and full of energy with a spring in my step; walking back to my home I felt so clean, refreshed, and alive I began to sing. I was greeted by another couple, who'd arrived in the night, and we got talking about motorhomes as we had the same type of camper van. Before long we were sharing travel stories, where they'd been, what they'd seen.

It was Maureen's and Kate's first time on the road as partners from Sydney, who were heading for Cairns via Perth as they circumnavigated the country. We swapped road stories as travellers do, and departed in goodwill, each wishing the other safe travels. I was in such a good mood; this is why I love travelling. I wandered back to the motorhome, and as I approached, Gordi was already standing there, fists clenched, his face red. He was already packed, the Getz idling.

'Hurry up, I'm about to get on the road!' he said impatiently.

It took my breath away how this man could be so damned infantile one minute, then an understanding adult the next. There was something wrong with him. He needed some sort of emotional help with this, I was sure.

'Come on, for God's sake! Let's go, and stop talking to those two,' he commanded, giving the two ladies in the distance a filthy look.

I knew the answer brewing in me now, was going to make him pop his cork, but I was not prepared to travel anymore with this angry man. Yesterday he was my caring friend, today he was a bad-tempered moron. I just could not do it anymore.

'Gordi, you go on your own. I will see you in Sydney at the airport when we fly out to Bali,' my happiness gone with his constant mood swings.

Gordi's look of disbelief only confirmed my feelings.

He took a step towards me.

'I meant what I said, let's go, now!'

So now he was trying to bully me. I held up my hand as he opened his mouth to argue and hurl insults.

'Enough, Gordi. Go away. I mean it. You're too hard to travel with.'

My two new friends Maureen and Kate wandered over, both standing beside me.

Kate asked, 'You alright, mate?'

I let go of the biggest sigh and shook my head.

Maureen walked over to Gordi. 'On your way now. This lady has asked you nicely, now I'm telling you, on your way before I ring the cops.'

Gordi stared at me, anger convulsing in his neck veins. He got in the Getz, put his foot down, and tore off a patch of dirt as he took off; gravel clattered against the side of my little home, and the only emotion I felt was enormous relief. Normally, I would try to please to make things better, but I was changing. This trip was about me now, and that meant telling it like it is. I did not need the stress, and, so far, I'd been letting stress dictate to me again, so enough was enough. My new golden rule, if and when I sought a future travelling companion, it would come with a clause; stress-makers need not apply. I thanked the girls.

'No worries, Darl.' Kate said. 'Are you okay?'

'I certainly am Kate. I've never been better.'

Sydney is only four hours away, and I'd four days to get there. I asked the manager if I could have another two nights' stay at the park, to which the office agreed. I paid the fee, then went for a swim, excited at the thought I could now tour some more; now I'd the freedom to go wherever I wanted again, and I decided this time to go north of Cowra to Woodstock, ending the trip at Orange. Breakfast was the first order of the day. I was starving and made boiled eggs, tea, and toast, all the while googling interesting things to see in the townships, I'd planned to explore between Cowra and Sydney. I was about to book a tour when my phone rang.

'Mum, I need your help.'

CHAPTER 38

Just when I thought I was in the clear, simplifying my life, something else always complicated my plans. I imagined throwing my phone out the window and leaving for the bush for good, ignoring them all. Instead, and like I always did, I answered as all mums do when they're needed.

'Hi, honey, what's up?'

'Mum, I wanted to announce this at a better time, but I have to tell you now. I am pregnant again, but my pregnancy has sent Jess off the rails, and he wants to run away,' she said, the stress in her voice rippling down the line.

'Well,' I replied, 'You gave us both a rough time when Rose was born. It's hard to blame him for being upset. And I know this is not the answer you want to hear right now.'

'Mum, can I send him to you? Just for a while, just till we all meet in Bali?'

'What?' My brain quickly assembled a picture of a grandmother travelling with a fourteen-year-old, hormonal teenager, and it didn't look pretty. Was God undecided whether he liked me? Did I have a death wish? Why was this happening again? Now I was feeling upset myself. I hadn't been told when Rae discovered she was pregnant. She'd left me out of the picture, and I had to ask, 'Why?'

There was a pause. 'Because we knew you would be upset as well,' Rae said slowly.

Fair enough, but I was determined to say my bit.

'I think this is a bad idea, Rae. Jess and I do not get on anymore.' I told her about Gordi and his anger and that I'd sent him on his way again, too. 'And now you want me to look after Jess?'

'I know, Mum, but we have had a talk to him, and Jess said he would absolutely love to join you.'

Yeah, I bet he does.

'Let me talk to Jess before I make a decision,' I said firmly.

Rae handed the phone over to Jess, and his greeting sounded bright and full of hope that I would agree to this.

'Jess,' I started calmly, 'I believe you want to join me?'

'Yes please, Nana,' he answered quietly.

I had to admit, this young man stole my heart the day he was born, and I wanted to help, but I was so afraid of the mess it might turn into. Jess waited patiently on the phone while I struggled with my answer.

'OK, buddy. Promise me Jess, you'll be on your best behaviour?'

'I promise! I promise!'

He sounded so relieved, as did Rae.

I could hear them all talking excitedly in the background and pictured them all sitting on the couch Russ and I'd bought together, smiling at my agreeing to have Jess on board with me.

Dear God, what had I agreed to?

So it was all set. Jess would fly out to meet me and catch the shuttle to the bus that would bring him to me in Cowra. I wasn't sure whether a fourteen-year-old could do all that by himself and I offered to pick him up from the airport, but Jess seemed confident enough. He had a phone, he knew to ask questions of where, how, and when so I left it in his hands.

I went into the town's camping shop and bought him his own swag to sleep in, stressing and half expecting to get a phone call to say he'd gone missing. I knew I'd missed a chapter in the growth of my grandson, because when he arrived, I was not too sure who the young man was standing before me. He wore the biggest smile in the world. I knew who this young man was though because he was just like me. He was a traveller.

My heart skipped a beat when I saw his face; he was so much like his grandfather, Russ. When had he grown taller than me? When I'd left Perth, I'd left a sulky little boy, who I thought was spoilt. Was this the same moody Jess I'd left behind? This kid was smiling and waving at me.

He hugged me, then went to the back of the bus to retrieve luggage.

'All done Nana, or can I call you Tara?'

He roared at the shocked look that crossed my face.

'Nah! You're my nana, always have been, always will be.'

Back at the camp, we settled in, putting up the swag, talking quietly about family. His concerns about Rae expecting another child were no more than what I felt. We had lunch, then I suggested a swim and a rest for us both, followed by a quick look around Cowra. Jess loved Cowra, loved the huge Peace Bell he just had to gong.

We bought hamburgers for dinner; Jess loved the pool, then he found the TV room and asked if I minded his staying there watching telly till bedtime. I was impressed. It felt as though he'd grown up in leaps and bounds after I'd left. I wandered over at about nine-thirty to remind him they closed the TV room at ten p.m., but he was not there. From the pool area opposite, I could hear low murmurs. There I found Jess in the pool his arm about a girl's shoulders.

I knew then that this young man was going to be more than a handful. I knew, too, that today's young ones met, mingled, and so much wanted to handle their own lives and passions. I was young myself once, too, but mischief was not happening on my watch.

I stood there until Jess saw my face. He quietly got out of the pool and walked back home with me.

'It's okay Nana, really, we were just talking,' he said.

But this Nana was not born yesterday. Once we were back at my camp, I sat Jess down.

'Okay, kiddo, this is how it works. I'm not prepared to be part of what you consider being an adult. I'm not prepared to give you so much freedom that you have no adult supervision. Now, you either like it or lump it. There is no discussion to be had, okay? Next time you do something like that, I will be having a discussion with Kane, understood?'

Jess nodded, looking sheepish. I made him realise he was not here to run amok. He was here to tour, have fun, enjoy himself, try to behave and be of help when I asked him for it. Jess nodded in silence; and so, our journey together began.

We woke about the same time, Jess knocking on my door saying he was off for an early morning swim. He also wanted to know whether I would mind if he went next door to the aviation museum.

'Are you meeting your friend on your travels?' Jess's face flamed red. 'You know the rules, Jess. Be home by ten am please. We are off for more sightseeing,' I reminded him. I tidied up, did the washing, and went for a swim in the camp pool. Jess was nowhere to be seen. I hung the washing out, and, sure enough, at ten o'clock, he loped back looking suntanned and happy, like the proverbial cat that got the cream. I did not enquire why; we'd discussed my expectations, and that was that.

Jess was my navigator and read the road map like a professional, entering directions into the Nav-Man, and gauging the miles we'd to travel before we reached a destination. Jess was the one who filled up the tank at the gas station. He was the one who bought the sandwiches for morning tea. He also programmed my radio to play the tunes I loved and then showed me how to use my new camera correctly. This kid was a blessing in disguise.

Our first stop, Woodstock, was one pub and one shop. I stopped at the pub for a cold drink. They were cooking a pizza. It smelled fabulous I looked at Jess. We ended up eating hot, cheesy pizza with ice cold lemonade. Not good for the intestine but so dammed yummy. We talked to the three locals, informative about what the tourists don't get to see. There was not a lot to see in Woodstock except the old shops that had been turned into homes, but they'd kept the old shop frontages as they used to be. It all looked Olde Worldly, so I snapped a few photos. Jess looked bored. Then, it was off to *the town that time forgot.*

In this little township, there was only one shop, and it was open, run by an old lady who encouraged us both to look around. The building was so old the floorboards creaked in protest. Cobwebs hung off many of the items on the shelves. There was everything here from old lambskins and wool to ice blocks and everything in between. It was a treasure trove of old, antique, and downright crumbly.

Across the road from the village centre was a small bed-and-breakfast, a pub and down the road was the mill pond where ducks paddled; small kids splashed about under a huge old tree. The whole place felt nostalgic.

On the shop's stoop sat an old man. While Jess charmed the old lady in the shop with his stories of his home in Perth, Jack, the old man, patted the dusty stoop for me to have a seat. HE wanted to tell me the history of his tiny village.

His story was full of bitterness and hate for the sheep farmers who'd ruined the place, and for the old lady inside, who he said was his bloody wife. Apparently, she inherited the haberdashery store from her folks, but he was not wanted by her or by the townsfolk. How he had to live in one room while she'd the whole house to live in. As he spoke, I could see the unhappiness in his rheumy old eyes.

When he finished his tale of woe, a young man walked out of the pub opposite us.

Jack looked at him, waved his walking stick in the air and shouted, 'Bloody publican.'

The man stopped in front of us. 'Don't believe all this mongrel tells you,' the publican warned.

'Piss off, ya dirty bugger,' he bellowed back at the publican.

Time for us to go. I did not want us to be in the middle of a heated argument. The one good thing about our stop there was that Jess had been given information about a haunted house by the shop owner.

'Can we go and see it, Nana?'

Why not? By now the insults were flying freely between the two men, and I did not want to be the one in the middle if they took to each other. Following Jess's instructions, we drove to the other side of town and there it was an old carriage house that looked just like a haunted house.

CHAPTER 39

It was a bed-and-breakfast, apparently quite popular for the séances held there and all sorts of weird goings on at night-time. And it was up for sale. We were shown through by Elspeth, the daughter of the couple who owned it. I asked the normal questions such as, 'Why are you selling? Where will you go?' And most importantly, 'how much?' Her answer to my last question was, 'Five hundred thousand dollars, or nearest offer.'

The inside was beautiful. It was well laid out and had a stained-glass window shining onto carved golden wood banisters that led up to the private quarters. And a two-bedroom granny flat with everything one needed to live a quiet life.

Everything else was for the comfort of the guests. The breakfast bar was on the street front, and a recently added attraction was the window on one side which had been made into a takeaway coffee bar. Mulled windows from the guest lounge clouded the view of outdoors, but once one was in the garden, it was stunning.

Large tubs of water hyacinths had blossomed into a blushing pink, agapanthus, daffodils, and jonquils, offering us a riot of colour. An abundant passionfruit creeper grew over a long trellis that led to a gazebo, and, in the gazebo, a round table sat with cushions and smaller tables scattered around it. I could hear water flowing.

Elspeth showed me the old water wheel in the small creek that flowed through the grounds. It was so peaceful to be amongst the birdsong and butterflies everywhere. I could hear my brain adding up the pennies. I really wanted to buy this haven, haunted or not. Then I looked at my grandson and watched his eyes widen with horror. He was white and could not tell me what was wrong. He just shook his head and made for the mobile home. Making my excuses to Elspeth, I had to beg an answer from Jess. It came out in a rush.

'Nana, it's awful. The whole place is creepy. There are devil signs carved into the wood, and it smells awful.'

Just as I'd gasped with pleasure at what I saw, he'd gasped in horror at the feeling he got.

I decided there was something going on here, and I was not prepared to leave it alone. I asked Jess to show me what he saw, and we asked for permission to walk through the property once again.

This time, I saw it through his eyes as he pointed out the hexagrams carved into the wooden posts. We followed the signs upstairs. I now saw what Jess was afraid of. He was right. Everywhere we looked, there were signs of witchcraft. We walked into the garden and this time Jess pushed aside the vines; two moulding gravestones were in plain view. How had I missed them? I'd no idea. The place was full of signs and symbols. Jess and I stood outside this bed-and-breakfast both shaken by the experience. Suddenly, Jess moved me aside.

'Nana, look at what you were standing on!'

I looked down. Ancient wooden doors with the sign of horns on one side, while on the other a huge hexagram had been carved into them. He then pointed to the front door that had a brass door knocker; a fat bellied gargoyle leered at us.

Why hadn't I seen any of this? Jess hurriedly got back into the mobile home. For some reason, I still felt it was our imagination working on overdrive. Feeling foolish at being so easily spooked, I walked around the back to inform Elspeth we were leaving. She called out to come upstairs in answer to my call.

Why hadn't I seen the large portrait of Matilda before, as I'd climbed the stairs? Elspeth was standing beside the portrait now, and the resemblance to Matilda was obvious. Now, I was really spooked. Elspeth saw me staring at the portrait.

'This is granny, buried out there,' she said, pointing to the backyard where the gravestones Jess discovered. 'They say she practiced witchcraft.'

Ahh, the penny dropped. So this was why I was drawn here.

First, I needed to calm Jess down, which I did, with a promise to be a bit more lenient when it came to his bedtime. We agreed on an hour later. I'm sure this young man had kissed the Blarney stone; he certainly had a way with words. He curled up on my bed with a book he'd found in a shop and the rest of my gingernut biscuits.

Once back inside the haunted house as they called it, Elsbeth made a hot cup of tea as I told her the tragic love story between Matilda and another. This young lady sat entranced as I retold Matilda's story. She cried, and I held her tight as she finally understood Matilda was the victim of mistrust and misunderstanding. That the love between these two women was a lesson to us all, that love will transcend gossip and lies.

Maybe one day Elspeth would write that all important book to right wrongs and tell the story as it was. I felt honoured Matilda's spirit had chosen me to be the one who could wrap my arms around this young one while the story was told. Today, people would have accepted that lifestyle. I pointed out to her that someone had cared enough to lay a small headstone for both women. They'd known the true story and had cared. We took time to cut roses and lavender, Elspeth wound ribbons from her hair around the bouquets, laying them beside the ancient headstones. I left her sitting beside them, the sun on her hair, warming her back as she talked to a member of her family.

We were halfway to Orange when I finally felt my chest expand with air. Jess, beside me, was still shaken. I chuckled. Jess looked over at me, then he couldn't help himself and joined in. Soon laughter filled the cab as Jess attempted to describe my face when I'd come nose to nose with the gargoyle on the front door.

'Nana,' Jess spluttered, laughing, 'You nearly choked. Your eyes stuck out like dog's balls!'

Well, that was it for me. I'd never heard my grandson say anything even close to crude in all of his fourteen years.

I pulled over into a lay-by, cut the engine, and bent over the steering wheel as tears of laughter coursed down my face. I was laughing so hard now that my ribs ached.

'Jess, that's not nice,' was all I wheezed out. Jess was doubled up beside me, his deep chuckles contagious as his body shook with laughter.

'I know,' he howled, 'but it's true!'

The afternoon was hot and dry. I would make a camper out of this young man yet. I pulled over into a small lay-by. The bush smelled so nice and cockatoos squabbled around in the treetops. Every time we looked at each other, we would giggle. I showed Jess how to light the gas stove inside, and Jess offered to make us an instant coffee. I could hear him rattling the gingernut biscuits round in the biscuit tin. I set up two camp chairs in the shade, keen to find out what country Orange could offer us. Jess had Googled it already and had a request. He wanted to see the movie, *Life of Pi*, and I did as well, so I immediately booked seats over the phone.

We both studied the tourism places. Apparently, Banjo Paterson, the famous Australian poet, had been born close to Orange in the year 1864. Jess and I thought that might be a good thing to check out, and afterwards, we'd pay a visit to the museum too. The only concern was the museum closed at four-thirty while the movie started at six-thirty. I saw his eyes light up when I suggested we find a place to park and camp just outside of town in the bush overnight, that way we could stay longer and do whatever we wanted.

'Can we do that here?'

'Sure, can honey,' I replied. 'That's the beauty of having a home on wheels.'

The museum was first. Finding a park was so easy; the streets were wide and clean, and the shoppers were finishing up to go home for the day. Temperatures had dropped to a cool and pleasant twenty-eight degrees, nice enough for Jess and me to wander around the buildings, learning about Banjo Paterson. Banjo had been a great Australian poet, most famous for writing Australia's unofficial anthem, 'Waltzing Matilda' (there was that name again). But Banjo was also a composer, journalist, and author, and he also wrote 'The Man from Snowy River,' which was internationally recognised. His work embraced Australian life, in particular rural life in the Outback.

Reading to Jess, 'Banjo came from the name of his favourite horse. And that he wrote Waltzing Matilda for his *girlfriend*.' Jess had also picked up on the name Matilda.

'Nana, I wonder if...'

I interrupted him. 'Let's not go there, Jess.' I did not bother to mention that in the display case with some of Banjo's personal effects there was a sepia photograph of Matilda. The same one I'd shared a mug of tea with back at the Cowra camp. Suddenly it all jelled. I'd the feeling there was no harm meant, just a lonely, troubled spirit joining me to tell me her story, so one day I could relate it to her great granddaughter.

CHAPTER 40

'Let's get some fish and chips before we pick up the tickets to the movies,' I said, changing the topic and hustling Jess out of the building.

We sat in the car park by the movie theatre with the promised dinner of fish and chips. I'd read the book, *Life of Pi* when I was a teenager; Jess was not too sure what it was about. I was sure I'd read it to his mum and to him when each of them was young, so I tried to fill in the storyline without ruining the movie for him. The theatre was a cool respite from the forty-degree day outside, my eyes taking in how beautifully decorated it was. White colonnades spiralled upwards into a tiled and mirrored domed ceiling; it reminded me of an Indian temple. The smell of fresh popcorn and carpet cleaner had always intrigued me; it seemed this was the universal smell of all movie theatres.

Jess was keen to get in and claim our seats and special glasses for the 3D movie. This was a novelty for him as over in Western Australia you buy a ticket and sit wherever you want. However, this was an old-fashioned movie theatre that had allocated seat numbers. Then it was off to the candy bar for Jess, my grandson-slash-bottomless pit, to buy a chocolate-topped ice cream and a large packet of those infamous Jaffa lollies. The lights went down, the credits rolled, and we were transported into a magical 3D movie for the next two hours.

The first thing he did once we were back on the road was call the family to rave about it. My promise to this young man about an overnight stay in a lay-by or the bush was still in my mind, so as we left, I kept an eye out for somewhere to stop and camp. If I could not find a safe place, then perhaps a farmer would not mind if we used his driveway overnight. A sign showed a road sign with tents painted on it, which meant 'overnight camping allowed.' It was dark out, but we found a water tap and a built-in barbecue. I cut the motor and the quiet of the night immediately surrounded us.

Making hot drinks for us both, I built a small fire in the barbecue pit while Jess put out two deck chairs. I sipped a cup of tea and Jess slurped back his milo and we both stared into the fire. We'd done this before when he'd been a small boy, making up stories about the flame pictures we saw; flames tinged with red and yellow now grew into castles, dragons, wizards, mountains, and unicorns. It was a wonderful to relax and let the mind wander, and we both enjoyed being mesmerised by the dancing flames. Soon it was time to put up Jess's swag. This young man's moods seemed to have moved over for more smiles now, and he had always had a wonderful sense of loyalty towards his family and a naughty sense of humour to boot; I could see it re-emerging ,the one thing bugging him was Rae's soon-to-be-born baby. I brought up the question about his mum and the baby.

'I cannot believe that she wants another baby so soon; the last time she nearly died,' Jess said, kicking at the dirt.

'Whoa, Jess. Why so vehement?' I asked.

Jess just stood there trying to find the words. 'It split us up, Nana.'

I had to disagree with that. 'No, Jess, you split us up. Instead of talking to us or asking questions, you got angry, and you took it out on me. Rae has Kane for support now. Things are a lot different. Plus, if need be, I can always fly back to be there with you.' That seemed to settle him.

We both sat in silence watching the flames holding hands, as if doing a tango dance. I knew there were a zillion questions rattling around in Jess's head, so I took a big breath, and I gave him some adult advice.

'Jess, honey, it is what it is. There is nothing we can do. This is your mum's body, and she knows the risks.'

It seemed to work, with a big yawning goodnight Jess trundled off to bed. The cool night wind wrapped itself around me as I lay there thinking of Russ. I knew he would have so enjoyed seeing Jess grow into adulthood. Taller than me now, his body frame was changing so fast, he was so much like Russ too. It was incredible. I could hear that familiar deep chuckle when Jess laughed. I still considered Russ my husband even though he'd been gone from us for over three years, and I still missed him so much. I missed his clean smell, his massive man hugs, my harbour of safety on so many occasions. I missed being part of his life as he was part of mine. I

THE CUPPA TREE

always had mixed emotions those times when family or friends would ask, 'Remember when Russ...?'

Maybe, I reasoned, that was why I was finding it hard to settle down, hard to accept another man in my life. I missed the deep friendship and trust we'd built together over the decades we'd shared in our married life, and nothing could replace that. I went to sleep crying softly and hugging a pillow, pining for my deceased husband.

One lone kookaburra woke me, its voice on surround sound, echoing through the bush. Jess stumbled out of his swag, his annoyance at being woken written all over his face.

'Clear off,' he yelled, waving his arms like a crazed windmill.

I got up ready to start a new day. I'd no need to go back to Cowra, so Bathurst was my next stop. Jess was sitting out on the grass, texting someone, his manner surly. 'What's up now, Jess?' I could feel my patience wearing thin.

'I want to go back to Cowra. I want to say goodbye to my new friend.'

Good lord, he sounded like Gordi.

'Jess,' I could feel my voice getting higher. 'Just text her please. We are on our way to Bathurst now.'

His face lit up. 'Bathurst? Where they have the international car racing?' Jess scrambled into the cab, yelling out, 'Yahoo!' his friend soon forgotten.

It seemed car racing for Jess still took priority over girlfriends.

Bathurst is not a small township, but a city growing in leaps and bounds since it first settled in the 1800s. Once, famous for its farming, it was now known around the world for its international car racing scene and for its Holden, Ford, and Chrysler rivalry, not to mention the super V8 race car. Peter Brock and many other drivers found fame and fortune on Bathurst's speedway, and Jess could not believe we were on our way there.

The world-famous entrance welcomed us into Bathurst; and as we drove under the signage, every picture I'd ever seen of the Bathurst racetrack came true in an instant. It was all right there in front of us. The sheer thrill of driving on this track gripped Jess and me both. I did not expect the speedway would be a real tar-sealed road with road signs and traffic lights open to the public and in use throughout the year. In the middle of this racetrack that, once a year invited race cars to hurtle around it at breakneck speed, sat at least an acre or more of domestic dwellings. People actually lived in the centre of the racetrack on properties with gardens overflowing with an abundance of flowering shrubs, trees, green manicured lawns, and outdoor picnic seating areas. It was just like driving down a street in suburbia, except I was driving on one of the most famous racetracks in the world.

Jess was beside himself. He was 'actually' on the Bathurst racetrack, which he kept repeating to himself as he snapped hundreds of photos.

'Do the Ton Nana. Let's see what this bus can do!' he shouted excitedly.

I smiled at the irony of it all. Here I was in a slow, rattly home on wheels, doing the required sixty kilometres per hour on a super international track. We drove two laps of the circuit, me ogling the homes and people doing their normal everyday things. Meanwhile Jess was craning his neck to impossible angles for a glimpse into the pits, hoping to see evidence of any race cars or drivers. Sadly, there was not.

Leaving Bathurst was a bit of a letdown for us both. Adrenaline had kicked in big time. We'd done it. We'd cruised around the famous mile-long racetrack together. We gave each other high fives, a special and cool moment shared between grandmother and grandson. I think Jess thought his grandmother was much cooler now, too. After all the adrenaline rush, however, I felt quite flat.

A bakery on the outskirts of town advertised fresh bread rolls. Signs on its window read, 'pick your own filling,' and since it was nearly one p.m., and since Jess claimed he was starving, I pulled over. We sauntered in, ordered, salad sammies with everything ,Jess devoured his waiting for me to finish mine drinking from the water bottles I'd tucked in the cab, then it was back on the road again. Katoomba was the next stop on my to-do list. I was so looking forward to seeing this little town. I'd heard about the quaint little coffee shops, art shops, and tourist bits to do and see. The most famous tourist attraction was the Three Sisters, a formation of three huge rocks that looked out past rolling hills towards the sea. My plan was to stop there and find a safe camp for the night, en route to Sydney.

CHAPTER 41

Jess's head rolled peacefully as we drove along, his earphones blocking out the noise of the humming motor. It was certainly making me feel sleepy too. Time for a quick coffee. I stopped on the side of the road, the heavy trucks and traffic now passing me by, making my little home sway. I drank a half-cold mug of strong coffee then was back on the bustling highway, one long seam of metal glinting in the sun, huge trucks, cars, caravans, boats on trailers and tour buses.

The fact the roads were getting fuller and busier was a clear sign Sydney was not far off. At times, I felt overwhelmed by all the busy traffic that sped past me. They were clocking way over one hundred kilometres an hour. I knew I should put my foot down and keep up; the days of plodding along between sixty and eighty kilometres had disappeared. Getting older was a bit like that, too. One either had to keep up or get left behind. So for safety sake and no other reason I'd decided to keep up.

Katoomba has always sounded so exotic to me, a bit like some place in India. The turn off was just up ahead. I moved across the traffic into the far-left lane. At last, I'd arrived and wound down my window, taking in the fresh air. That's when I got the first whiff of a hot engine blowing in the breeze. I looked at my temperature gauge. Sure enough, the needle was edging its way up into the red zone. It had been no more than a minute when I looked back again, and Katoomba had become shrouded in a blue-grey sea mist. It was so thick it was sticking to my face. Jess loved it, holding his hand out the window as the heavy blue-grey wisps snaked between his fingers.

The one thing I dreaded was a breakdown on a busy arterial road. Pulling over into a large, shiny modern garage, I called the information centre.

'Sorry, Ma'am, we can't help you,' a voice answered.

Katoomba was packed with tourists, locals, and everyone else on his way to celebrate the Christmas holidays. Standing in line for at least half an hour, I finally enquired about a mechanic.

'The next available mechanic is two days before Christmas,' the lady advised.

'You're kidding, right?' came my dumbfounded response.

The good news was that the mechanic was available if I wanted to have a quick chat with him. I did so, his only advice being to add some sort of green goop to the radiator once it had cooled down.

'That should help. It's most likely an old pipe that has decided it's had enough,' the mechanic said, rubbing together two of the worst oil-stained hands I think I'd ever seen.

Mechanics are a breed unto their own; they're beyond me. I can change a tyre, check oil, change oil if need be, but a busted pipe in the radiator? No idea. Jess was getting impatient and wanted to explore. Trying to batten down a teenager while finding a place to park so the engine could cool down seemed like stress was never too far away. That, plus making sure I'd enough in my account to pay for everything. I could feel that damned headache returning at the base of my cranium.

First, we needed to find a place to park; then I needed to think of what would entertain Jess so he would not wander, and I could jump onto my laptop to do some banking, transfer some money over. The only place I could see to park, though, was by the air pump. Once again, I stood in line at the desk to ask. The young lady on the till shook her head.

'Sorry, ma'am; we need that area open for our customers' use.'

'I *am* a customer,' I argued. 'And the mechanic is helping me.' She glared at me.

'Next please!' she shouted.

She dismissed me altogether, which was not nice. Stuff it! I would simply park there and check my tyres, and if they waved me on, I would claim engine trouble.

'She won't bloody start!' would be my excuse.

I gave Jess one hour to walk around the township; he knew what I expected of him, behaviour wise. He took off like a cut snake. Unlocking my van and yanking out my laptop, I punched in my bank code number, changing money over. As I was about to shut it down, I saw I'd one email marked urgent. I had to re-read it, an offer from another publisher I'd sent the manuscript to. They would love to publish it, and an editor and proof-reader would be provided. This company had a long list of credentials and they'd come to me, not the other way round.

I read it with disbelief. Then I sat there looking around where I was, lost at dusk in the high hills of Katoomba with a grandson who'd just gone A.W.O.L. and no one to share my big news with. After all I'd fought for and achieved, all the anger seemed a bit flat, I felt the tears prickle behind the eyes. The mechanic knocked on my cab door, pulling me out of my reverie.

'How's it going?' he asked, popping the bonnet for me.

He poured in the green goop, instructing me to start the motor and to leave it running for half an hour.

'Then you should be good to go!' he whistled a Xmas tune while rubbing his dirty hands on the proverbial oily cloth and walked away.

I rang Jess, who ran back to meet me. I paid for the green goop and the mechanic's half hour, just about passing out at the enormous fee. When I questioned the bill, the cashier shrugged, 'It's Xmas lady.'

Then we were off to Sydney, merging into the line of tourist's cars, caravans, and huge, red double-decker tourist buses as they all wound their way in and out of Katoomba. It was awful. Everywhere I looked there were crowds of tourists, lines of pedestrians hopping in between heavy traffic.

I was so disappointed the one tourist destination just outside of Sydney I'd so looked forward to seeing was one huge jumble of beeping, jostling, tooting, screeching, yelling tourists. I felt extremely irritated I did not get to see any of it or,

Was it really the traffic and tourists that bothered me right now, or was it the fact I'd no one who cared whether I was being published?

Katoomba was not what I'd expected, and I did not want to be part of it, so I followed a tour bus to the lookout point of the famous Three Sisters. It was almost dark out, yet crowds of noisy tourists all jammed the fence line and were still taking photos of everything from the litter bin to the darkening horizon. Jess saw the look on my face, which mirrored with his own thoughts.

'Nana, this place is a circus, I just want to go to Sydney.'

I couldn't have agreed more. So we set off in the fog of Katoomba now turning to drizzle, large caravans and four-wheel drives passing us and driving water up onto the windscreen, making for poor visibility.

Driving was now a real challenge. Panicking, I took the wrong turnoff and found myself down a one-way street and facing the driveway of a block of apartments; it nearly impossible as I tried to reverse out of the tight space, what with other cars trying to squeeze past me. I took deep breaths, trying not to get overwhelmed, muttering 'Shit!' to myself with every crunching sound the gears made as I shifted the motorhome back and forth to edge my way out.

Sydney's main roads at night-time are not for the faint of heart. It was now met with the new challenge of driving her on the old, narrow suburban streets. Meanwhile, my ears readjusted to the chaos of urban noise of cars whizzing by while horns beeped, and trucks tooted all around me. It was just noise upon noise.

Jess found the campground on the GPS. Finally, we arrived at the Palm Beach Campground on the outskirts of Sydney, attaching ourselves onto another long line of campers, all waiting to get in. An hour later, we'd parked the mobile home and set up a rudimentary sort of camp, fixing a quick meal of warmed up leftovers and fried eggs. It had been a long day, and I hoped a hot cocoa would be the magic potion we needed to send us off to sleep.

It wasn't to be, however, because this campground was super hectic. The sound of people and new arrivals whacking in tent pegs or motor homes beeped their backing lights into camp sites carried on till well after midnight.

Problems were mounting. The temperature gauge of my home on wheels was not healthy at all. To fix it might mean big money and finding someone on such short notice to work on it was impossible. Mechanics were not just in high demand around here; they were also all closing down for their Christmas breaks.

I will blame stress overload here as the reason I mistakenly booked seven nights, not twenty-four hours with the campground. I explained my error to the manager, explaining the next day we were expected to meet family at the international airport in Sydney to fly out to Bali.

My small site was overpriced, and Sydney was expensive. It was an awful lot of money to waste on a careless mistake. If I'd been religious, I would have prayed for super strength right then. Instead, I fell into deep sleep, where I let my brain and heart do all the hard work of having problem-solving conversations and finding the answers for me.

CHAPTER 42

Jess had already been up and out the door long before me, and he smelled of fresh air and youth as he came hurtling through the van's entrance, his eyes wider than an owl's.

'Jess, it's only seven a.m.,' I complained, however, that meant little to him.

'I've just been out for a walk, Nana. I went down to that river near where we're parked. and I saw some disturbance in the water. I thought it was a big fish, but then I got the biggest surprise, Nana! A huge lizard walked out. These beasts are everywhere!' he exclaimed excitedly, trying to catch his breath.

'Well, they're actually called water dragons, Jess, and they're common around rivers and creeks.'

'But Nana, you gotta see them! They're huge!' Jess said, throwing his arms wide for added emphasis.

'Just don't touch them,' I warned. 'They will take your finger off, Jess. They are carnivores. Please, be careful.'

It took the patience of a saint to get Jess to sit and eat breakfast because his ever-busy legs had other ideas. He stuffed cereal hurriedly into his mouth until it was jammed full, wanting to get back down to the riverbank. To his disappointment, they'd gone.

I explained, 'They're pretty shy creatures, and it's full daylight now, they'll be reluctant to come out. Maybe if you sit patiently without making any noise, they will reappear, but you must sit quietly, no chasing, jumping up, or trying to catch them. Okay?'

Jess begged me to leave him there, promising to wait for me by the river. His plan was that I could chat to the office staff while he watched for the lizard's return. As a grandmother, I realise there are some things you should never agree to, especially when it involves a teenage boy. Reluctantly, I agreed and went to have a chat to the office manager about rearranging my week-long booking I'd made in error. To be honest, I'd half expected an argument or dismissal, with the old, 'you've paid for one week, and that's it' type of scenario. To my surprise, however, my cancellation was accepted with joy.

'We have so many people trying to get in to stay,' they said. We agreed on half the amount I had originally paid and they happily gave me a refund in cash.

In no time at all I was backing my little home that Jess had nicknamed Wayward a into its resting place behind the office block for the next ten days. There it would safely stay put while we ventured off to Bali. They returned my original camp fee to my bank account. It was painless and the staff professional.

Jess was exactly where I'd left him, now totally fascinated by the water dragons that lay not even five feet away; both intently staring each other out. I felt like I could read Jess's mind.

The look in Jess's eyes said, 'capture and tame.' I could also see the look in this rather large water dragon's eyes. 'Yum! Finger lickin' good.'

'I can just see the headlines in tomorrow's paper. Young teen's hand bitten off as he kidnaps protected water dragon.'

Jess said nothing though, deciding to inch closer.

'Jess,' I said nervously, his name sounding like a gunshot blast as one disappointed and the hungry lizard took off slithering into the cool shallow waters below.

One annoyed grandson stood up. 'I was only going to pat him.'

'Yeah, right, Jess. I wasn't born yesterday.'

With the motorhome securely packed up and stored, we could finally look forward to meeting up with the family at the airport for a week's holiday. I knew once we returned, the motorhome would have to go into a repair shop in Sydney. It was a must if ever I was going to finish the remainder of my travels up into the Northern Territory and all the way safely back to Perth.

Christmas Eve in Sydney is mayhem with so many national and international tourists. It's jam-packed, to say the least. Buses, shops, malls, bright lights blinking on and off, Christmas tunes being belted out in every direction. Everywhere there are people bustling, trees with every conceivable decoration dangling from every nook and cranny. Christmas sounds more like a jangled mess that hurts one's ears. It's as busy as New York. The bus we rode on had tinsel and reindeer antlers hanging in every window. Santa was driving to the digital remix of Rudolph the Red-Nosed Reindeer and We Wish You A Merry Christmas on repeat.

I found that dumb tuneless song stuck in my head all day long as we wandered around the Palms Shopping Centre making purchases. I got all my shopping done in half an hour. The rest of my shopping, I figured, could wait until we were in Bali. I was happy with what I'd bought Jess. I purchased a small games laptop that would be perfect for him to play till his heart's content. Especially given that most nights in Bali he would be trailing behind a group of adults who'd prove to be as boring as bat poo for him.

I also bought a pot of Rae's favourite skin cream, Rose from the French body store, L'Occitane, and I found a book on Australian snakes for Gordi, and a bush knife for Kane. Jess had become bored. Shopping was clearly not his thing, but he'd discovered the mall had a movie theatre in it. His brown eyes begged as he pleaded with me to go to the movies. The Hobbit was playing, so we stored our backpacks with the office staff, and bought tickets. Why not? We didn't have to meet the family at the airport until five o'clock.

By the time we'd seen the movie and collected our backpacks, it was time to catch the bus which connected to the airport shuttle that dropped us off at the International departure doors. Phew! By the end of it we both just looked at each other, dazed. As we entered the airport doors, I heard that voice I love with all my heart say, 'Hey, Mum, over here.'

My arms opened like airport doors, and I held my daughter in my arms. No words are ever needed when the one you love returns it to you, holding you tight. Jess sprang up in the middle of us.

'Come on, you two! Break it up! My turn, Mum.'

Kane stood back, his greeting to me friendly with a quick peck on my cheek. We did not know each other well; and then suddenly, in the background, I spied that annoying, bothersome, infuriating, irritating, smiling Gordi, whom I realised I was still attracted to in some weird way. We hugged, and he leaned down to whisper in my ear.

'Over the knot in your knickers, are you?'

This man was impossible. I smiled, not knowing what else to say, then walked away asking the Universe or whoever was listening that Bali prove to me to be the calm and peaceful holiday I intended. I did not need 'Eat, Pray, Love.' I needed Eat, Swim, Sleep. Rae picked up on my feelings towards Gordi.

'Let it go, Mum. You're on break now.' If only she knew.

Our flight was being called, so it was time to line up, get passports checked and file into the duty-free lounge like cattle. Then Rae and I begged for some time together in a close-by café where we could chat man free for fifteen minutes or more, if we were lucky. The men, meanwhile, shuffled off to have a beer, two doors down. Jess was quite happy to follow the two adult men in his life, who I knew he really liked.

Rae and I sat down with our coffees to talk about the pregnancy and how well she looked and felt; then talk soon turned to my time with Jess. I had to admit he was the light of my life, but to be honest, I found being on the road fulltime with Jess was tiring. I also admitted we'd had a fantastic time.

'Imagine that, Mum. He left home a mixed-up teen only to be quite the young adult when called upon. I guess my little boy is growing up,' Rae stated, the pride in her voice palpable.

Our flight boarding number flashed on the board then, and Kane, Gordi and Jess stood outside the café and chorused, 'Time to go!'

Bali, here we come! All five of us; it was the greatest birthday gift ever. Our destination, Sanur at the Bumi Aiyu Hotel, a poolside cottage. Heaven. Russ, Rae, and I'd made this our holiday home on the many previous occasions we'd been to Bali, though it had been a while since we'd been back. Believe it or not, they even remembered us and our names, the management asking about Mr. Russ. It took my breath away. For a minute I stood there feeling unbalanced; the ground tilted as I tried to take a deep breath.

It was Rae who answered for me.

'Mr. Russ has passed away.'

The management staff's eyes filled with sorrow and an awkward silence filled the air as bags and cases were lifted from our hands.

We followed the concierge to our room as I tried to gather my wits. I entered the familiar bungalow we'd stayed in as a family, its window overlooking the green jungle in the hotel's backyard with its old stone idols saturated in moss and vines. Rae came into my room to see if I was all right. I nodded. She was not at all happy about the sleeping arrangements. They'd given us a Two-room apartment as requested; two bedrooms with queen-size beds and a pull-down settee in the lounge, which meant two of us had to share. I could hear the loud discussion going on behind us in the lounge room between Kane and Gordi.

Jess had already made a dash for the pool, keen to hang with other teenagers his age. I gave up a prayer of thanks he was now back under his mum's care because, from what I could see, some of his new friends were curvy.

Rae and Kane wanted to be together, understandably, and Jess certainly would not want to share a room with any of us. He was still mortified if we even mentioned underarm hair. That left Gordi and me to sort it out, and I took a sidelong glance in his direction. I could swear he was smirking the whole time. I rose to the challenge by dialling the office number myself and asking for a spare cot to be delivered to the room. I hung up the phone, ready to make my point to Gordi.

'You can sleep in my room but not in my bed, okay?'

The next phone call I made was to the hotel massage parlour. Undressing in my room's ensuite, I put on a pale blue sarong, brushed my hair off my face and slid into a pair of comfortable sandals.

'See you all later!' I sang as I waltzed out the door. 'I'm off for a massage.'

I could hear Gordi muttering as I closed the door behind me.

'See ya, Mumbo. Enjoy!' Rae called back, laughing as Kane turned on the telly and collapsed on the couch.

Walking past the pool, Jess waved. He was happy. I could literally feel the stress lifting off me. I was back in the place I loved, beautiful Bali.

As my body relaxed, my mind refuelled. My heartbeat quickened with renewed energy, and with every long deep stroke and every single knead of her expert hands on my back, I felt my strength return. The masseuse knew exactly which pressure points to work, and my muscles responded. The warm scented oil of fresh lilies and frangipani evoked a sense of calm, and the only sound I could hear was water trickling through a pebbled stream just beyond the doors of my room.

After working on my back and thighs she asked me to roll over. She then began her massage on the tops of my thighs, working her way gently down my tired muscles, then onto my arms, neck, and shoulders. I must have drifted off to sleep, because she came back to wake me an hour later.

The Cuppa Tree

'Miss Tara, your herbal shower is now ready,' she said.

She spoke in such a soft, soothing, and dreamlike voice. I walked to the shower where another woman waited for me, and she washed and brushed my body under tepid water; then I was free to go. She took my hand, her thumb tracing across my palm, following my heart-line.

'Welcome back!' She smiled serenely.

Her blind white eyes and age-ravaged face told me we were old friends from way back.when we came here as a family.

I felt like a million dollars. When I returned, Rae wore the most mischievous smile.

She whispered, 'I told Gordi the massage guy was pure male, you might be a while.'

I got the drift immediately, looking over at Gordi who was scowling. I hoped he could cope with some gentle teasing, because I did not want my family to witness his temper tantrums. I was here for a real break from stress and arguments and hoped he understood this. Rae offered me an iced mint juice and Bin Tang beers to the two men.

So far, so good.

CHAPTER 43

Life in Bali never stops, and it amazed me how it had grown since my last visit. Shops had sprouted up everywhere and the place hummed with life. Scooters were the norm as they zipped by us, carrying multiple bodies or produce from the neighbouring farms. I had to laugh seeing chickens in large bamboo cages hanging off the sides of one scooter; on another, a bar fridge attached to the back of the scooterWe soon found a small family restaurant and ordered their famous fried rice dish.

My personal favourite dish when in Bali is the black rice pudding. Jess and I shared a bowl, asking Gordi if he wanted any, but he just wrinkled up his nose.

'No thanks. It's much too sweet for me.'

Jess slurped as he ate. Gordi commented on his lack of table manners, and Rae looked shocked that Gordi would say such a thing. That feeling you get when one shoe drops and you're waiting for the other one to follow, that's how I felt.

To be honest, I could feel myself putting off going to bed as I could sense what was coming, so I began searching desperately for ways to avoid bedtime. I wished I were a betting woman; if I'd been, I would have won. No sooner were the lights out, then Gordi got up and lay on the bed next to me.

'Feeling better after the massage?' he asked softly.

I pretended to be asleep. His hand reached for my shoulder.

'Tara, come on we're mates, aren't we?'

His hand then reached under the sheets, cupping my breast, lightly pinching my nipple.

'No, Gordi,' I whispered as his lips tried to seal over mine.

I pushed him away, and he stopped, seeming to understand. Finally, I hoped he would leave me alone to fall asleep.

I woke the next morning with the sheets tangled around our bare limbs, my intentions of a quick escape thwarted by a large hand holding me down by my arm.

'Let go, Gordi. I'm heading to the pool for a swim.'

'I'm coming with you,' he replied.

And that's how my mornings went for the entire time we were in Bali. If I went somewhere, Gordi followed. I went shopping after the swim and Gordi not only came with me, but he also had to step in and bargain for me, arguing the price down so low it became plain rude. As we walked up the street afterwards, he put his arm around my shoulders again, trying to pull me so close I could hardly breathe. It seemed the more I struggled against this demonstration of ownership, the tighter his hold became on me. I felt so smothered I became cross with him, because in my mind there was just no need for such a display of domination. What on earth was Gordi's problem? Once we were back in our rooms, I think my face must have told Rae the whole story. I just could not get away from him. Rae took me aside into the bathroom.

'What's going on, Mum?'

I had to be honest with her, but did not go into detail, not now, saying, 'He has an ownership problem.'

'You're going to have to lose him then, aren't you?'

'How?' I asked. 'He's keeping such a close eye on me. Watch this.'

I left the bathroom and walked from the bedroom across the lounge and opened the front door; Gordi was beside me instantly.

'Where are we going?' Gordi asked. I looked back at Rae.

Rae had a word with Kane, who then got up to say something to Gordi. Gordi nodded and within seconds they were both out the door in search of cold beers.

'Quick, grab your gear, Mum,' Rae said. 'We're off to the zoo.'

We quickly snuck out the back way, grabbing Jess on the way.

The hotel driver opened the car door with a flourish, not understanding why two weird Aussie ladies were now doubled up in laughter. Even Jess was confused. We were off to spend the day at the Bali Safari Park. What a treat! The weather was awful humid and overcast, so what better way to spend the day than wandering around the airconditioned zoo? There were no long lines to get in and two cute Balinese girls who took Jess's breath away greeted us at the entrance. His eyes glazed as he took in their stunning natural beauty and flawless brown skin.

From early days, we'd loved a day at the zoo; the four of us when Russ was alive when we'd first come to the Bali Safari Marine Park about five years before, and it had grown so much since then. We were impressed. The young trees planted then , were now shady, towering giants. The stone fences were covered in that vibrant green moss that creeps up and over everything and anything that stands still for too long.

We had a quick bite in the main food barn, with no Gordi to give blow by blow accounts to, I could feel myself relaxing and enjoying the camaraderie of just the three of us. I couldn't wait to tell Rae about my new publisher.

'I'm so proud of you, Mum. I knew you would work it out. Have you told Gordi yet?'

I knew what Rae was saying, because Gordi had been such a big part of helping me resolve things with Mike and getting my publishing deal back on track. Guiltily, I shook my head. It was time to explain.

'Rae, since we have been on the road, Gordi and I haven't really seen eye to eye. I am struggling with his constant insecurity and unpredictable mood swings. I have already told him I can't travel with him anymore, and twice already I've asked him to leave, but he rings you and before I know it, he's back. We eventually make up, then he thinks our relationship is all hunky dory again and cemented forever, telling me we belong together, which brings us right back to square one.'

I could tell from the look in her eye Rae was putting two and two together. How lucky was I to lay my cards on the table and be completely honest with my daughter! Rae's face turned from thoughtful into beaming; she has always had a smile that lights up her face.

'So, what you're saying is you find him attractive?'

'Yes.'

'But as partner material, it's a no?'

I nodded. I did not want insecurity in my life again. Russ and I'd been there and grown together. Since becoming a widow, I'd enjoyed rediscovering myself as an adult, answerable to no one but myself.

Jess broke the conversation between us, sighing and patting his little fat belly.

'Right! What's next?' he asked, wanting us to stop chattering and get a move on.

'OK, Jess, lets check out and watch the Bali Agung cabaret show its about to start. The Bali Agung is the stage show of a Bali fable. I had purchased platinum tickets and got us front row seats, and we sat down in the air-conditioned theatre just as the lights went down. The Balinese orchestra started up, banging their bells and gongs flat out which I figured made sense to them. To our western ears it just sounded like a lot of clanging and like someone had forgotten to tell the conductor to show up.

The show started, all three of us transported to another world of make believe. Their singing and dancing enraptured us, the drums and rattles depicting the bad guys as lightning flashed and sea monsters roared. Then the vibrant colours of beautiful women in long silk robes entered on stage, drifting towards the handsome men who'd fought against the bad guys, while well-trained animals and birds circled overhead. Their coloured history dazzled us as they paraded before us, and I can honestly say that of the many shows I have seen in my time; the Bali Agung tops the list.

All too soon it was time to leave. However, unknown to Jess and Rae, I'd also booked the day Safari ride for the three of us. It filled up quickly with Asian tourists, then we took our seats in the enclosed ten-seater bus and we were off. All manner of jungle animals were on display from tigers, lions, hippos, and camels to orangutans and zebras, doing their own thing.

The young Balinese tour guide did her best to talk above the noisy tourists. They were screaming and shouting excitedly as they banged on the windows, trying to attract the animal's attention, and then laughing at the animals that responded to their antics. I was glad when it ended. It was hot, and the noise was overwhelming. I think the guide knew this as well, because she sighed when the noisy tourists got off and invited us to do another tour, his time with a quieter elderly English couple. This time around we could actually hear her narrative.

We arrived back at the small bus station and the guide told us there was an elephant show to see. I do not normally like to see any animal trained to do silly jokes, but these performances told the story of their survival in the forests of Burma. I surprised myself by how much I enjoyed it and clapped vigorously at the end and joining in the applause to show my appreciation. There was one more thing I wanted to do, and that was to go on a night safari into the dens of lions and tigers. But our Jess was once again hungry, and Rae had that pregnant tired look, and I was thirsty, so we headed back to the Zoo's foyer Rae called Kane, telling him of our plans.

'Book us a table at the hotel restaurant, will you, honey? We'll be home in an hour.'

I saw a look of surprise cross her face as she passed on that Kane informed her it would now be just the four of us. Gordi had passed out in the lounge: too many Bin Tangs under a hot sun.

'Mind if Kane joins us? He wants to do the night-time safari too.'

'Of course,' I answered. 'I'd like that as well.'

CHAPTER 44

We had an hour to kill, so we stopped by the display in the foyer where we saw two of the most magnificent birds: a native Balinese Hawk and a Macaw parrot. Both rested on their trainers' leather-wrapped wrists. On command these birds would stretch their wings out wide, modelling the most stunning wingspans that caused them to double in size. The Macaw's brilliant blues and yellows had the eyes of a clown surrounded in white feathers tipped in black. The Hawk too, was a handsome and striking creature, its brown flecks covering snow-white feathers on a proud head with the sharp unrelenting eyes of a predator.

We ate in the silver service restaurant and they treated us like royalty. The ladies' toilets had a large, plate-glass window that looked directly into the lions' pit. I could hear the roar of the biggest male lion as he posed on a rock directly in front of me, his yellow-green eyes piercing mine. The fear that was suddenly written all over my face amused the towel attendant. Thank God for the glass that separated us. He was the most magnificent male lion I'd ever seen, sporting a huge black mane that he wore about his shoulders like royalty. He was indeed the most majestic and royal king of all the animals, and his presence in the bathroom made me want to pee even more.

Once I was back at the table, I told Rae and Jess, who immediately took off to the men's toilets. I could just imagine him, face pressed to the glass, challenging the lion from his vantage point. Unlike Rae, Jess was fearless and loved the adrenalin rush. Rae, however, declined, thinking it better to stay calm in her pregnancy than engage in thrill-seeking activities. I was concerned the night safari might prove too much for her and Rae readily agreed, preferring to sip a milkshake and wait for us at the end. We were disappointed that Kane had not arrived when it was time to board the safari truck. I left it to Rae to sort out.

The night safari guide escorted us to the safari truck, Jess and I like two excitable, bumbling kids. We could just make out some of the animals as they rested at night, hidden amongst the foliage in their natural habitat. Just then I wished I could camouflage myself like that, hideaway in plain sight, away from Gordi's eagle eye. I felt the truck come to a stop mid-way as the guide turned off the vehicle's lights. Suddenly we felt a soft thud above us even before we saw it; the guide then turned on the soft lights so we could see. One amazing adult male leopard sat on top of the cage. I swear that leopard looked back at me through the mesh, its green eyes flickering over every one of us as morsels of fresh meat.

They warned us not to put our hands outside the cage as large cats circled us, all vying for a nibble of chicken or the stray finger. I looked up to where the leopard lay, studying his oversized pads. They were as big as plates, the claws not quite fully extended, yet still sharp and dangerous. As the truck slowly backed up, the leopard refused to budge. Then, it was all bright lights and action as beeping horns and guides shouting stirring the cats, who were the first to take off into the dense foliage. All except for the leopard that lingered there still, its languid body sprawled lazily atop the truck. I could smell its breath as it panted and dribbled long strings of saliva down into the cage, probably dreaming of us as food.

What greeted us back at Bumi Ayu was not dissimilar. I could hear Gordi's train-like snores from where I stood. As I passed him on the way to the shower, I could see his long drunken dribbles were all over the couch cushions, long strings of saliva frothing forth at the corners of his mouth. His face was a florid red and the smell of rank, boozy sweat permeated the bungalow. To wake him I realised would only make him grumpy , then we would have had to put up with a sobering drunk, so we decidedly left him there in all his dribble . The family was sitting out by the pool enjoying a cold drink before bedtime, so I threw on some shorts and a tank top and rummaged in my backpack for some hairclips.

As I did, my hand closed around a large parcel. Suddenly remembering it was Christmas Day, I realised I still had the gifts I'd brought for everyone. I dug into my bag for more gifts, pulled them out, then strolled past Gordi the sleeping beauty to deliver my Christmas cheer in colourful wrappings of all shapes and sizes. We all opened our gifts, each of us grinning from ear to ear as Gordi's snores ripped through the night.

Soon we discovered the hotel staff in the Bumi had gone to a special effort for us, leading us down to a poolside table surrounded by candles that sparkled in competition with the starry moonlit sky. They'd seen Rae was pregnant, and they knew Russ was no longer with us, and it was the first time they'd met our Jess as a teenager, so they'd a surprise in store.

In the Bumi, they waited on us like royalty as they delivered tall, frosted glasses of alcohol-free fruit juice. They then served us fresh crusty bread and soft goat's cheese on a handmade bamboo basket, all set out on a snow-white tablecloth. I was still a little reserved with Kane. I did not know him all that well, so it was a complete surprise when he ordered two glasses of Champagne and two glasses of orange juice. He held his fizzy glass up to me in celebration. What happened next surprised all of us. Kane stood up, and glass in hand, walked around to where I sat. He knelt beside me, formally asking for my daughter's hand in marriage. I heard Rae let out a gasp as Jess shouted, 'What!' and then I too choked up, overcome with emotion. All I could do was nod.

The tears streaming down Rae's cheeks said it all. My daughter stood up to hold her man.

'I Love you so much,' she cried.

The love in her voice melted any reservations I had had about this relationship.

'Kane's gonna be my Dad!' Jess announced happily to the world.

Now smiles shone out from every face as Kane said, 'Well, that's the intention when I marry your mum.'

If it were at all possible, Rae outshone the sun and the moon and everything else in the night sky in that moment. Jess whooped and jumped in the pool, fully dressed. As I was sitting closest to the pool, I was the one who ended up with a huge puddle in my lap, looking much like a drowned cat. Rae spluttered, Kane let rip with a belly laugh, and Jess lay in the pool.

'Move over, Jess,' I shouted as I jumped in beside him.

We arrived back at the rooms, soaked and smiling, a team of happy people, Gordi still fast asleep on the couch. We decided we would leave him there for the night and Jess would have the spare bed in my room; an arrangement I was happy with. It was bedtime for us all, and we all exchanged soft goodnights and hugs between the four of us. What a peaceful, loving way to end the night!

Bali wakes early. The sound of scooters grows from a mumble to a loud grumble, hour by hour. Waves of noise seem to flow over the tall stone wall dividing the city street and our hotel. I found it hard to sleep, and the pool looked like an inviting, peaceful exit from our room. I slipped into the pool and did some serious swimming. The desserts would kill my waistline if I were not careful, and we still had a few days to go before we left Bali.

I was on my fifth lap, feeling my muscles stretch and release, when I saw a watery image of Rae standing beside the pool waiting for me. I trod water, greeting her.

'Morning, honey.'

Rae held out her left hand which flashed a small diamond and pearl ring at me.

'I'm engaged, Mum! I'm actually engaged!'

I wanted to hug her, but it was a bit hard as I was in the pool, so I patted her arm instead.

'You deserve it, Rae. You deserve all the happiness in the world!'

I knew I was going to cry in that moment, so did she. My chin wobbled, and I ducked under the water to carry on with my swim. I wanted to cry with a strange loneliness that hurt deep in my chest, but I also wanted to sing with my heart full of happiness for my little girl. As I dried myself off, the sun warming my back, I could see Rae resting there in the shade under the balcony. Next to her were our rooms; the lounge window faced the pool, and when I looked up, I could not believe what I saw next. Gordi stood there in full view, calmly scratching his scrotum.

Kane had already gone out for an early morning jog, he pulled up next to me poolside, equally dismayed by the view.

'Not a pretty sight,' he said. 'Oi, mate, we can all see you! Put your bloody undies on!'

Everything about Gordi annoyed me.

Kane had organised a family day at the Bali water bomb park, but I opted out, preferring to do a little shopping, followed by a facial and manicure. But all our plans left Gordi on his own, so at breakfast we encouraged him to go on a tour up to the mountains to see the sights before all meeting up again for dinner. I think we all sighed with relief when Gordi finally agreed to go.

At the Bumi, they do everything for you, which means no housework. All

The Cuppa Tree

I had to do was get dressed from togs to cotton sarong and walk out of the hotel and down the street three doors to the beauty parlour. Again, the staff all remembered me from my last visit.

'Welcome, Mama Tara,' they chimed in welcome, the girls all looking lovely in their hot pink sarongs.

After my facial, they massaged my hands in softening creams, my nails soaked in scented water while Keechi, the owner, was busy telling me how her Aussie husband had built a new house for holidaymakers. She showed me a photo of the house and immediately my opportunity antenna went up. It would be a perfect holiday home for us all! She said they were considering renting it for three months or longer, and they were discussing the rental with their agents tonight, which in Bali means bargaining, and is what the Balinese excel at. She knew I was interested and promised to show me around after my nails dried. Keechi brewed ginger tea; . When I was finished, she asked me to wait out the back under the frangipani tree. There she would pick me up. I should not have been surprised when she arrived on a scooter and gave me a helmet.

'Get on!' she yelled over the sound of a thousand other scooters on the road.

This was going to be fun. Fear and excitement are such a heady mix. Off we went, whizzing in between cars, past scooters and people, downside roads, around tiny shops that were no more than openings in the walls. We zoomed past skinny dogs, fat babies, happy families playing. The Balinese are used to the mad tourists, the locals wave and smile as you fly by. I am not sure why we tourists think the Balinese are awed by our bravery, since the mad scooters and zero road rules are a normal part of their daily life. I was no different though, and I got caught up in the spirit of it too, waving and smiling back at them as though I were a superstar.

I could see why Keechi wanted me to see the house. It sat on the edge of a lush forest and was an entertainer's dream with indoor and outdoor kitchens, a spa and a lap pool, and a private movie theatre that would make a grown man cry. I wanted to rent it then and there, but there was only one problem. I told her I would talk to my family and meet with her again. I loved the slow life and the Bali vibe and knew I was smitten. This would be perfect for us as a getaway. The other option was, I could live here permanently.

CHAPTER 45

There is no rushing to anywhere in Bali because your time is always yours to do what you please. I wandered back through the shops, and enjoyed engaging in the bartering dance, where in Bali it is customary to have bit of haggling, and, if not happy, we both simply shrug, smile, and move on. This was why I loved Bali. Everything was always easy.

This time, though, I found Bali was becoming more frantic than ever. The old Bali that used to live on its own clock, where one could take the time to shop, have a cup of tea, chat to a neighbour or customer, was fast disappearing. I lay down in the sunny room of the bungalow and curled up into a nana nap, relishing the quiet time I had with a good book and a lie down. The family and Gordi had gone out exploring what remained of the old Bali and I hoped they would stay away for another hour or two.

I was fast asleep when I heard the front door open. I carefully opened one eye to see who it was. If it were Gordi, I intended to get up and spend some time with him. I'd been feeling guilty for not spending any time with him lately and thought perhaps we could go out for a drink. If it was family, I was going to stay right where I was, like a cat curled up asleep in the sun. Gordi sat himself down on the edge of the bed where I lay. Before I could get a word out edgewise, Gordi interrogated me about my day; where I'd been, why, and with whom.

This man could drain my energy in five minutes flat.

I got up to move into the lounge. When I tried to slip by him, he gave me a peck on the cheek.

'That's for Christmas, babe,' he explained.

Then he tucked an envelope under my arm as I quickly escaped through the door to the lounge.

'Thought you might like this.'

My heart sank, I did not want gifts or kisses from him. Opening the envelope, I found a brochure with a deep mauve sunset printed on its cover; inside were two tickets for dinner on a ketch.

'Gordi you shouldn't have, really. It's too much.'

Gordi flapped his hands at me.

'I wanted to give you a combined birthday and Christmas gift, and to apologise for my behaviour last couple of months.'

To decline would be childish, so I accepted. 'Thank you; it's lovely.'

My gift to him lay on my bed, giving it to him seemed flat, after looking at his gift to me. Gordi simply tucked it under his pillow and said 'Thanks Tara"

Gordi joined me in the pool, and although swimming is not for him, he enjoyed dunking me as I went by him. He still did not understand that swimming, for me, is necessary exercise. I know when my body needs to stretch out because of a lower back injury and whiplash in my teenage years, plus contracting a mild case of polio. These days with migraines and backaches as my bug bears, swimming controls it.

By the time the family turned up from their day at the water bomb park, I was once again tired of Gordi reaching for me as I swam by. I kept quiet, but a peacekeeper I am not. The older I get, the more I seem to lose the will to mix with toxic and stupid behaviour. Jess and Rae joined me in the shallows, while Kane opted for a lie down, and Gordi continued to act like king-sized dope in the pool.

I told Rae about the house I'd just seen, and my plans to meet Keechi again for lunch and the scooter ride. I also told Rae about the dinner for two on the ketch.

'Good luck on that one.' She chuckled.

Gordi slowly swam past me again almost touching me. For some reason it was the last straw. I was having a conversation with my daughter and he kept swimming between us. When his head popped up out of the water, I blurted so loudly.

'Enough, behave, or go to your room!'

I could not believe the words that escaped my mouth. Gordi stopped mid-slither. My family also shocked that I would yell in such a tone to anyone, but this man was driving me nuts with his constant need for attention.

Dusk had settled on the beaches of Bali. Gordi, now chastened enough to be an adult, was ready and waiting. I'd deliberately dressed down: no makeup, no perfume, no jewellery, my hair pushed back, tied into a small ponytail. Long skirt and long-sleeved t-shirt. Rae came into my room, putting her arm about my shoulders.

'Are you sure about this?' she asked.

Then she stood back and took stock of my attire.

'Good God, Mum, you've dressed as if you're going gardening.'

I explained tonight was the night I would tell Gordi the truth about us. It was friendship only. I'd tried many times before, but he, for some reason, thought he was God's gift to me.

'Mum, you don't do things by halves, do you?'

The ketch looked like they'd taken it from a storybook. Moored in a private dock, this was not one of the party boats which had left already to do their nightly cruise. Those with disco music and coloured strobe lighting ramped up full throttle while shrieks of laughter filtered across the bay. No, this was a private, chartered forty-foot yacht, a beautiful, two-masted sailboat. And she just sat there, gently rocking in the dark deep waters, waiting for us to board. A crew member assisted me on board. Dressed in black, gold braid hung off one shoulder. Making sure we were comfortably seated, the motor started and as we got to open ocean, the motor was cut. We glided across the soot black Indian Ocean, a full moon glowering in a silver path, we seemed to follow.

It was just Gordi and I, seated Indian style on the deck, glittering silver and red pyramid cushions supporting us. They served dinner Moroccan-style on low tables spread with fruit and spice, platters of food to dip and eat to our heart's content, and golden wine served in paper-thin, gem-encrusted glasses. The conversation was pleasant enough; Gordi and I chatted about othe day at the zoo. I told him how excited I was about Rae and Kane's engagement, and then about my scooter ride around Sanur. Gordi told me about his day up in the mountains. He'd taken the tour up the volcano, eaten at the volcanic restaurant, and still hated black rice pudding. He noted how the rice paddies looked like sea grass as the wind flowed over them. The haranguing of roadside sellers annoyed him, and he didn't quite get the whole thing of bartering. He'd also been to Turtle Island, where he said there was a catch and tag program for saving the sea turtles.

'That's when I spotted this tour on the ketch, and I immediately thought it was for us,' he said.

He smiled hopefully into my eyes. I looked at this man who desperately wanted to be part of my life, and here I was, thinking how I wish he were the Gordi who'd looked after Rae and me last year. Where had that man gone to? That Gordi was sexy, with a healthy attitude towards mind and body. Where had he gone? This Gordi was obnoxious and full of anger, and all I could think was how hard my news was going to hit him.

'Gordi, we need to have this talk,' I bravely began.

His hand locked around my wrist.

'Tara, don't send me away, not again. Because this time, I won't come back. I do have a life without you. I have a loving family without you involved. I also have a wonderful friend in New Zealand who is waiting for me to go back and wants to start a life with me. She wants marriage and kids.'

His words shocked me. Emotions clunked and gathered around my chest cavity, and it surprised me to discover envy was one of them. 'Then why me, Gordi?'

His reply shook me.

'Because I fell in love with you the first time we met. I knew that in my heart and my soul, I loved you.'

I heard myself gulp as the beautiful food stuck in my throat and the wine turned sour on my tongue. I knew in the depths of my soul I did not love this man. There was too much I found wrong with him. Antics that, while in all probability made his sweetheart in New Zealand smile and perhaps encourage, his behaviour drove me mad. His red-faced temper tantrums made it hard for me to be patient with him. His dripping sarcasm made me shudder. On the flip side, I loved his male strength. He had never once said, 'I can't do this,' or 'I won't help.' Consistently, Gordi had dropped everything to come to my aid. And yet I returned his love by picking out his worst faults. He had given me his heart, and I was going to break it. I did not want this job at all.

As I held onto his hand, my eyes smearing over with unshed tears, I was about to tell him I did not love him. I was about to hurt this man who'd always done his best for me, the only way he knew how. But the chef appeared from the galley just then, and we applauded them in admiration at the banquet they'd prepared for us.

Following the Chef, three Balinese men emerged from the galley, two guitarists and a violinist. They played songs on request. Gordi requested *Save the Last Dance for Me*. Soft music enveloped us, and the mood turned decidedly romantic. Gordi and I held hands. Maybe this was the right way to say goodbye. The black ocean water was calm now, the ketch almost stationary. I stood, holding my hand out to this man who'd just poured out his heart to me.

'Dance with me, Gordi.'

CHAPTER 46

I asked the band, 'Can you play Pokarekare Ana?'

The violinist took up his bow, and the music swelled around us, over us, circling us, grieving for what could have been, as a warm wind bound us together. The moon was now high in the sky, its night journey almost complete, as was ours. Gordi and I rocked together slowly, and for once we were in complete harmony. Suddenly the tears I felt in my throat became an outpouring of emotions as I buried my head into Gordi's shoulder. Something told me he was crying too.

'Is this goodbye, Tara, or…?'

Gordi's unfinished question just hung there, suspended in the air, dancing between us like a question mark, waiting for me to answer.

Bali in the early morning is serene. The ketch had just docked, and as their custom, they carefully placed offerings to their Gods before altars, whispering prayers of peace and love. Incense, thick and heady, burned from every corner as hands small and large came together in supplication. I paid for a tiny basket of rice and frangipani flowers placed so creatively in a small bamboo basket, and I laid the basket before a roadside temple of Shiva. My prayer was for my decision to be the right one: to lead a life of travel, fun, and love, and I asked for my family to be protected and loved in the spirit realm. Gordi knelt beside me then and placed an offering as well.

To respect him in his moment of prayer, I stepped away, my mind replaying my youth with Russ. Images flashed before me of our first trip to Bali. Holding hands down tiny streets, laughing over dripping ice cream under a scorching sun, making love, and declaring our love for each other with every chance we got. My heart ached remembering how he would pick me up, hug me tight. I knew that within this circle I was safe forever. Russ called me his lady, and I could feel his hand on my shoulder even now, as he'd done in the past. I knew he was there, only I could not see him. I prayed I'd made the right decision.

Gordi stood beside me, his eyes soft in the altar's light, and I noticed how they were not the hard, demanding eyes I'd seen lately. The woman who was selling the offerings handed me a single frangipani flower. I bent down so she could tuck it behind my ear, and she blessed me. Gordi had given me his heart, and it was time for me to be grateful. I had to stop comparing him with a ghost because there was no comparison. Gordi was here, now, and he was here with me, wanting me, ready to be part of my life and my family's life.

We held hands as we walked along the sandy beach, and I tried with all my might to explain how I felt, but in the end it all sounded so trivial and ungrateful and selfish. The truth was, I'd once experienced a deep love. Russ and I had grown up together, we'd played and stayed together, and we'd built a family together. If I accepted Gordi as my partner for life, then I would be asked to do it all again. The thought terrified me.

Gordi's immaturity worried me. His wild temper concerned me. His ability to think I simply had to accept his behaviour because he was who he was, were my biggest concerns. As we reached the entry to the Bumi Hotel, the night watchman welcomed us. I reached up behind my ear, removing the frangipani and placing it on the hotel's stone idol in the foyer. Gordi's eyes searched mine. It was time to give him an answer. I'd done my best to explain with as much love as I could muster, that I was not here to destroy this man. On the flip side, I was not here to be instructed, owned, or commanded either. I took his face between my hands, placing a soft kiss on his lips.

'Gordi, you're my friend, and that's all I can offer you—my friendship.'

Jess was playing on the iPad, his hair still ruffled from sleep, at times looking so much like Russ my heart smiled. Rae and Kane emerged from their bedroom.

'Hey, you're home. How was the sailing trip?' Rae asked, giving me a hug.

Kane winked at me and gave Gordi a high five, and immediately I knew what he was thinking; that Gordi and I were a couple.

'It was wonderful, wasn't it, Gordi?' I said smiling, giving nothing away. 'I'm ravenous, what's for breakfast?'

Today the family planned to visit the elephant park, and I'd booked at the hotel office for all five of us. My plan was to get out and see these huge grey mammoths, then get back in time for another massage in the afternoon.

The Mahouts had two sturdy elephants all ready and saddled up for us. Gordi and Kane got on the first elephant, then Rae, Jess and I clambered onto the second one. Then the Mahouts gave the order, nudging them with their bare feet to get going. It was utterly fascinating to hear the rumble and squeak of the elephants communicating with each other. Together they swayed in unison through the forest floor, stuffing huge bunches of fresh green cane into their mouths as we began our trek.

A baby elephant stuck close to its mum's side, its little trunk flopping in half circles around its face, not knowing what to do with it. It looked so cute. The other tourists let go oohs and aahs as the mother gave it a cuddle, wrapping her big, gentle trunk around the tiny baby body, guiding it in to suckle. It was a peaceful family scene. We all enjoyed it, ending our day back at the Bumi Hotel for Dinner.

As I lay down on my bed that night, Gordi lay on his cot, I heard him get up, my body stiffening as he moved onto my bed.

'Don't stress Tara; I just wanted to hug you before I leave. I've booked a midnight flight back to New Zealand.'

I did not say a word, I just held him close.

'Bye Gordi, think of us kindly, and thank you for being there when I needed you.'

Gordi picked up his swag and slipped away into the night. The next morning, I woke with a full-blown migraine.

'I think you should spend a day in bed.'

My room was definitely where I was headed. Rae pulled the curtains tight, blocking out the sun.

'Try to sleep. We will check up on you soon.'

At noon, Rae came creeping back into my room.

'You awake, Mum?'

I nodded. At least the nausea was gone. They'd brought back some fresh ginger tea. Once heated, it certainly helped. I told them that Gordi had gone back to New Zealand last night. Kane's reaction was what I expected, as he did not know Gordi.

'That's a shame. He's a good bloke.'

I did not reply or defend myself. What was done was done.

We'd twenty-four hours left to do anything else we wanted to do in Bali. Kane wanted to go on a tour, but all I wanted to do was curl up in bed. Rae was undecided, wanting to stay back with me till I said, 'Let's go.'

A tour over the mountains in pouring rain to a Pearl farm had looked interesting. Kane booked for four. Did I enjoy the tour? I hardly saw it. The deep sadness in Gordi's eyes stayed in my mind.

Dinner was a quiet affair that night. We ordered curried prawns and rice made with coconut milk, but I found it hard to eat, and nibbled only on a salad. Rae's eyes were full of concern for me, while Jess just hooked into his meal. Oh, to have the innocence of a teenager.

Sleep was again jagged. I kept waking every two or three hours, my head throbbing again, and I wanted to cry so badly my chest hurt. Morning was well and truly in the sky, heralded by a beautiful orange Bali sunrise.

I sat out on the porch, watching the early morning cleaning staff go about their duties, sweeping paths, placing small offerings of flowers and fruit before their stone idols. I longed for that sort of faith; a faith where I could put my trust in something, then just walk away, leaving the problem sitting on a stone idol's knee. Problem was, I was too pragmatic and nosey for that. I wanted to know the ins and outs, the workings of things.

One of the kitchen staff came up to me and offered me a gift basket to place before the idol by our door. It was rude to decline, so I placed it on the stone's knees and raised my hands in prayer. Then I asked whoever it was up there listening, that Gordi be kept safe and my family and friends to be safe and loved.

I have no idea of the power of prayer, and I have never been a religious sort. I have only ever kept believing in what my gut has always told me was right to feel. I am, however, a great believer in the power of Mother Earth, her herbs, her solid presence. I guess in my faith I believe that we as humans eventually disappear, but this planet Earth, our home, will always be here. I also believe in reincarnation as too much in my life has not been coincidence. Overall, I was quite happy with how I saw the universe.

I guess what was bothering me most was the sorrow I felt about Gordi. From what he'd told me, he was a much-loved member of his family. He was his mum's boy. To learn he'd a sweetheart waiting for him hurt and surprised me. Time to mind my own business; get on with my own life.

Wayward, I'm coming home.

My massage time arrived, and Rae pushed me to keep the appointment. The massage room was quiet and dark, and the therapist's opaque eyes told me she knew by touch what I needed. She poured warm oil over my chest; her hands then started kneading my muscles. Then she did something a little different. She placed warm stones on my groin and sternum in the shape of a cross, pushing small black stones into tight circles, and then placing them back in a bowl of hot water. Her hands massaged the air a fraction above my skin. I asked her why. She shushed me.

'Reiki, there is too much energy in the heart chakra.'

CHAPTER 47

I wanted to buy some pretty gifts for my friends in Perth, so, slipping out of the hotel into a side street, I found a stall that sold sarongs in delicate, detailed pastels with fancy sequin work on them. I bought four; then I spied a large one in lime green that would look good over the bed of my little home that was still perched in a corner on the outskirts of Sydney.

My family was due back soon, as late that afternoon we were all catching the seven-thirty flight to Sydney.

We all snoozed on the flight back to Sydney and spent the night at a hotel in the city. The next day we were to go our separate ways. Jess desperately wanted to continue his trip with me. I left that decision up to Rae and Kane.

Rae's pregnancy was going well. She was in good health and had a good man who really cared for her. It was soon decided that Jess could continue to stay with me for another three days in Sydney, then fly back to Perth as school was starting. They'd booked to fly out that next afternoon.

I was touched when she and Kane presented me with a pair of drop pearl earrings from the Bali pearl farm. 'This is just to say thank you for taking care of our boy and for being the mum you are.'

That was a big compliment coming from my daughter.

I booked into Sydney backpackers and was lucky enough to be offered a room for two, with all amenities. I booked and paid over the phone. Jess and I spent the next three days exploring Sydney. It's such a busy place, cosmopolitan, so we got down to sightseeing. Every morning when we woke up, Jess would boil the jug to make me a cuppa and himself a milo. By then, I had the map open, the guidebooks out and a pencil and notebook in hand. I'd called the campgrounds, and they assured me the Wayward was fine where it was. It was time to explore the Harbour Bridge, The Docks, The Opera House, Sydney's Open Art Museum, Taronga Zoo, and The Botanical Gardens.

Every day we left the hotel at eight am and toured around, either by the free metro bus, train or to the zoo by boat. Three days flew by. Too soon it was time for Jess to fly back to Perth. We both dragged our heels, both of us not wanting our special time to end. I had this feeling to treasure every moment. My grandson was growing up fast.

As I walked Jess to the departure gate, I realised he was not a child anymore. A young man now walked beside me, and he was tall, well-muscled and good looking. Jess gave me a super strong hug before boarding, then reaching into his backpack gave me my travel diary back. Jess had been my official note taker through our travels together.

'Bye, Nana, thanks for the amazing holiday, love you, take care, and take care of the Wayward.'

Where had the years gone when I would lift him up to kiss him, tickle him till he would run away, snuggle with him on the bed, rough and tumble with him on the lawn? This young man now met me, eyeball to eyeball. It was so hard to walk away. It was hard to wave goodbye. If only Russ could have stood beside me now, to see our future board the plane.

It's not like me to be maudlin, but, faced with my mortality, I suddenly wanted to cover as much ground as I could and write as many books as possible, and photograph and paint beautiful places. With this renewed outlook, I wanted to pack as much fun and travel into my life as soon as possible so, where to next? I was excited to think what interesting conversations lay ahead, what new strangers I might meet, who would pass through my life? A range of emotions kept running through me. Excitement filled me as I thought about where I was heading next.

I felt a slight pang of sadness as I packed away the tour diary Jess kept for me. His messy handwriting, his scribbles, and doodles in red ink of funny faces drawn beside comments made me miss him even more. I felt sadness about Gordi too. Time to move on, Tara; time to pick up the Wayward. Time for more travelling; the Northern Territory beckoned.

Finding my way back to the Palm Beach Camping Ground took two hours and two buses. Everywhere I looked, I thought I saw Jess. Finally, I was unlocking the door to my motorhome. I put my backpack inside and went to inform the camp office I was leaving. Turning onto the main road in Sydney in Friday midday traffic was no mean feat. I could not have chosen a worse day to head north. The queue into any gas station was long, so I chose the last one I could see before dusk. I found it had a dirt field behind it for campers to park overnight. Perfect. My phone had many messages. One at five a.m. one week ago, my great aunt in Adelaide had died.

I felt incredibly sad and old; I was the last remaining woman in the female line. I wondered if she'd left her story behind, somewhere, so others could read of her struggles and triumphs. Or maybe? that's what I was meant to do.

I filled up with petrol and oil and checked the tyres with the pressure gauge. I made sure the water system was all filled.

Making myself a toasted baked bean sandwich and a most welcome hot cup of tea, I sat back and thought about Bali, my great aunt and Gordi. I cleaned up, putting away the plates in the sink. My hands shook, in fact my whole body sagged with grief and loss. Sitting on my small bed, I cried for loss of family and friends till there were no tears left.

CHAPTER 48

It was time for me to settle down under a starry night sky and get a good night's sleep. Tomorrow would be a long day and Alice Springs was a long way, so I needed to head out to the highway at the crack of dawn. The map showed I could drive two ways; one way would take me through some dry, out of the way places. The other was via the Stuart Highway, which seemed the more sensible route and main artery to Alice Springs, some 3,000 kilometres away.

The next morning, I followed two large caravans out of the layby. They say Australia runs on road trains, and that is the truth. Before we could even get onto the highway, we all had to wait for three road trains to go past, each one carrying various amounts of mining equipment. Each road train had three trailers loaded to the brim. I love the bright lights some trucks have. At least you know when there is a large truck bearing down on your tail. It can be scary though when you're doing your best to keep the speed limit and you're stuck in between two huge road trains that are not mucking about. Driving alongside these long haulers who practically lived for the road certainly took courage This time I found myself sandwiched in between a caravan and a five-wheeler. I felt so small in comparison, my little motorhome doing its best amongst these road beasts. The temperature gauge was fluctuating madly on my dashboard, and I was getting more and more uncertain about what I should do. I'd been driving for about three hours when I finally had to pull over, flashing my hazard lights. Steam was now erupting from the radiator. It didn't look good. The five-wheeler stopped behind me. A young family had their faces pressed against the window as their dad got out, offering me assistance. The nearest roadside tavern was about an hour away. He kindly rang for assistance from the RAC, the Australian roadside guardian angels. They towed me an hour to the tavern where a young mechanic looked at my little engine. Even from where I stood, it looked old and tired. He stood there shaking his head and sucking on a toothpick like some lead character in an old cowboy movie.

'Lady, you've got a big problem here. Your square O-ring is shot. I can jerry-fix it until you get to Alice. They will be able to help you there.'

I am no mechanic, so I agreed with the man and he did what he could. He charged me a small fortune for applying green goop to the radiator while I bought and filled two large plastic containers with water.

'Where're ya headed?' he asked, looking concerned.

'Alice Springs,' I said, trying to remain hopeful.

'Well, I wish you all the good luck in the world, lady. Be safe aye, the roads are hard out there in the Outback,' he warned.

I thanked him and got on my way. Alice Springs was on my GPS and, according to its fine navigation system, I'd approximately another day of driving ahead of me.

I took it quite easy, stopping every hour or so to let the needle drop from going into the red and lugging plastic cans of water to refill the radiator. I could see green goop now seeping from tubes and mesh as another roadhouse came into view. I pulled in. Concern for my home on wheels was now paramount. No one ever wants to break down, especially not out here in a desert where the weather was climbing to well over forty degrees. I asked the owner of the roadhouse if I could pull in around the side to stay overnight, and he agreed for a small fee. Talk about taking advantage of a traveller in trouble!

Hot, weak instant coffee and a stale hot chicken roll from the food bar was my unsatisfying dinner. The Asian boy behind the counter was the only other person there. Harsh neon lights drew massive brown bush moths that clanged and banged against the window, trying to get in inside. The boy was trying so hard to be friendly and start up a conversation with me, but all I wanted was to get to Alice Springs so I could find out what was wrong with the Wayward, I'd little to say. His pidgin English was limited, so our conversation became stilted. I wished him goodnight.

He replied in his broken English, 'Watch out for big brown snakes!'

Just what I wanted to hear.

Morning in the desert is cold. I filled up every container I could with brackish water from their one and only water tap. There were signs that

The Cuppa Tree

kangaroos, emus, and snakes had all been visiting the campsite because the water puddle from the tap attracted them as the only water source around. The landscape was so dry that everything left a footprint, especially around the damp sand beneath that leaking tap. I added mine to them.

The sun was just rising as I backed out and headed for Alice Springs. The young Asian boy stood at the roadhouse window waving me off. I'm sure if I'd stopped and offered him a ride out of there, he would have accepted; he looked bored and lonely. Out here, way out in the back and beyond, they employed anyone who would work, often advertising for young ones to come from overseas. They tempted them with the promise of a good salary and the chance to see Australia. Poor sods don't know what they are in for. This can be one of the loneliest places on earth because Australia is a huge country with pockets of barren land yet to be discovered.

It took another five hours of slow driving, pulling over for road trains and other folk with more modern transport and accommodations than mine. My little home seemed antique compared to some of the monsters flashing by. The whole time, my motor was in trouble. The temperature gauge sat in the red. 'Alice Springs camping grounds: turn left,' was the first sign I saw as I drove through the entrance into a gorge.

I pulled in, the engine barely coughing over, and the camp owner came out to greet me. He could smell how hot the engine was and directed me to a campsite way in the back of the camp under one lone eucalyptus tree that provided little shade from the burning hot sun. I cut the engine, which was still making horrendous sputtering, hissing, and clanking sounds. She was one sick engine. I did what any female would do. I burst into tears. The last twenty-four hours had been total crap.

I called the RAC, forgetting it was New Year's Day. One loses all sense of time out here, where time seems not to exist. A tinny female voice informed me that only emergency crew was on duty; she asked for my details and said they would be in contact. There was nothing for it but to stay put and sort it out when I could. A pool is an excellent way to get rid of stress, as had been proven to me many times. This camp had a brand-new pool. I swear I wore it out. With nothing else to do, I would catch the campground shuttle to town, do a bit of sightseeing; have a swim, then collapse in the Wayward while I waited for the RAC, to get back to me.

The temperatures soared sky high into the mid-forties. My little air conditioner gave up the ghost, and all I had was a small fan at my disposal. At least the nights were cool, but I did not like Alice Springs at all. I was uncomfortable with what I saw around me. There was obviously a big alcohol problem in the town.

I succumbed to eating at a local pizzeria, its air conditioning cooling me off. The temperature outside was still in the forties, and small black flies, the bane of the Aussie Outback, stuck to sweaty bodies, faces and eyes. Directly opposite my table was a park, and as the night brought on cooler temperatures, so too did it bring out its indigenous people. All I could see around me was a race of lost souls. The word 'lost' written in their large, hollow brown eyes. I was glad when the camp shuttle bus came to pick me up.

At night, they locked the camp. Big iron gates with heavy chains across the entrance kept the unwelcome out. I'd never heard of a gated camping ground until Alice Springs. It was hard to go anywhere without my own transport. I did, however, find an air-conditioned movie theatre. I could have hugged the ticket lady I was so happy to just sit in the comfort of air conditioning. Another day, I was shopping for food for the Wayward when by chance, I walked into a didgeridoo shop. This was a magical place. The clerk kindly gave me a demonstration, playing the instrument which raised the hair on my arms. It was a tribal sound, and I was surprised to learn that he was not Australian but was in fact European.

That night, I ate at the local hotel. It was across the road from the campground, but upon arriving I immediately saw the negative effects of how alcohol fuels an argument. The cook had just finished his shift, went outside, lit a smoke, and it surprised me that no one even acknowledged the violent brawl going on not ten feet away.

'Leave it alone, lady,' the well-meaning cook warned, looking over at me.

One of my mother's sayings flashed through my mind then. 'If you can't fix it, leave it alone.' You did not have to warn me twice.

CHAPTER 49

What a relief to hear my phone ring on my fourth day. It was the RAC calling to see how they could help. I popped the hood in expectations of a miracle cure, but nothing had changed. I could still see green goop oozing through the radiator. The RAC mechanic arrived. His inspection over, he announced, 'Ma'am, you need a new radiator.'

I wanted to laugh; I could have told him that.

'So where do I get a new radiator?' I asked. I must add here that nothing in the Outback is ever fixed in a hurry; but I was from Perth, which meant I wanted it fixed today.

'I will see what I can do and let you know,' was all the mechanic could promise me. I asked about the square O-ring they'd informed me about earlier on my drive here. He looked at me, his eyebrows raised.

'You're serious, right? I have no idea what you're talking about, as far as I know there is no such thing as a square O-ring.' Then he explained, 'Well, lady, you see, the pressure from another tube has made an indentation on a rubber ring that connected the radiator…'

He lost me at the word 'tube.' As I've said before, I was no mechanic. Instead, all I could hear was that song that goes, 'the knee-bones connected to the thigh-bone,' which ran through my head as he yammered on about crucial attachments to engines. Then, I became more interested in the fly that now crawled over his face as long mechanical words came out of his mouth. I'm sure it was the heat making me smile as he lectured on about the dangers of driving alone 'in this heat,' and 'a woman in the desert.' The more he droned on, the more delirious I felt.

He was not wrong about the dangers, and the question.

'What the hell are you doing?' skittered again through my overheated brain.

The RAC man promised to scout around to see what he could do for me, and I was grateful. The pool was calling to me in the high heat of day. This time, two other couples were there enjoying the cool relief the pool afforded. We began talking as people do when you're all cooling off in a pool. They invited me for cocktails and nibbles at seven p.m. I felt rude declining. We all need friends, especially when on the road, but all I really wanted to do was to have an easy tea and fall into my bed. The evening heat was still overpowering, and I politely declined, saying I was expecting phone calls from family.

I wasn't wrong, even though I'd fibbed. The phone was ringing as I rushed into the cab. The green light winked signalling a voice message was there for me. It was Kane. They'd admitted Rae to hospital for a rest. Her blood pressure had been a little too high for the medical team to be happy. Otherwise, all was well, and I was told not to worry. Everything was under control.

How do you not worry when your daughter is in hospital? I called back. Kane sounded subdued. I spoke to Jess, and I could hear the fear in his voice. I wanted to project calmness, love, and hope, even if I was stuck in a godforsaken city, but all I really wanted to do was scream, 'stuff it I'm out of here!' I calmed myself with a silent 'Breathe, Tara, just breathe.' I put my heart into reassuring Kane and Jess.

'She's going to be all right. This time, she has both of you there to help her.'

My sleep was restless. I'd been back in Australia for nearly three weeks and there was so much more for me to see, but my little home had given up the ghost and Rae was not well, Was it insane for a woman in her mid-sixties to say, 'I want my mum?' Because in that moment that was all I wanted. I needed a big hug from the one person in my life who'd always made things go right when I was a child.

The sound of the phone woke me at seven a.m. Feelings of dread enveloped me as I thought a phone call this early could only mean trouble. This time, however, it was good news. The RAC man had found a radiator for the Wayward. He and another mechanic were going to call by and replace it in the morning. Yahoo! I hoped this meant I could be on the road by late afternoon. I wanted to kiss them both as they finished up the job and wiped their oily hands on the paper towels I supplied. (That seems to be what mechanics do when they talk to you. Maybe it's a ritual they learn at mechanics school.) Anyway, it was all done and dusted. I had a new radiator. The wallet was two thousand dollars lighter, but I was back on the road. I thanked the campground manager for his concern, and, looking over longingly at the pool, I drove out of those formidable iron gates and down through the Hevitree Gap out of Alice Springs.

My motorhome and I were now back on the Stuart Highway again, heading south to the famous opal town of Coober Pedy. With the sun boiling down on my little home, temperatures climbed again into the high forties. The scorching hot weather had moved in and was expected to continue for the next three months. These conditions were proving a little too hot for me, and the air conditioner in the motorhome stopped.

In fact, now it seemed to only be blowing warm air, not cool air into the cabin. I turned it off and wound down the windows on both sides, figuring it was better to have even a warm wind in my face than none at all. The flies had a lot of fun; finding an opening like an open window was like inviting them in for a great big party. Everything was pumping along nicely, and I stopped for a couple of photo opportunities, expecting to arrive in Kulgera around two pm. With any luck, I would make it to Coober Pedy by nightfall and rest up there for a couple of days. I had to keep reminding myself to slow down. This was not a race.

Kulgera is a one-shop, one-stop in the middle of the Simpson Desert. The deep red, mineral rich sands of the Simpson are in a constant state of flux, where hot desert winds are constantly moulding and shifting the dunes, and the landscape changes almost hourly. As I drove in, the strong afternoon sun beat down on one of the quirkiest Outback pubs I'd seen, a large red dirt encrusted building out in the middle of the desert. Nothing, and I mean nothing grew out here beyond the red sand hills and scrub. However, I am not diminishing this place at all, because if not for Kulgera, I would have died out there in the desert that night.

The first thing I saw as I drove into the first parking bay in Kulgera was this place called the Shoe Tree. It was a huge, dead tree, its age unknown, covered in tourists' shoes, thongs, work boots, dress shoes, sandals, and sneakers. I smiled because it was such an unbelievably quirky sight to see way out in the middle of nowhere. The story goes that, if your shoes fall out of the tree, you will not be back. If they stay up on the branches, you will be this way again. I did not tempt fate, my shoes stayed firmly on my feet. It was one photo I definitely had to have to send off to family and friends.

About two p.m., I pulled up outside the roadhouse where outside sat a group of Aboriginals peacefully eating their lunch. I took a couple of painkillers for the headache sitting at the back of my eyes and sloshed them down with half a bottle of tepid water. Time to check everything again: gas, oil, water, and tyres. Everything was looking good.

A tour bus with fifty grinning faces pulled in; grinning that was, until they got out snapping photos of the tree, the pub and of me. God knows what I looked like. The searing heat hit them, along with the flies that quickly invaded them the moment the bus opened its door. The tourists all scampered back onto the bus again and back into air-conditioned comfort. I could hear them all complaining as they swatted away at their new travelling companions.

I climbed into my cosy home on wheels and headed back out to the highway, meeting up with enormous road trains again, but I was feeling confident I would reach Coober Pedy by nightfall. I think I was about an hour into my road trip when suddenly a pipe burst. A geyser of steam erupted from the bonnet, and the Wayward screamed in agony at it ruptured. Turning the engine off, I'd just enough power to drive into a spacious lay-by, coming to a stop behind a large sand hill.

Phones don't work out here. Nothing worked out here. I was in the middle of nowhere. My only link to civilisation was the long stretch of empty road ahead. I knew I was in trouble.

The temperature was now hitting over fifty degrees in the late afternoon, and with nowhere to go and no one to call, there were only two options I could see. I could either stay put and sleep there overnight, (which I felt would be alright apart from the heat), or I could try to flag someone down to give me a ride back to Kulgera. Fear of the unknown and being out there alone in the desert had me choosing the latter. Packing a backpack with all my wallet, phone, laptop, camera, and water, I walked up the sand hill onto the road and attempted to flag down any vehicle that passed me. A minivan and a mobile home roared past first, ignoring me. Then a car full of teenagers screamed past, one giving me the F off sign. Flies crawled everywhere. In my ears, eyes, nose, down my shirt, sticking to my legs. I was dehydrating fast, and if someone did not stop soon, I would have to stagger back to the caravan and sit it out for the night. I could not believe my luck when, out of nowhere, a three-trailer road train slowed down, its air brakes screeching in protest.

'What's up, lady? I can't stop, I can only slow down. Think you can get up here with me?' the man yelled out through his window.

If it had not been so awful it would have been comical; so, I ran as though seven devils were at my back, my backpack crashing painfully on my spine as he swung open the passenger side door. With a desperate leap like nothing I'd made since high school days, I hung onto the bottom step, which had to be at least three feet in the air. The man held out his hand through the open door and I grabbed on to him as he pulled me in.

I was breathless, but I'd made it. I was finally in the cab.

My back growled in pain, but I was so grateful he'd stopped to offer help. His name was Bill, and he was driving to Alice Springs and said he would drop me off, back at Kulgera. Silence is golden, so they say, and we did not chat the whole way. As we drove along, I silently reeled in shock at what I'd just done.

Approaching Kulgera, Bill explained I would have to jump off again, and since he could not stop and could only slow down, he prepared me for my exit. As we approached the shoe tree, Bill slowed the road train, downshifting gears while telling me what to do, the air brakes screaming. I opened the cab door and then he said, 'Go!' and I jumped, landing in a heap on the sandy, red earth.

The staff in the roadhouse came to my rescue. They gave me cold water to drink and cleaned up my scraped knees, but there was nothing they could do to fix my pride. I gave the publican details where I'd broken down and he offered to go out there and tow my home back to the tavern after the rush of customers died down. I looked around the quirky watering hole. There were perhaps four people in total standing at the bar.

As I have said before, no one is in a hurry out here in the Outback. The publican's wife offered me hot chicken with gravy and vegetables, but I had to refuse because I found myself on the verge of throwing up. The roadhouse had a motel out the back, and I gratefully accepted their offer to stay. As I approached the reception to pay for my accommodation, the publican's wife shook her head.

'You's old birds shouldn't be travelling alone, especially out along this road.'

I looked at her blankly. I'd no idea what this woman was on about. It was then that the horror stories came out.

Her tales made my blood run cold. Kulgera was known for its night-time massacres, and mobs roamed the deserts, raping and pillaging folk just like me.

'Recently,' she said, 'a man and his wife had been attacked and cruelly beaten. They'd then been robbed, and their car burnt out.'

The stories just kept coming. I knew the publican's wife could have gone on all night, so eventually I stood up, feigning tiredness ,I retired to my room. As I settled in for the night, I knew it would be morning before I would see my the motorhome again.

It had all become too much of a nightmare to think about. It was amazing I slept at all after that. I think my body and mind simply shut off for the night, because all I remember was collecting my key and finding my way to my motel room, falling face down on the bed.

The rattling of tin buckets in the room next door woke me. They were obviously cleaning. It was then I realised the time. It was ten-thirty in the morning. I'd slept as though there were no tomorrow. I felt groggy, but a hot shower helped. My scraped knees were scabby, stiff, and a little swollen. My lower back was giving me hell, so I let the water cascade over me, praying I was suffering only aches and pains, not some real injury. That was the last thing I needed out here. Out here there are no medical facilities. Basic first aid is available, anything more serious would mean a trip to the closest hospital. Alice Springs was nearly three hours away, so for life-threatening issues, The Flying Doctor Service were on call.

It was time to face the day. I hated putting on clothes I'd worn all day the day before. Red dust had stained my t-shirt and shorts. I looked like a drifter, albeit stiff, sore, and grubby. I noticed even my hair was stiff from the hard water out there, too. More seriously, my lower back was telling me something was wrong. It pinched and sent off shooting pains, but I hobbled out the motel door anyway into the searing sunlight and there was my Wayward parked in the middle of a large, sandy red paddock. 'Welcome to the Kulgera campgrounds' was written on a rusty tin sign above my mobile home. It squeaked in protest against a light wind, and I looked at my tiny motorhome It looked beaten up and sad, like me.

CHAPTER 50

Advertised in the dark, cool lobby was an all-day breakfast. All I wanted was a slice of toast and a pot of tea, which the short-order cook did his best to fill. Two pieces of cold toast, no butter or jam, plus a pot of black tea, no milk, all served up on a sticky tray. I gulped back the cup of tea, and, refilling it, asked to speak to the owner. Now getting familiar with the slow pace and the fact that no one, anywhere, was in a hurry, I waited with as much patience as I could muster. When the publican arrived, ordering two cold beers from the bar, he sat beside me, sliding me the second beer.

'Here ya go dear, you might need this.'

City Tara would have looked shocked. No one in my circle even thought about drinking alcohol before five o'clock. But the worn-out, in-pain Tara sucked back the cold heavenly brew, its white froth leaving a drinker's moue on my top lip. The owner looked at me and said 'Cheers' but there was nothing that could mask his frown.

'Your little bus is buggered, lady,' he said.

Which should really have come as no surprise. I knew it was but hearing the words out loud truly stung. When the temperature gauge went over into the red mark at the same time as a red water geyser shot out the sides of the hood, I knew then that we where not going any further. I had to be grateful no one ransacked it or burnt it to the ground. I wanted to at least salvage some of my personal things before I decided what to do.

I knew I had to sort out what to do, but my brain would not work properly. I knew I should have called my family in Perth, who clearly had no idea of my dire situation. They probably thought I was in some camping ground enjoying the company of others, touring around amazing places, and taking midnight dips in cold pools. I nodded sadly, acknowledging the owner and drank my beer as he commiserated with me in my misfortune.

I booked the room for two more nights. I could have stayed in Wayward but with no air conditioner, I knew it would be as uncomfortable as all hell, since forecasted temperatures would be in the high fifties. I wandered over to my little home on wheels, my lower back on fire as I unpacked what I needed and carried those items back to the room. I still had no idea of what to do with heror myself, but at least now I'd bought myself a couple of days to sort it out.

I had to be honest with myself. I was getting low on cash, and the money machine was broken in the roadhouse, a large black sign posted over the screen saying, 'expected to be fixed within the month.' Another sign in red over the bar read 'No credit given, so don't ask.' Everywhere I looked around here there were warning signs, broken or don't ask. And now I was stuck in the only place for miles and miles around in the middle of a red desert. I was fast learning that, out here, one either obeyed the rules or got shipped out on the next bus. That was when an idea formed. If I could sell the Wayward for a cheap deal, I could catch a bus out of there in two days to Coober Pedy. And If that went to plan, then I could buy my flight home.

The one burning question was: whom I should approach about selling the Wayward? Kulgera had six people that were permanent residents living quite simple lives in the Outback. Who would buy a broken-down motorhome that needed some love that badly? I placed an advertisement in the roadhouse, borrowing a felt tip from the barman, also begging some A4 paper from the office.

'Motorhome for sale: price negotiable,' with my room number beside it.

It wasn't till I walked out the back of the roadhouse that I discovered my nirvana; a huge, totally enclosed pool lay before me, covered in garden netting to keep the bugs out. It was my heavenly oasis in the stifling heat, and I stripped down to my bra and undies and plunged into the coldest pool on earth.

My back went numb in the icy water and I found myself alone, not another person in sight. It was just me and the deep russet red desert and I felt as though I were one of the last people on earth, which suddenly made me feel isolated and lonely. I soon found out you can't swim and have a good cry at the same time.

I surfaced from the pool feeling half-human and, wrapping the warm and toasty towel around me, slipped on my sandals and collected my undies and a sarong I'd pegged out on the community clothesline. Everything in the Outback was so dry. So dry I reasoned that, out here, one could literally sit and watch paint dry. My lower back was now becoming a real problem. Pain was now coursing down my right leg, shooting across my lower back and up into my left hip. Every time I walked, I limped, which was obviously not a good sign. It was time to face facts about my jumping from the truck the day before. I'd torn a muscle or jammed something. The only thing I could think of that would help was a back rub, cream, painkillers, and rest.

In fact, I ended up staying in Kulgera for a week. Every time I walked, the pain caused nausea, and the painkillers were causing me to be vague about everything. I think they call it brain fog. I was in such a fog that when the cook at the roadhouse offered me fifteen hundred to take the my motorhome off my hands. I shook on it, deal done. It felt as if my dream holiday had ended abruptly. Alan, the cook, wanted to travel. He had the time and the roadhouse garage out the back to fix the her up, I was happy with it. I booked myself a seat on the next bus out to Coober Pedy, intending to fly back to Perth from that point on. I could just see the look on my family's faces when I told them the news. 'It is what it is' was always my mantra, though. For the first time I realised I was homeless, yet in a strange way, the thought tickled my fancy. I was footloose and fancy free, and I liked the idea of not being beholden to anyone or anything, even though this situation had never crossed my mind before.

Alan gave me the cash the following day. I emptied the Wayward of my personal gear, leaving anything else for the new owner. I handed over the keys to Alan. In just a few hours, I would be on the bus leaving Kulgera. They'd been kind to a point, but they'd also charged me for every kindness they'd offered. For the one week I'd been there, I'd paid a small fortune towards keeping myself safe. I would have called my family, but there was no phone coverage, so I decided it would just have to wait till I got somewhere where there was enough reception. The bus pulled up, and with my backpack loaded on board, I and four other people were on our way. I had a towel rolled up for back support, and painkillers at the ready. There was no looking back, for the Wayward now sat inside an old tin garage, its little motor scattered about the place in pieces. I cannot lie. It hurt. It felt as though I were losing an old friend.

Maria was my next stop, and I could not wait to get up, get off, and stretch my legs. Mail and groceries were all delivered to this outpost. But as soon as the bus door opened, the flies hurtled inside. Outside it was even worse, and my face, arms, and back crawled with them. This was the Outback. It could be so beautiful and so worthwhile to visit, yet so damn awful at the same time.

At Maria, my phone finally beeped into action. It was a great time to call family, connect and tell them what had happened. I also had messages from my friends and one from Gordi. I only had a few minutes to make calls, so I dialled my family first. It rang out. I tried Jess's mobile. He answered, but his voice was faint and scratchy. I tried calling my friends, but there was nothing except for a strange whistling sound. nothing. I was on my own.

The universe has such a droll way of saying, 'You asked for this adventure, and guess what? It's all yours.' Bloody typical.

We'd another two hours to go before we hit Coober Pedy, but even as we drove along, I could already spot mounds of white rock coming into view. They belonged 'to the hobbyists,' according to the bus driver, who announced points of interest over his microphone. The mounds reminded me of little pyramids. Then, as the landscape changed and bigger opal mines appeared, there were huge mounds that were miles high and a brilliant shade of white, just like the Pyramids in the Chiza Valley of Egypt. It was truly breathtaking.

They dropped us off at the Coober Pedy Hotel, but I chose the cheaper option: The Sands Motel and Caravan Park. The bus dropped me off at the door.

The Sands is owned by a Greek family that came here in the 1800s to run the camel trains from Coober Pedy to Port Augusta, or so a plaque on the foyer door would have it. I booked for four days. Once I settled into a room, I ordered the house menu of hot pepperoni pizza and a cold beer. After a day on the bus, it was a slice of pure heaven. I lay on the bed and ate my meal. My lower back was over the painkillers, and I sensed it needed some attention, and soon.

CHAPTER 51

Numbers on my phone suddenly appeared, flashing up on the screen; among them was Gordi's. The harsh sound of the phone's ring jolted me after days of silence; I was finally back in contact with the outside world.

Gordi instantly knew I was not telling him the full story. He knew I was skipping the serious parts. When I finally got up the gumption to tell him I'd sold the Wayward, he gasped in disbelief.

'Tara, what else are you not telling me?' Gordi asked, point blank.

It was time to own up. I was in trouble. I hadn't felt the full impact of the danger I'd been in until this moment, so I told him everything. It all spilled out in a jumbled heap. I was so used to bottling up my emotions that when I did let it all go, Gordi copped it all. The tears, the snotty hiccups as I sobbed, the anger, the shame of feeling that I'd failed.

Gordi's next comment cemented all those feelings and more in my chest.

'You stupid woman!' he yelled.

This, I did not expect at all.

'Why? Why did you not ring Kane, or me? We could have helped in some way!'

His yelling set me off again.

'I felt that it was all too much, Gordi. Kane is stressed about Rae, and I did not want to bother anyone. And I did not want to intrude on you and your new life.'

This was my truest and only excuse I could offer.

The tears flowed long after we'd said our goodbyes. I'd made Gordi promise not to tell the family. Now he knew everything that happened, and I felt happy and relieved someone else knew. I needed to find a masseuse before I ended up at the doctors. My brain wasn't functioning right, and I became vague as I muttered to myself: masseuse or doctor? With this question swirling around in my head, I fell asleep.

The decision was made for me once I woke up. Walking to find a massage place was not an option now. I phoned for a taxi to the hospital, my lower back feeling as if it were broken. Thank God for medical insurance. Once the taxi driver laid eyes on me and saw my condition, he called ahead to the hospital. I was barely crawling; the pain was too much.

A hospital gurney waited outside an old, rundown building. This was just a small country hospital and a team of three orderlies came out to greet me, carefully lifting me onto the gurney, all the while supporting my neck in a brace. I was a possible spinal case and with spinal patients, it was imperative not to move any part of the spine. They tied me down securely and transported me to the examination room. The waiting was the worst part. Lying on my back, tied down, the ache in my back only growing worse. Finally, a young doctor approached me, clipboard in hand, his white starched coat flapping at his sides. I thought he looked no older than sixteen.

'Tara; can you tell me what you have done?'

'Jumped out of a moving road train,' I grimaced, wincing in pain.

The doctor's eyebrows raised. He rechecked his clipboard and immediately ordered a lumbar CT spine scan for me in the radiology department. I lay on the bed in traction, unable to move as tears coursed freely down the sides of my face. I wanted to move, but my arms were still strapped down to the bed, my brain not accepting the awful situation I was in.

'Tara never gets ill,' I muttered, but nobody heard me.

My doctor was a lovely South African man and a new immigrant to Australia. He would stop by on his rounds to chat about my travels. Apparently, two discs in my back were bulging. I surmised all of this caused by a jump from a slow-moving road train. The doctor disagreed with my own prognosis. What had really done damage to an already inflamed and injured spine was that I'd continued sitting down for so long. I admitted I'd covered hundreds of thousands of kilometres in the months I'd been on the road, and now I was nothing more than a road-weary traveller. I felt old and useless, disappointed my life of travel was over. I could just imagine hearing the comments from friends and family already, saying 'We told you so!'

I'd been in the hospital for four days and in that time, I couldn't sit up or stand up for more than a half hour to shower, then it was straight back into my bed. They'd injected steroids into my spine for pain management and my body hummed with anger at my situation, while my brain, operating in its own drugged zone, asked, 'What pain?'

My job now, the doctor said, was for complete rest. All I could do was sleep, but my eyes felt puffy and sticky all the time. I drifted off into sweet dreams, dreaming lovely soft dreams of better days as Gordi's voice floated in and out of my consciousness. Jess and Rae were with me too. Occasionally I came to, feeling my face being washed with a cloth as a hand rested on my forehead while some far-off whispered conversation continued between two people I couldn't make out. Wanting to see what was going on around me, I tried to open my eyes and focus on the grey hospital wall, waiting for my vision to clear. Whatever drugs they'd given me, they were working. I was not with it at all and felt myself slipping back into warm, fuzzy pain free darkness.

On day four, the nurses came and gently shifted me back onto the gurney to be wheeled off for a second CT scan. My unfocused eyes landed on the radiologist's face as nearby technicians buzzed around him. He looked down at me and nodded, letting go the faintest hint of a smile. My spine was out of permanent danger. I was to stay in the hospital for another two days to come off all drugs they'd been injecting into me; then I would undergo more tests. by that afternoon, I could almost focus properly. My vision shuddered with the effort. The excursion to the scan room had left me limp as a rag, even though I'd been wheeled everywhere. I was still in some stiff plastic brace that clipped around my lower back, but I wasn't moving or going anywhere anytime soon. After all the exhaustion of the scan, I fell asleep again. It was Gordi who delivered my meal to me that next lunch time. Just the shock of seeing him standing there left me speechless.

'Geez, Tara, cat got ya tongue? That's a first!'

'Stupid Kiwi!' I mumbled back. 'Your mum let you out for the day.'

Gordi reached out and held my hand in his and his voice became low and serious.

'I'm staying with you, and I won't take 'no' for an answer.'

I didn't have the energy to argue with him and fell asleep with his hand in mine, feeling safe for the first time in a long time.

I woke with one burning question in my head. How on earth did Gordi know about my hospital stay? I soon learned they'd called Gordi to the hospital. He'd been the last phone call I'd made, so the hospital staff had called the number in case it was family. Gordi immediately told them he was my partner who'd been on holiday with me from Perth and he was flying over to take care of me. They'd reduced my pain relief, and tested my blood pressure, sight, and kidney function. All signs were great. Gordi could finally take me home.

Home was now the Sands Motel, where I would remain for as long as it took for me to bear sitting for more than an hour at a time. The taxi ride there felt like a camel walking over me; a smooth ten-minute ride proving much too painful. A normal bed, however, had never looked so good.

Gordi did all the arranging and organising of things, right down to having our breakfast delivered. Suddenly his nursing skills and background as an herbalist and masseur kicked into high gear and I became his sole focus.

People and places were contacted, orders placed, and Gordi even had the motel owner, George, chasing down a stiff board for extra support under the mattress. Almost overnight the room filled up with herbal rubs, heat pads, some sort of electrical equipment, and a massage chair. Gordi asked around for a rental car because he wanted to pick up some herbal medications, he'd ordered express from Sydney. My laptop, he said, was out-of-bounds because of it involving too much sitting.

I simply could not believe the planning that went on; and under his supervision, it all fell into place. This was not the Gordi I'd come to know; this man was powerful and assertive and in charge of things; if someone said no to his requests, he simply thanked them for their trouble and called another..

Where had the hot tempered, rude, sarcastic, impatient Gordi gone?

Gordi had just given me my first massage, and the herbal rub was warming its way into my bones. He made me a cup of tea, arranging the pillows so I could lie carefully on my side to pick up the cup. That evening, Gordi coaxed me to try a short walk with him to the pool.

'Just some light, gentle water exercise. It will be good for you,' he suggested.

He supported me by my elbow. I must have looked doubtful because Gordi stopped to assure me.

'If it hurts, we stop. It's that simple.'

This time, the conversation flowed freely between us. We'd so much to tell each other, and it was exciting to relate the ways our lives had gone since we'd parted in Bali. I asked about his family and his sweetheart.

'Nothing's changed, Tara,' he said. 'She is still on my case, wants to marry me, to settle down close to our families, and my mum wants me to supply her with 'A grandchild or two

'Mothers,' we both said at the same time.

I told Gordi of Waywards overheating problems and her last, sputtering gasp when I ended up stranded on the road outside Kulgera. We agreed that that had been a near miss for me. I'd dodged a bullet. I hadn't taken that ride, who knows what or where I would be? It was a place that neither of us wanted to go. Needless to say, I got off lightly.

Tears fell when I told him about the pub's cook buying my little home. Gordi, too, felt sad.

'You know what, Tara? Sometimes, if you can't fix it, you have to walk away.'

I'd walked away, but it still left a sad ache in my heart.

Gordi said how his mum tried vainly to put him and his ex-fiancée together.

'But she was soon stunned to learn that my ex was now interested in another gentleman. When that whole ruse failed, she claimed it had all been too much, and she took to her bed, feigning illness. So all the attention was now aimed at her and her failing health.'

Gordi rolled his eyes in that comical way he'd about him.

'Families!' we both cried together, though we both had to admit we wouldn't be without them.

I looked up then into Gordi's soft brown eyes and couldn't help noticing the tenderness in them. I had to admit, something in me had missed him. This time it felt right; our close friendship felt right. We'd both been to hell and back, yet here we were in Coober Pedy of all places, laughing at our experiences, and enjoying each other's company. I was so grateful it was Gordi they'd called. He wanted to make everything so much easier on me, and the swim had proved medicinal too. His thoughtfulness overwhelmed me. My body was now tired enough to sleep without pain relief through the night, and I could feel the herbs and herbal teas comforting my body instead of drugging it. It felt good.

For the next five days, although both of us were itching to get out and explore this place for its underground homes and opals, we postponed it all, as my health came first. For two travellers, however, this was no mean feat; but we stayed inside, rested, and watched TV. I progressed in my swimming and could soon breast stroke a length of the pool by myself, and do some light water aerobics to stretch my cramped muscles. I took a long list of herbs from magnesium to Vitamin B, D, C, Manganese, plus that one other rare herb that money can't buy: Trust. There was no more jealous anger that I could see because what was growing instead was a healthy respect for each other and our differing personalities. We were finally equal.

On day seven, Gordi asked if I was well enough to take a ride out to the underground Greek Orthodox Church that was known for its sandstone sculptures. Now it was more a matter of whether I could withstand the sitting. I really wanted to tour again, but Gordi warned me fiercely.

'Feel even more than a slight ache or tiredness and we are coming home to rest.'

CHAPTER 52

Gordi bought me a hip brace online a small web belt I buckled up under my clothing to support my lower back. It was maybe a ten-minute ride, over hill and down dale, finally reaching a hump in a hillside. They'd carved the dwelling out of the sandstone hill. Its builders had carved into the rock, creating altars and carved marble doves that hung suspended in alcoves as if ready to fly away. The intricately carved domed ceiling looked more like a lace tablecloth. It was so delicate. Everywhere I looked there were magnificent carvings and sculptures; it even had two separate floors, one dedicated to its worshippers, the other for tourists.

We stopped at the Miners Hotel for afternoon tea. Every mark made by the massive boring machines was on display under artificial lighting, and touristy boutiques and a casino. I felt sad that this once holy place had turned into a place full of one-armed bandits and booze. I could also see the greater tragedy of the indigenous people, who were now taking part in a world that was highly addictive for them.

I waited for Gordi in the car as he went into a local store for groceries, watching as two aboriginal families carted their grubby bedding around a small dirt park, squabbling over who was to sit and sleep where. I watched the local bus pull in and a European woman get out, greeting a well-dressed aboriginal girl with hugs and kisses. You would have to live here to understand the complicated strings of this society. Gordi was taking ages, so I stepped out of the car and stretched my back. While I was stretching, the European woman walked up to me.

'Strangers here, are you?' she asked.

I nodded. *I wonder if she is going to tell me off for staring?* Her intentions were quite the opposite.

'Welcome to Coober Pedy,' she exclaimed brightly. 'My name is Mani.

Would you like a tour? No charge. I can show you what an underground home looks like.'

By this time, Gordi was back by my side and we looked at each other, both of us wanting to say yes. Gordi was concerned because it was my first day up and about, but I nodded.

'Let's do it. We may never be back this way.'

We followed her car, which headed for one of the three hills where three pipes could be seen poking out of the top of each hilltop. We were told it was someone's home. Mani owned three, renting out two to the local miners. She winked at me when she said, 'We call it a unique experience.'

We toured her own home, and it was beautiful. They, her husband and friends had bored a large cave out of the hillside, and from there, bored each subsequent room. There were two bedrooms both with an en suite, a study, a large lounge and kitchen, the main bathroom and another room had just been started for a TV room. What amazed me the most was Mani's next sentence.

'If you need a shelf,' she said, 'start carving.'

Created as niches in the wall, they'd even made space for the bedside tables. It was all homey, cool, and quiet and I took some photos. Mani invited us to stay for dinner: kangaroo stew was on the menu. Gordi paled a bit, whereas I was ravenous, and we sat around her fireplace eating crusty fresh bread and Skippy stew, it was positively delicious.

Mani explained to Gordi that, often, the aboriginals didn't have the cash to pay for her husband's services as a local mechanic, so they would pay with whatever they had. This payment often came in the form of their dinner. The kangaroo stew smelled and tasted great; all the herbs were from Mani's shaded garden, along with fresh carrot, cheese, and parsley salad.

Gordi was becoming concerned I'd been upright too long, and I agreed with him. I was feeling a niggle of pain, and I thanked Mani profusely for her hospitality and kindness, then we made our way back to the motel, Gordi lightly admonishing me for being silly and pushing it too much. I knew deep down he was right. It was heaven to lie down, heavenly to feel Gordi's hands massage my back, and heaven to fall asleep knowing I was safe.

The phone woke me at one am. I saw it was Rae's number.

'Hi, sweetheart, feeling better now?' I asked. Her answer came in the form of an angry, squealing cry.

'Meet your new granddaughter, Mum!'

I could not speak; tears of joy escaped me, and I so longed to be with her in that magical moment. I knew I'd asked Gordi not to tell any of my family of my goings on, and now was not the time to say anything, either. Instead, I cooed over the phone to my new grandchild.

'You clever clogs. How much does she weigh? What time was she born? What is her name?'

It all rolled out of me in one breathless sentence. Rae was as excited as I was as she rattled off statistics.

'2.8 kilos, two minutes past midnight, so that makes her an Aries baby, born on the twenty-seventh of March.'

For a moment, an eerie silence passed between us, then came Rae's most reverent words.

'Mum, I've got my little girl.'

'Her name?' I queried, dying to know.

'It's a tie between Shana Rose or Shauna Ray.'

'Oh, honey, either is perfect.'

'Come home soon please. We want you to be part of her life, Mum.'

I knew deep inside what an honour I'd just been given. Rae wanted me to be as involved with the baby as I'd been with our Jess.

'Let me sort some things out, honey, I will call you later today. Give baby a big hug from her Nana .'

How does one sleep after that sort of news? Gordi leaned over and held my hand.

'Congratulations, Nana. You're going to need all your energy now.'

There was only one problem stopping me from going home, and that was me. I had yet to see Uluru, the biggest, reddest rock in Australia, and I realised it was now or never. With all that had happened recently, I'd become a diehard pessimist. You never know what is going to happen tomorrow. Switching on the bedside light, I asked Gordi if he thought we were up to a road trip 'Where to?' he asked, scratching his head.

'To Ayers Rock, Uluru.'

Gordi sat upright in bed, excitement showing on his face.

'If you think you can, then I will be there to help you achieve that goal.'

He slipped over into my bed, putting his arms around me.

'I'm here for you, Tara. It's the only place I ever want to be.'

In that moment, I could see that Gordi was promising something I felt I'd no right to ask of him. He was asking for a permanent place in my life, to share our lives as one. I was unsure about the word 'permanent,' yet I knew that, in some weird way, he was meant to be here as well. We snuggled up together, but falling asleep took a while. I hadn't shared my bed for so long that I'd become used to being alone again.

When I woke in the morning, Gordi was still there, snuggled up beside me. I took my time to study his face. He was six years younger than me, loved kids, loved to travel, was independently well off, and had a large family that loved him. I, too, had all those things. My life had also dealt me a few emotional tumbles by now, and I was still asking myself if Gordi really was ready for such a huge commitment? Or was it me who was not ready? Did he understand how momentous a word 'permanent' was? Was either of us ready to commit? What was it that was holding me back? What was I really scared of?

I padded over to the bathroom, had a quick shower, dried myself off, and sprayed myself with a bit of perfume. Then I strapped on my hip support belt, (not the sexiest thing I'd worn recently) and threw on a fresh sarong, adding a little lip gloss to my lips. I ran a brush through my hair, noticing how long it had grown since being on the road. I then made our morning cups of tea, waking Gordi, who was surprised to see me up and about, as I placed his tea down beside him.

'I figured that, if we were going to go to Uluru today, I'd better get up and about. What do you say to a swim after your drink?'

Gordi looked sheepish, and looking down at the sheets, I could see why, his arousal obvious.

I followed his eyes downwards, realising what he was thinking, and to be honest, desire flooded through me too. It had been a long time since we'd made love. I pulled back the sheets, our eyes meeting. Everything just felt so right.

'Are you sure, Tara?'

I nodded quietly, putting my fingers to his lips. It took some adjusting of positions; it's hard to be sexy when limb placement becomes more important than arousal, however, we got there. I have no idea how, but we did. My lover and I rode that wonderful wave of passion together.

'Now, it's time for that swim,' Gordi said with a smile.

I could hardly breathe, let alone move, but Gordi sprang out of bed as I crawled, his lithe body snapping into shape. I struggled to pull on my swimmers; to stubborn to ask for help. Gordi walked ahead of me to the pool and dived in, while I took my time, sinking into the tepid water, the ache in my lumbar region begging for relief.

Gordi knew I was in a bit of pain. The grimace and wincing said it all. Back in our room, he layed out his massage oils and a thick padding of towels on the floor.

'Okay madam, I am at your service.'

I smiled at Gordi's corny humour, then grimaced again as I bent over, trying to get my swimmers off; it was too painful. Gordi stepped in and helped me, held me close, listening to my fears.

CHAPTER 53

'It's too late for us. I'm too old for you. You deserve someone young and able to have kids,' I blurted, sobbing. 'Even your mum doesn't like me,' throwing another fact onto the mounting pile of reasons we should not be.

'Hey, you're not alone in that one; she doesn't like any of my friends!' Gordi responded with a laugh.

He wrapped me up in a bath towel, sat with me, and hugged me tight.

'Tara, you're all I want. Give us a chance. Please. Stop trying to control us. Stop pushing me away. I love you. What is so bloody hard to understand about that? I have loved you since the day we first met. Since the first day I came to nurse Rae.'

This was not the first time Gordi had told me this, so why was it so hard to believe? It was time to make a commitment to him and mean it, not race away from it because I felt disloyal to Russ, or because I could find annoying things about Gordi. I was being offered a committed relationship right here, right now, and if the past few months had taught me anything, anything at all, it was to live in the moment. Be in the present. Gordi sat in front of me, looking back at me expectantly.

'Love me back. That's all I ask of you. Let me be part of your life. Let me be with you until the inevitable parts us.'

I looked at Gordi, then. His sincerity reached out, he held my hands with his, which were shaking. He meant every word he'd uttered. I knew I had to close the door on the past. Something in the air felt right this time.

Holding his hand, I finally said, 'OK, Gordi, let's give it a go.'

I realised I'd just said, 'I will' in the most unconventional manner, time, and place, as together we sat on a motel floor, towel half draped round me, my body sticky with oil and bits of fluff stuck to me. (How romantic!)

Meanwhile, my Kiwi bloke joyously whooped about the room in his undies.

We cemented our relationship with a hot cup of tea. I knew we needed training wheels on this bicycle built for two. It would be a bumpy road ahead, but after all, isn't it the journey that counts? A mental list was forming in my mind of what we had to do: then start writing a to-do list. How to get to Uluru became our priority, then factoring how to get back to Perth after that, given we no longer had Wayward plus, how to do and see all we wanted to on the way without too much pain involved for me. Gordi suggested we not tell family about Kulgera or Coober Pedy until we were safely back home. We would just tell the facts about how we'd arranged to meet up once I'd left Sydney. Gordi thought it would stress them to know any more details, and besides, as far as they knew I was safe, happy and with him, and this was enough.

I thought it best as well, and I rang Rae to say Gordi and I'd met up as planned and made the news of our relationship official. However, she met it with hesitation.

'Gordi, Mum? Are you sure about this? You don't even like him, do you?'

I could picture the frown crossing over Rae's brow as she spoke. Kane, on the other hand, was the typical male just happy for us. I asked to speak to Jess, who was not there, so they promised to share the good news when he got home from school.

Next was Gordi's family. His mum answered the phone and Gordi spoke quietly at first to make her understand the seriousness of us being together. I heard him call me his fiancée. My face flamed red when I heard her Scots brogue, loud and indignant.

'What? Oh no, not her! Do you know her history? Does she have children?'

Gordi took a big breath, looked over at me and spoke slowly and deliberately.

'Yes, Mum, and she has two grandchildren.'

'I think you and I should have a talk,' his mum replied.

'Mum, I'm an adult, and I make my own decisions. I will call you tomorrow. Give the gang my love,' Gordi said calmly but firmly and turned his phone off.

He then reached over to my phone, hitting the off button.

'Let them digest it for a while,' he proposed calmly. 'Now what about a coffee and some Anzac biscuits while we find out how to get to Uluru?'

He helped me up and onto the bed.

'You know what Gordi? I'll leave it to you to find out the 'what and how' of our next adventure.'

We discussed the merits of driving or taking a first-class coach, both of us opting for the coach as it may prove more comfortable for me. I purchased our return seats on the coach, while Mr Google found me the number of the Lost Camel hotel in Uluru.

Booking us a two bed back packers' room, it was all set. We were both excited.

Clinking our mugs together, Gordi said, 'To us my darling.'

Our future together as a couple had begun. Gordi packed for us both, placing most of our gear into his backpack, so mine remained almost empty.

We needed an early morning start to catch the eight a.m. coach to Uluru. The Greek motel owners were also up and about, the owner, George, sang out, 'Glad to see the Mrs. finally up and about!'

The taxi arrived and delivered us to the drop-off point for the coach. Gordi made sure I was comfortable as we waited for the other hotel guests to come on board. That first ten minutes I would soon discover was the only peaceful moment of our entire ride. For the next four hours, we endured the noisiest group of Asian tourists. From the moment they got on the bus, it was like living inside a smelly tin drum. They'd all ordered takeaway breakfasts, and they opened their food packages, swapping them and shouting at each other. If that wasn't bad enough, there were other noises, such as sucking food off teeth, clicking plastic cutlery, climbing over to each other's seats and generally being disruptive. This went on all the way until we made our first stop in Kulgera. When we pulled into the now familiar roadhouse near the Shoe Tree, it was Gordi who first spied the Wayward. She was still sitting in the garage out the back of the homestead, and she looked lonely. I looked over at Gordi and sighed.

Inside the roadhouse, the barman Mike instantly recognised me and came to pay a visit. I introduced Gordi and ordered a pot of tea and Gordi ordered a beer, while the rest of the passengers fuelled up on chips, coke, and every other quick fix. Mike and Gordi chatted about Coober Pedy and what to expect at Uluru. Then we were all back on board the coach again for another one and a half hours. The day was hot. The bus was really stinking hot in-

The Cuppa Tree

side, what with thirty excited people now all clamouring to catch their first glimpse of Uluru, this most sacred ground for all aboriginals throughout the land.

Turning off at Erldunda and onto the Lassiter Highway, I sensed we were not too far away. Our next stop was Curtain Springs, where the tourists flung themselves off the coach, overly excited at being in the Outback, only to be met by a great wall of heat and flies. It stopped them dead in their tracks and they all looked stunned. Gordi looked at me.

'Time for a walk?' he asked.

I nodded. I could not say no, my back was beginning to spasm.

Everyone headed for the shade inside the gas station, the tourists eating ice cream as though it were going out of fashion. Silly move, I thought. I wished they would read up on how to keep cool out in the desert. All the signs say 'drink tepid water and often.' But no, they gushed down pints of cold lemonade, ice cream and anything else that was ice cold and fizzy, which of course resulted in the more senior ones becoming travel sick. Soon, all the vomit bags behind the coach seats were being filled. Wonderful! On a fifty-degree day, as we rode over bumpy roads, now we endured the smell of stale food and vomit that filled the bus.

Soon we came to the first outcrop of rocks which looked as big and red as Uluru itself. The Asians got out their cameras and started snapping wildly from all angles, flashes popping. They'd mistaken it for Ayers Rock when it was in fact one of the thirty-six red-rock domes of the Kata Tjuta formation (colloquially known as 'The Olga's'). In front of us and alongside us was a jumble of arms, legs and camera cords before the driver's voice came over the intercom. He told everyone to please remain in their seats as Uluru was coming up next on our right.

Uluru is a statement from the heart. My first sighting of this magical place left me breathless as I realised, I was finally gazing upon the one and only Uluru. Its mammoth hulk mesmerised me as it glowed in all its majestic glory of deep russet reds in the afternoon sun. This; this was what I'd come to see. For a moment there was nothing but pure silence as we all drank in her sheer magnificence, then the fury of the camera brigade went off.

CHAPTER 54

This was indeed sacred land; the closer I came to the Red Rock, the redder she became. Off to one side were the marked trails, our guide waiting for us. This, I could not miss. Swallowing two mild painkillers, and adjusting my hip brace, which was firmly in place, we left the bus and made our trek across the vast dry land, her ancestral ties palpable. It was a bit of a hike up to the base of Uluru, but it was all worth it; it was amazing. The land itself spoke its own story, one of ancient mythology.

I spied a small cave, more like an overhang, biting deeply into the rock. Had no one seen it yet? I yanked on Gordi's hand, pulling him inside with me.

Aboriginal drawings three thousand years old unfolded before us. Handprints of ancestors placed on the walls, paintings of all the ancient animals depicted in story form in rich red ochre and white clay. I breathed it all in deeply; the aboriginal guide acknowledging my need to stay still, to enjoy where I was, while she carried on taking the group with her. The local people say dwellers leave their prayers here. Well, that day, I left all of mine there.

As we sat there, Gordi and I, tucked up inside this amazing rock cave, his arms went around me, and I knew then that I'd made the right choice.

My heart sank with sadness as, my moment of reverie now over, we sat watching the mayhem of tourists climbing, clambering, trudging over sacred soil with nary an ounce of respect for its history, flora, or fauna. Not once did I see anyone stopping to feel the spiritual feeling emanating out from Uluru; yet in sharp contrast I could feel her humming through my bones like the deep resonant sounds of a didgeridoo.

How could one not feel it? It made me sad to see it treated with such disrespect. Gordi had seen the look on my face as we rounded a corner, and I saw the deep azure pool in front of me. He touched my hand and walked on alone, giving me a moment to sit quietly for a while by the women's sacred pool. It was a deeply religious place for women only, for their ceremonies, prayers and to bathe in. It was stunning. A gentle waterfall cascaded into a deep, clear blue pool. The air was full of the wet bush perfume that only the rains could bring. It was time to reflect upon all I'd seen and learned. Seeing Uluru had been my greatest wish on this trip, and it had finally come true.

We then went to the Aboriginal village, where Aboriginal women were creating their Dot Paintings. It was fascinating to watch as an artist myself. The Aboriginal woman there demonstrated the dot technique and said they also ran workshops by day. Dot painting, she said, had started after watching Aboriginal men drawing symbols in the sand as they told their stories. Based on the technique being used, it was also possible to determine which culture and tribe the artist came from. However, in Aboriginal culture it was considered both disrespectful and unacceptable to paint on behalf of another's culture.

The dottting technique soon merged into the 'dot and drag' style, where linear lines emerged out of connecting dots with extended lines. It was a whole other language, and I fell in love with it. Time was ticking on. There were few people walking around outside now as most had already returned to the bus. Gordi broke the silence that surrounded us.

'We'd better get back,' he reasoned.

I shook my head, amazed that no one had even tried to look in the cave with us. Once we were back on the bus, I asked the two ladies sitting in front of us why they'd not looked inside the cave.

'Why? It was only some stick figures on rocks,' they said, and laughed. 'We just wanted to see the Rock!'

I could not believe what my ears were hearing. The two women then reached inside their pockets, pulling out little stones and fragments of rock they'd collected as souvenirs to take home.

I gasped inwardly and Gordi just shook his head. I felt so sad that these people who'd travelled all this way from many other countries like America, Asia, and Europe, did not seem to grasp what it was all about. The ancient history of Australia's first people and the deep spiritual connection with this land, with the belief we are all one, from eagle to ant, the trees, the rocks, the ocean, sand, and sea; we are all connected. And these people had taken two small rocks as curios? Did they not see, or feel, the enormity of where they were standing? How incredibly sad.

By the time we'd reached the foyer of the hotel I was exhausted, in pain, and needed to lie down. Gordi, by contrast, was on fire and still wanted to get out there and explore, his pockets now jammed full of every information brochure available. Gordi and I were told our room number. It was down a dim corridor of faded cream with old worn carpet; many doors faced onto this corridor. I had opted for the Backpackers to save some money, no frills, but they were clean and spartan. It was all we needed to be comfy for one night. The dining room was lovely. They'd arranged the Stuart pea a red desert flowers in white vases on pristine white tablecloths where we had the choice of a five-course menu or soup and cobbler, the bushman's special.

I ordered the soup and was served cream of leek soup inside a cobbler loaf. It was a stunning presentation and a first for me. Gordi had the Bushman's special, a hot cheese mix, with salad and chips. He was not impressed, commenting on clogging the arteries, but he soon emptied his plate. Afterwards, we wandered around the local shops that were doing a roaring trade. It was the glass gallery that caught my eye. Inside were enormous plates of glass made by a Western Australian aboriginal tribe, which had been on display in Japan and Germany. They were simply amazing. There was also an art gallery that displayed many local artworks in abstract. I was in seventh heaven as I took photos. The shop assistant, Tina, was a great help, telling me little excerpts about each painting. As we talked, I picked up on her Kiwi accent and she said she was from Auckland. I told her about my Kiwi bloke.

'So, you're newly engaged! Best wishes!' she exclaimed happily.

I realised it was the first time anyone had wished us well as a couple.

Tina told me how she'd landed this amazing job via the internet two years ago. She was about to leave Uluru and tour around this huge country. I gave her my business card.

'Would you email me your employer's name? I would love to exhibit my art somewhere like this.'

Tina happily popped my card in her back pocket as she closed the shop for her tea break.

'Might see you on the road, hey,' she said.

'You never know Tina, you just never know,' was my reply.

THE CUPPA TREE

Gordi wanted to play, see, and do. I was getting sore, and it was making me tired.

'You go for it, Gordi,' I encouraged him. 'I'm going to have a rest.'

He almost dived out the door. I felt a bit put out, but this was just Gordi being Gordi. It was not all about me. He'd planned this trip as well and had been just as excited to come here. The hot shower helped my back, and with two herbal muscle relaxants I was ready for a snooze. When I woke again, it was dark. I noticed Gordi had been back as there were leaflets by the bedside table with big circles around our tour for the next day.

I was up early; my back was not as sore as it had been. In fact, I was feeling really good. I woke Gordi up just as the sun came up over Uluru.

This place makes your heart acknowledge a spiritual meaning deeper than what we as Europeans will ever have. You can feel it as the sun rises out from the shadows, forming shadows in the rocks and crevices as the new day dawns. Everywhere there are shadows of all sorts, displays of light against dark.

I flung our windows open wide, the desert air still cool, Gordi pulling two chairs up to the open window. We our sipped hot Earl Grey tea, both calling out names of the shadows as the sun came up, from Lizard, Snake and Dingo. Then I saw an image I will never forget, the shadow of an aboriginal face.

'Gordi quick look,' I yelled, but he failed to see it. The sun climbed higher, and the image was gone. In the distance, grey clouds were coming in fast, the rains were setting in.

By the time we'd our continental breakfast and found our tour bus, the driver announced Uluru was crying. We were witness to something that rarely happens out here in the Outback. Waterfalls of tears were cascading down the sides of her deep red rock face, and I too shed a tear for Uluru. She was truly the most majestic and magical of monoliths.

We'd been on the road about an hour, zipping by Kulgera in a red heat haze, when a fence line covered in ladies' brassieres came in to view. The bus stopped, and the driver enquired whether any of the ladies wished to add to the ensemble on the fence. Quite a few did, and this started the crazy dance of getting your bra off under your clothes, something only we ladies knew how to do. I liked to think of it more like a chicken dance with a waltz mixed into it.

Husbands chuckled, cameras went off in a frenzy as four of the ladies each held up her trophy, placing it reverently on the fence. I decided my bra was to stay right where it was, on me. Coober Pedy came into view. I loved the way the white rock deposits looked like mini pyramids, becoming enormous white glistening art works the closer one got to it. The bus dropped off most of its passengers at the hotel and offered to drop us off at the motel, which we quickly and gratefully accepted. I was really feeling sore, and Gordi was concerned for me.

Gordi and I both slept badly that night, the recent trip having exhausted us both. Trying to fit in all we could in the twenty-four hours we'd allotted hadn't been good for either of our stress levels. By one a.m., Gordi was up. I murmured, 'Why are you awake?' He turned on his bedside light.

'Tara, how do you feel about staying an extra night in Coober Pedy?'

I know I looked a mess, my skin pale with huge bags under my eyes. My body ached so much that even the strong painkillers were not working anymore.

'Tara, this was not how I wanted to see Australia. I wanted to stop and have a good look around, not whizz by in a rush of time restrictions, stopping off for half an hour here, an hour somewhere else, then racing off to yet somewhere else.'

I had to agree. I did not think this was fun either. It felt like we were almost running on the spot.

'What's the plan then, Gordi? What are you up to now?' I knew he'd a plan. It was written all over his face.

He showed me an advertisement for a company that hired drivers to transport what they called 'returnable hire vehicles' all over the country, and his excitement was contagious; it was nearly three a.m. before we switched out the lights again. Our new plan was in action. Tomorrow we would phone the hire place and find out as much as possible, then take it from there.

The next day, Gordi rang around with a vengeance, his phone not stopping till we'd answers. We'd asked whether we could book the motel room for one more night, but they'd booked the whole place out for a mining company, so we'd no choice but to move on. Gordi's face looked haggard. There was no good news. It looked as though our only option was to drive to Adelaide in the hire car and fly home to Perth. I was sad to end the trip like this, but I was also excited to think that soon I would be reunited with my family and holding my little granddaughter for the first time.

Gordi's temper was fraying. His face was mottled red. He now snarled answers at me when questioned. Here again was the man I did not like at all, and all my fears of the past came rushing back into my chest. Did I really want this, to have to teach another person patience and stability? Or had I thrown in the towel of independence for the sake of having another to lean on when needed? Once again, I questioned my motives for accepting Gordi back into my life, knowing full well that if things did not go his way, I was his target. Rae's question, 'Are you sure about this Mum?' was now coming back to haunt me.

Maybe she was right to doubt me. Maybe I did not want the responsibility or have the time really for a full-blown relationship. I'd done my bit, and to be truthful, I was done mothering people. In the past, I'd often had the impression Gordi and I were in a competition instead of in a relationship, and I could feel my heart and hope for us slipping.

But with my experience of Gordi thus far, I knew once he was happy with the outcome then 'Mr. Sweetness and Light' would reappear. To answer Rae's question, I had to admit that, no, I certainly had doubts about this. I could only hope these doubts would eventually take care of themselves.

I left Gordi to his devices and put together a light lunch of cheeses and crackers, pickles, and some fruit. Then I made a cup of honey, mint, and ginger tea. My back was feeling better, day by day. I went to tell Gordi that lunch was ready. He was still on the phone with someone, trying to find out more about the hire company we'd read about last night. As I approached him, the scowl on his face stopped me, mid-step.

Stuff it. He can get his own flipping lunch. I'm not prepared to put up with this nonsense.

I was over him going from happy to crappy in mere minutes. It was unbelievable.

CHAPTER 55

I sat in the sunlight streaming into our room's windows, eating my lunch, looking at the build-up of emails on my laptop. Invitations to join this, be part of that, and create something or other, were all demanding my attention and wanting pieces of me. I had requests to be back in Rockingham for a festival; but to be part of any festival, one had to be there on certain dates. It was so tempting to just say, 'Yes, I will be there!' to all of them. And if I had been at home, I know I would have. How frustrating. Thinking better of it, I turned down most invitations and accepted just two: the Mandurah Stretch Festival and the Rockingham Castaways beach sculptor competition. Both festivals I'd done before, and it was fun. I'd loved being part of both, but this meant I now had just two weeks to get home to Rockingham.

There was one email from Jo in Perth, who was concerned about me.

'Where are you? We miss you, is everything alright?'

The last time we'd spoken was when I'd been in Alice Springs. I did not feel like explaining everything immediately, so I flicked a quick email off instead. 'I'm good, in Coober Pedy till tomorrow.'

It was time to tackle the bad-tempered man who was now outside, leaning against the hire car; still on the phone, still scowling. Gordi found it hard to admit defeat. I suggested we book a flight home and be done with it. We could always come back another time. My words seemed to sink in, and he turned off the phone.

'I think your right, Tara; I'm about done with all the stupid red tape. So be it. Let's finish our lunch and phone through to Adelaide and get us a booking to fly home.'

It was settled. Gordi's face immediately looked much more relaxed as the tension left his body; now he even had a smile for me.

'Sorry, love, I wanted this to be one last adventure for us.'

I put my arms around him, and we held each other gently. He'd come all this way for me, to help me, to be there for me. Surely, I could overlook the way he dealt with stress sometimes. Now we were homeward bound, a rush of excitement flooded through me. I suggested a quick swim then to pack up our backpacks and make the plane booking to Perth so we could relax for the rest of the afternoon. We'd just changed into our swimmers and put on our fly screen hats when Gordi's phone buzzed.

'Ignore it,' I said, turning away. Gordi dived back into our room to retrieve it.

I was in the pool by the time he'd finished the call. I could just see him through the fly mesh around the pool. Slamming the door and ran out to me by the pool.

'Tara, we got it, it's ours! Woohoo, honey, we did it.'

I'd no idea what he was going on about. 'What, booking flights?' I asked.

'No, we have been given the contract to drive a motorhome back to Perth!' Gordi explained the terms. 'We pay for the gas, plus a dollar a day for the use of the motorhome. It's being delivered tonight from Adelaide. This, my lovely, solves our accommodation problem!'

He climbed down into the tepid water to join me.

'See? I told you: persevere, and it will happen.'

I splashed him in the face.

'You mean, tear the world apart till it's yours.' Gordi put his arms around me.

'Well, I got you, didn't I?' he said with a wink.

It all sounded crazy, but that was the deal. We were now driving a motorhome back to Perth. We climbed out of the pool and had a simple dinner of warmed up meat pies and a slice of chocolate sponge roll from the motel's little shop. The motorhome was to be delivered at nine o'clock, but that soon came and went. By eleven p.m., we were ready to admit it wasn't happening, both of us thinking something had gone wrong. We went to bed gutted, wondering where we would go next without any future accommodation or travel plans. At midnight, we woke to someone knocking on our door.

'Anyone here for a motorhome?' the driver shouted through the fly screen window.

Gordi sprang out of bed. I took my time. There it was, parked outside our room. She was a sleek, white fourteen-foot motor home. Both of us signed the insurance papers, agreeing to the contract in fine print. It had to be delivered to Perth within ten days. Perfect. We were both too excited to stay in the room any longer. Home was now calling out to me, louder than any other place on earth.

I'd packed both our backpacks during the day. Gordi had packaged anything else we had brought into the room. We'd already paid the bill, there was nothing keeping us there. We decided to get on the road. Then we stored all the gear in the new motorhome, suddenly realising we still had to return the hire car. It made us feel like two little kids who'd just had their lollies taken off them. We looked at each other, mutually agreeing to stay in the room for the night. Climbing back into our cold beds again, waiting for the morning. Waiting for eight-thirty was so hard when all we'd wanted to do was to get up and go. It was an agonising wait, knowing our new wheels that were to carry us home was parked just outside the door! Just when I thought we couldn't do it, we both fell into a deep sleep, the sleep so solid it took the cleaning lady to knock on the door and wake us.

'You guys goin' or stayin'?'

'Going!' we yelled in unison.

Gordi drove the motorhome to the hire car office, and I followed him in the hire car, giving him my bank card to pay for it. Oh, the joy of being back behind the wheel of a motorhome once more. The seat fitted into my back perfectly, the steering wheel was at the right height and arms' length for me, no hunching over. The brakes so smooth, the motor hummed with precision. We both fell in love with this little beauty.

Gordi quipped, 'This is a little bit different to .' Wayward

That stung my pride. My little motorhome had done its best to keep me safe and take me to places I'd not seen before. It had been my home for over eight months. I was grateful for that opportunity. I knew I would never be compensated for what I'd spent on the Wayward Or for what I sold it for. So far, it has been the trip of a lifetime, in every way, one of memories and experiences that money could never buy.

However, he was right. Inside was a fully kitted out modern kitchen and a bathroom with a big double bed. Last night I'd thought this day would never arrive, but here we both were, grinning as though there were no tomorrow. On the way out of Coober Pedy, Gordi pointed to a signpost: *The*

The Cuppa Tree

Painted Desert Look Out.

'I want to have a look at that,' Gordi cried.

I turned the wheel to where he'd pointed. We were soon bumping slowly along down an uneven track to be greeted by an amazing view. This is how we loved to travel, seeing, and doing what we wanted to do, not what the tourist guide told us to.

The Flinders Ranges is a huge desert in a semi-arid zone of Australia. It was formed millions of years ago, as evidenced by the pink and cream layered rock with shelves of russet red sandwiched in between. In some places, squeezed in between the cream and the red was the sage green of the native saltbush plant. It all complemented the backdrop of an endless, azure blue sky that stole a little piece of my heart. You know you are the smallest, most insignificant dot on the planet when you try to take in the vastness of such an incomparably arid landscape, such as this. Gordi just kept saying 'Wow,' his heart also in awe by this experience. This was not the township of Coober Pedy; it was not the opal grubbing, tourism pushing money-making face of the Outback. This was just pure, untouched beauty. Gordi put his camera down.

'Photos just cannot even do this justice,' he uttered.

He was right. Before us lay the most picturesque, raw and God given beauty; it was a gift to us all. I felt so protective of this land to keep the sparse rawness beauty of this place safe from the footprint of man before he had the chance to walk on it and ruin it because of his own greed. We sat there like that for an hour, drinking it all in, but then it was time to go, time to get back on to the highway, time to head home.

We'd planned to stop in Woomera overnight, which was about a four-hour trip from Coober Pedy. That was until Gordi spotted an opal mine that was giving tours. When Gordi wanted something badly though, I noticed he'd look a bit like a wounded puppy.

'Ok,' I said. 'I get the hint.'

I pulled into the parking lot, where we spent a good one hour talking to the owners. For five dollars each they gave us a hard hat and told us not to go into any of the corridors marked off with tape, otherwise we were free to roam. We walked from room to room, Gordi fascinated that someone would drill so far underground to find opals: it was cavernous. Gordi had thought opals were small stones and was amazed when the mine owner showed us what a fire opal really looked like. A large stone, on the outside it was rough rock, but on the inside lay the trail of red fire through milky white stone, or blue stone with green and pink fire deep within. All the colours caused by pressure, volcanic action, sea water and age. The female of this team placed a plain silver ring in the palm of my hand, the opal in it was exquisite. Its age was the most fascinating aspect of all, for I now had countless millions of years winking back at me. I saw the price tag and happily gave it back.

I became fascinated with the jewellery a couple from Germany made and sold on site. Robby, the owner, worked in the mine by day and as a silversmith by night. Toni, his partner, washed and packed the gemstones when not by his side, mining for the main trophy, a perfect seam of opal. Inside these massive dugouts in the ground, it is a calm, silent twenty-two degrees Celsius. When I'd last checked, it was a stinking hot forty-eight degrees outside. Robby and Toni were so hospitable, offering us freshly brewed coffee with homemade ginger cake. Robby and Gordi had an hour-long conversation on opal mining. While Toni and I discussed how they came to be living here, it was not the normal thing couples do. Gordi became mesmerised by the whole idea of owning a mine and living underground, opals aplenty; I could tell he was getting the Opal itch. It was time to move on. Woomera was waiting for us.

Woomera was the first place in Australia to test nuclear rockets. The gateway to the region displayed these defused bombs as a memorial, with the word 'Welcome' painted on them. There are many stories to come out of Woomera about the desolation and destruction caused by a government experiment gone wrong. People have written many books about the damage it did to not only the Aboriginal people, but the army and staff working here. I had to wonder at just how many people had never fully understood what 'nuclear' really involved? If you ever had the chance to visit Woomera, then you could see it firsthand.

The entire landscape had the look of brown sand; even the campgrounds were brown. The hills were bare, a bleached landscape. There were warning signs posted everywhere not to drink the contaminated water, the whole area felt like it was in some brown/black void. I looked around for signs of life, there was nothing. No trees, bush, plants, animals. The entire place was completely soulless; the only life was in the campground where two permanent male residents lived. Two old diggers, one at each end of the camp, had

The Cuppa Tree

made it their home. The park ranger only ever called in to collect overnight fees from one-nighters like us.

A grey storm was brewing overhead, and strong winds were whipping up desert willy-willy's waist high, that began whirling across the ground in front of us.

'Buckle up for the night, people. Big storm coming in,' the ranger warned in a gruff voice.

We'd nothing we needed to buckle up in our mobile home. We hadn't extended the motorhome awning, so we felt as safe as brick houses.

Speaking of the motorhome, I'd not yet had the chance to explore inside our little home on wheels, so I went off to explore. It had one big plush double bed sitting in the middle of thick grey pile carpet. A small kitchen with all the pots and pans a cook could need. There were tea towels and bath towels by the shower and small bottles of body wash and shampoo. The mystery was, where was the toilet? While I heated baked beans for our dinner, Gordi continued the search for the missing loo.

'Found it,' Gordi yelled.

He'd found the toilet, a pop-up porta tent with a small port loo. The pop-up contraption was like a tall, domed tent that expanded as he pulled it out of its carry bag, kind of like a mini circus tent. The Porta loo: a plastic cube, you filled with water and after you had finished, you emptied it yourself. Me, I would rather use the abolition block, but Gordi wanted the full-on experience of Outback camping. So with winds now howling at thirty knots or more, I watched my Kiwi bloke struggle with a tent and toilet that did not want to go outside. I tapped on the cab window to say dinner was ready. Gordi waved at me, his face beaming. He'd erected the tent, fighting the wind. As he stood there looking so immensely proud of his achievements, a huge gust of wind tore the tent away from his hands. It rolled off across the brown dirt to rest beside one of the old diggers' caravans.

CHAPTER 56

I dissolved into fits of laughter as there sat the Porta loo, all alone in the middle of the paddock, all ready to use. The sight had me in stitches. My humour clearly was not appreciated by the Gods above, for right then our power point blew up which caused a complete blackout. The wind howled around us as the rain burst out of the clouds, shooting like wet arrows, each one hitting the ground with a spurt of dust. Lightning forked its way across the field next door. I rummaged around, finding a torch. What is it that gives man such pleasure in seeing that lone beam of light? I was grateful.

I became aware of the possibility of being hit by lightning considering I was sitting in a plastic bubble, next to a gas bottle that was tucked away somewhere under the stove. This was not my idea of fun. The drama of what might be unfolded before me. A sudden flash of lightning on the motorhome and I would be toast. Literally. Gordi dashed inside, dripping wet, while I did my best to mop up brown pools of muddy water he'd bought inside this beautiful motor home.

It's true I'd admired a fierce electrical storm coming across the Nullarbor when we first started out on this journey, but this storm was mere inches from my face, and much too close for comfort. I went to sleep to the sounds of thunder rolling around overhead, but I couldn't wait to leave this godforsaken place, full of ghostly nuclear memories.

'Come on, sleepyhead! Let's go!' I called out to him in the morning, revving the engine. 'Let's have breakfast in Port Augusta.'

With that, I drove away from this godforsaken campground just as Gordi made it into the seat beside me.

'For God's sake, Tara, what's your problem?'

I gave him one of my best smiles. 'Don't argue, Gordi: just smile and nod. That's all I ask.'

We did not talk for an hour or more until I found a small café in Port Augusta. The café was a real find, called the French Teapot. It was 1930s with a splash of haute couture about it. Bright plastic red geraniums spilled out of bronze painted ceramic vases, grapevines of green plastic festooned about the walls, and antique, faded paintings of voluptuous, scantily clad Grecian ladies carrying the obligatory water jars. But the freshest croissants, all flaky and golden, were piled high on the countertop. I drooled at the fresh wholemeal scones with parsley and feta cheese, baked pita breads sprinkled with black pepper and Turkish goats' cheese.

It looked so nice, I wanted to stay and eat there. Gordi wanted to be on the road, so we settled for takeaways: A French Vanilla coffee, two parsley and feta scones to take with us. Plus, two croissants filled with cream custard. We were on our way home. And what better way to travel than with good food, good company, and good music by my side? What more could a girl want?

We cruised along with Andrea Bocelli singing Celeste Aida. Wundina was four hours away and had a proper camping ground with a pool. Gordi was busting to drive the little motorhome, which we had now nicknamed Winnie (It was, after all, a Winnebago.) I was happy with the plan. All I wanted to do was take photographs and relax while we drove. Gordi was impatient to see and do as much as possible, and in his frustration to get there quickly, he stamped his foot down on the accelerator. Still, we reached 65kph, and that was it.

Frustrated our new motorhom wouldn't go any faster, Gordi pulled over on the side of the road to examine the accelerator. The hire firm had applied a speed governor, which was a small bump welded beneath the accelerator, and Gordi's frustration was palpable. Me? Although I was eager to get home to see and do all the things I'd promised, I knew I was coming to the end of my trip. I was happy to go any speed.

In roughly four days' time, I would finally be back in Perth. I also knew I'd given my home to Rae to bring up her family in, so what I referred to as home was no longer my home. I knew once we were back and handed the mobile home over to the hire firm, our life may be in one room. The thought of renting a new home with Gordi scared me a little. Gordi's reactions to my questions were often already mixed with annoyance, so, while he drove along, albeit impatiently, I knew it was time to open another can of worms.

I waited till we'd pulled into the camping spot we'd booked at Wundina. This was a up market South Australian roadhouse compared to Kulgera. Nevertheless, a roadhouse it was and charged typical roadhouse expenses. While Gordi put petrol in the tank , I bought a few necessary items for dinner: bread, milk, butter, a little cold meat. The price made me look twice at what we'd bought. Unless they capped the milk bottle in gold leaf, there was no way it could have come to Eighty Dollars. I stopped mid-swipe of my credit card.

'This is wrong,' I said, looking at the attendant who re-added it on her till.

'No, Ma'am it's correct.'

Out here in the middle of nowhere, you pay what they ask, or you don't buy at all. It is what it is. It was basically highway robbery. So, I asked to pay only for the gas. We would use up whatever food we still had.

'No, sorry, paying for gas only.'

Gordi looked horrified as I pushed it all back at her and paid my bill of fifty dollars, walking back out into the forty-degree heat. The use of the pool came with the campsite, and right then I thought that was just what I needed, a long cool swim. Gordi declined my offer to join me. He lay on the bed, reading a book, obviously not happy about my decision not to buy any groceries. I'd been in the water about twenty minutes when I noticed Gordi frantically waving at me to come out. I looked back at him quizzically, as if to say, 'what for?' Apparently, a wedding party had booked the whole place out, including the pool. Management had asked Gordi to remove me from the pool area, so their guests could start their celebration.

It was not exactly what I'd imagined, but twenty minutes was better than nothing. Plus, Gordi was warming up some massage oil, the smell of geranium and black pepper oils filled the motorhome. I did not need to be told to get my swimsuit off and lie on the bed. Gordi started at my heels. By the time he'd reached my shoulders I was far away in dreamland, my intention of asking about living arrangements in Rockingham long forgotten.

When I woke up, Gordi had made a light dinner for two from the salad fixings in the chilly bin. He served them with chilled soda water with a slice of lemon zest on two small plastic plates lay those yummy croissants. I lay back after dinner, feeling relaxed and happy to have time to read. I was right into a book and it was just one of those books you can't put down, and I read well into the night.

The music from the wedding party took over the night, the sounds of Greek dance music thumping through the ground beneath us. It sounded as if Mad Max and a tribe of woad-painted tribesmen were trampling through the campground. There was not much one could do, and I realised this was just one of those times when, as a camper living in and sharing close quarters with others, you just had to accept it. While I tried to master the skills of breathing and patience, my Kiwi bloke snored peacefully in dreamland.

Gordi was first up. He looked refreshed and full of pep.

'It's time to go, Tara,' he announced.

He handed me a coffee. I was still taking things easy. First, I clipped on my hip brace. We were becoming firm friends. Buckling myself into the passenger seat, leaning across and giving Gordi a morning kiss on his cheek, we were off. Gordi wanted to make Ceduna for the night. It was only a four-hour drive. I remembered how our first motorhome struggled with the radiator way back then and me struggling with Gordi's moods then too. None of it pleasant but a big learning curve.

There is not much else to see in Ceduna, but for the views of the ocean, which is spectacular and the rise and fall of the sun and moon. I suggested we buy groceries once over the border, that way we wouldn't waste anything. In Ceduna there was a proper grocery store where we could stock up on basic food without the huge costs. This time the Ceduna camping ground asked if we would care to park around the back of the camp, not the grass and sand dunes as before. Its prettiness, a canopy of trees in between each camp bay, which afforded us plenty of shade, surprised me. The summers in West Australia are extreme, so although it was April when it's supposed to be cooler, here it was still extremely hot.

In front of us lay the sand dunes with board walks that made for an easy walk down through the sand dunes to watch the sun set. On a cloudless night you can really see the moon. It glows on the ocean, forming what looks like a walkway to the sky. Poets and songwriters have tried to capture this moment. *Plein air* artists have lined up to copy it onto a canvas. To be honest, there is nothing that can compare to the real thing. On a windless night when the ocean is a whisper as it softly kisses the sand, it feels surreal. Gordi offered to carry the bottle of cold white wine, compliments of the motorhome company, and the wine glasses up to the top of the dunes. I followed close behind, carrying a small box filled with crackers and cheese plus a rug for us to sit on.

We sat and chatted about the time we'd spent on the road, the thrills and pitfalls and crazy adventures we'd had, including the heartache and goodbyes. As the sun sunk deeper and deeper, it became a magnificent sunset of orange, yellow and peach so strong it coloured us in a bronze hue. It entranced Gordi. He'd never seen a sunset like it. He turned to me, cupping my face in his hands.

'I just want to live in this golden moment forever,' he said.

Then in a flash it was gone. The night sky now in full display, a velvet blanket of deep blue. The stars showed off their beauty, and behind us sat a pale lemon half-moon. Gordi and I sat in awe, taking in all the natural beauty that surrounded us.

'I love you Tara, and this trip we have shared together has been the trip of a lifetime,' Gordi said softly.

Reaching for my hand as he delved into his pocket, he pulled out a silver ring, slipping it onto my ring finger. It was the opal ring I'd admired. He'd purchased it at Coober Pedy from the two opal miners we'd had a bite to eat with. The ring I'd admired and gasped at the price was now on my finger. There were no speeches, no bended knee, no poetic sayings, no fanfare, just the two of us sitting on a sand dune, watching the moonlight dance peacefully on the rippling water.

Gordi put his arm around me, and I snuggled up into him; no words were needed. We simply knew the time was right for us both.

The day we spent in Ceduna gave me the time I needed to have a conversation with Jo back home, to tell her the news.

Her only comment was, 'What took you so long?'

It took the wind out of my sails a bit. Then I called Rae. I could hear the baby crying in the background.

'Mum, I'm so glad you're okay. Where are you? And when will you be home?' Then Rae said, 'Hang on a minute, Mum. Shauna's crying.'

So, they'd called her Shauna. It was a beautiful name. Its origin was *Irish*, its meaning *God is gracious*. Yes, he is. My family was living proof of that statement.

Rae gave the phone to Jess. 'Nana, when are you coming home?'

It had been such a long time since Jess and I'd spoken.

'In about three days, Jess. Any room for one Nana and a Gordi at the house?'

Jess laughed. 'No worries, you two can have my room.'

It erased any doubts I'd had about our welcome. I realised then that these doubts had been haunting me ever since we'd decided to drive home to Perth.

CHAPTER 57

Packing up this tiny home on wheels was a breeze. Everything in one or two cupboards. We placed any clothing or bathroom gear under the beds, then vacuumed the floor with a mini-vac. Within minutes of my finishing any housework, Gordi was calling out, 'Ready to go?' and I was clambering up into the passenger's seat as we headed for the border.

We stood to the side and waited while the border patrol took the inside of our motorhome apart. Gordi was as impatient as ever, wanting to know what the border patrol were doing, and why. I guessed they were immune to impatient tourists by now because they just simply carried on, ignoring Gordi. They took everything in the way of food. That's one reason I'd been skimpy on buying fresh produce. Then they asked me if there was anything I wished to declare. Once they were satisfied with the inspection, they waved us across the border.

'Woohoo! I'm home!' I said excitedly as our wheels crossed over into my home territory and state of Western Australia. I was so excited.

After an hour or two on the road, we pulled into the Eucla coffee shop for a morning fix of tea and huge, toasty fresh scones with jam and cream. Then we were back on the road again, driving across the great expanse of the Nullarbor plain. Gordi had done a little shopping at Eucla; just enough for a couple of nights of free camping in the desert. This was what Gordi had been waiting for: free camping. When you're driving along and spot a lay-by that suits you, you can just pull over and stop wherever you like. To be honest, I think the appeal of it all is just the sense of freedom that comes with it. Some places are full of bush and trees, which have exceptionally large globe spiders living in them. However, the larger spaces have already been cleared out of overhanging branches by people camping regularly in them.

Gordi knew of my aversion to eight-legged critters that fell into any category between big or hairy. Globe spiders can be as big as your fist, and are fast, which leaves one (me) as in a terrified trance. They're not poisonous, just damn ugly, hairy, and huge, so Gordi kindly found larger spaces with no overhanging trees. I had to admire this man. He'd gone from being a city wimp into a budding outdoorsman. He took charge of everything, and I happily watched as he went outside, expertly setting up the pop-up toilet. Then, he pulled out the small barbecue that came with the motorhome and set that up, ready to cook up a batch of sizzling sausages and eggs that night for our dinner.

I was told to rest up while he made me a cup of tea. I was disappointed as I was going to show Gordi how to make damper bread over a fire pit and billy tea. It's a skill every bushman or woman should know, and tasty. Because it was the dry season, there were huge red signs all over the place, *Do not start campfire,* promising a huge fine if caught.

How peaceful it all was! The bird life was quieting down at dusk as cicadas said goodnight to each other. Then that twenty-second hush between day and night I love so much when the chorus of birds and bees switches over to hoots of owls, night frogs and night insects. Green and brown bush moths, some as big as my hand, flew around the outside light of the motorhome. I lay my journal down on my knees, my heart feeling so full of gratitude for all that I'd done and seen. If you can't relax out here, then you can't relax anywhere. I looked up at the sky; it was a stunning, star-filled canvas of beauty, and I took a moment to inhale the clean air into my lungs, the perfume of gum tree sap all around me.

I looked down and studied my opal ring, admiring the way the soft light winked across it. The red veins within the marble of it leapt to life as though fire lived inside the opal.

'I knew that ring was for you the moment I saw it,' Gordi said.

He watched me as I admired it.

'It's a rare stone, smooth and beautiful to look at, inside it's as fiery as hell!'

'You think you know me, do you? Have I got news for you Gordi, you don't know the half of it.'

Now with us so relaxed was as good a time as any to talk about where we would choose to live.

'Do you have any plans?' I asked, nonchalantly.

His reply was not what I'd expected.

'What about moving to Coober Pedy for a couple of years and go opal mining? We could rent an underground home there, and I could use my herbalist practice as a wage earner. You could teach art if you wanted to, and we could mine for opal, or just sit back and put your feet up for once.'

My insides quickened. The possibility of another adventure was on the horizon. But still, I needed to persevere with my original question.

'Yes, but where would you want to live when we are back in Rockingham? With family or another caravan? Rent somewhere?'

I could sense both of us were still undecided. We agreed to wait. Gordi knew I wanted to see and hold my new grandchild, catch up with friends, be part of the local community festivals again. Plus spend some quality time with our Jess and Rae. It was important to me that Gordi did, as well; he was part of the family now. We agreed home first, see how we felt and then decide.

We went to bed both feeling a little sad that soon all of this would be over. Our arms around each other as we settled in for the night, I was happy to reflect and admit I was learning there was no hurry to anything anymore. Only the delightful building of love and trust, now confident that we'd a together.

In the early morning, when the mist had not quite unwrapped from around the trees, we drove out of the overnight campsite and onto the main road. We knew we had one more night travelling along on the long stretch of the Nullarbor, then maybe two more days after that, and we would be home.

We drove for four hours at a stretch, passing through areas of desert that hadn't escaped the recent bushfires. With camera in hand, I snapped photos of what was left of the tall and stately trees that had been reduced to blackened stumps; short and broken branches now lay covering the land like a war zone. I also saw regeneration. Delicate signs of new life peeped out from the hollowed, burnt-out trunks. Everywhere I looked around the cindered, blackened ash contained the spirit of survival. Already, fuzzy green shoots were forming along tree branches, while other branches appeared to throw their arms up in the air towards the sky, celebrating the gift of life itself.

By four o'clock we'd both had enough of being cramped up in the cab and needed to stretch our stiff bodies. We pulled up into a lay-by where I spied a big red bus, the name 'Bull' written across its front and rear. Instantly I recognised the van. It was the couple I'd met months ago when my journey had first begun. I asked Gordi to park alongside it. Sure enough, it was Doug and Marion. Marion quickly recognised me in the new motorhome and came running over, her arms enfolding me as soon as I was out of the cab.

'Tara, we were only talking about you the other day and wondering how you were going on your travels!'

We all hugged each other warmly, happy to see each other well. I introduced Gordi to them both, Doug and Gordi immediately bonding.

Soon we'd our deck chairs alongside theirs outside their bus and we added two tins of baked beans to Doug and Marion's bush tucker. Well, we called it that. I felt Gordi might have blanched as he did in Cooper Pedy if I'd explained these folks also lived off the land. Instead, we ate and talked about our adventures, mopping up the rich brown gravy on our plates with the damper she'd made. We laughed all the while at the mishaps and stories we'd to share about life on the road. We washed down our tucker with Marion's heady home brew.. I shared my story about the Quaker family, and the Otto debacle. That particular story had the three of them laughing.

CHAPTER 58

It also made me wonder what they would think now if I turned up again with a new man by my side. I could just see Ceri's my Quaker hosts face if I had arrived unannounced with Gordi in tow. It would have mortified her, proving her point to the family that I was nothing but a temptress, or maybe she would have approved. Who knew?

Marion and I washed up dishes. Admiring my new ring, she said she was happy that Gordi and I were a couple.

'Everyone needs someone, Tara.'

Maybe she was right. I made a confession to my outback friend.

'All this time I never thought Gordi and I were compatible. I did not know it then, but I guess I was still not over Russ, my husband. I wasn't ready. I was holding onto my past. And I was comfortable doing so.'

'I couldn't ever imagine losing Doug. That must have been so hard on you,' Marion said, putting away the plates. 'But at some point, we must move on. We have to heal, we have to forgive, and we have to let love back in. Right?'

'Right,' I said, nodding. I told her about my new granddaughter, Shauna.

Marion's eyes lit up. 'Oh, what a year you have had! Now there's another thing to celebrate! We should be popping a bottle of bubbly! Home brew will have to do.'

She gathered all four battered mugs, then beckoned us to follow her to the roadside where there stood a gigantic old grey gum tree. Raising her mug to the night sky she said, 'To life, to love and to the new baby.'

Then each of us taking a sip of potent home brew then placing our mugs one at a time on its thick branches.

We christened it 'The Cuppa Tree.' I took some photos and quickly texted it to Rae and Kane.

'Mum, we love it! Thank you!' they messaged, sending through a photo of my beautiful family. There was Rae, holding her baby girl, Shauna, with Jess and Kane sitting either side of them. I immediately showed it to Gordi and my two friends.

'Meet our family,' I said proudly.

We settled for the night knowing we'd soon be home. Gordi's idea of Coober Pedy had me rattled, yet also intrigued. I decided in that moment to leave it all to fate. If it was to be, then so be it. First though, I would have to have my fill of everything I loved in this world before I could move on again.

By the time we awoke and had breakfast, there were more road-weary travellers pulling into rest. I got the surprise of my life when I stepped outside of the motorhome just after dawn. Low and behold, they'd added four more cups to the tree! Just like the Shoe Tree in Kulgera, the Bra fence in the Northern Territory, and the iron horse fence in Western Australia, we now had a Cuppa Tree on the Nullarbor.

We said our goodbyes to Marion and Doug, preparing ourselves for another long day of driving ahead. We were headed for Salmon Gums, where we would set up at another free camp that night. After driving all day, by late afternoon, we felt hungry, tired, and gritty. I longed for a strong hot shower, but the water read low on the tank gauge. So, I boiled the jug instead, filled up the tiny basin, soaped the flannel up and gave myself a quick wash. It felt liberating to stand there in the nude, a warm breeze blowing through the window, washing off the day's grime.Gordi knew by now there was nothing even remotely glamorous about life on the road. He sat outside the door on guard, and then it was his turn.

We were at the end of a lay-by, surrounded by pink salmon gums which shed their bark in long paper strips. Under the paper-thin bark they have salmon pink coloured bellies. They glowed a light honey colour in the late afternoon sun, turning a deeper shade of pink as dusk settled on the horizon.

Wild Quails ran around the gum trees, their plumage so intricate, like their mum had knitted all of them identical grey and white jumpers. Gordi sat down next to me and I pointed over to a branch of a tree, the biggest, hairiest caterpillar seemed to hang in mid-air, Gordi trained his camera lens on it.

'It's not a caterpillar, Tara. Be quiet and come with me.'

We ducked around the side of the tree. There, in the hollow, was a tiny possum curled up and fast asleep, the only telltale sign of it being here was its furry little tail, hanging out of a hollow. Gordi snapped a few photos of it until it turned its back on us in disdain, its plump backside facing out as it pulled it's tail up and around itself. Its message to us was clear; it said, 'Bugger off! I'm sleeping!'

The drive from Salmon Gums to Esperance only takes about an hour, but the brochures do not do this place justice. Esperance is truly one of the most beautiful places in the world that you just have to see to believe. For the two nights we stayed in Esperance, I drank up everything from its stunning, turquoise-blue ocean to its golden and white sands. Everything here is so clean and crystal clear. It is truly a paradise. However It poured with rain the whole time. Gordi grumped about feeling chilled and damp, but I revelled in the rains and thought it a godsend. I imagined the trees and the parched landscapes drinking it up in the soil and growing strong until their leaves shone. After the many months of heat, dust, and dirt, I loved the smell of rain and how it turned everything green. The lush grass growing wild as Mother Nature giving up an enormous sigh of relief from the heat.

Leaving Esperance, we were now on our last leg home, and I could sense Gordi was digging in his heels. If we hadn't signed a contract to return Winnie, I know he would have kept going; the travel bug was well and truly alive in both of us. We passed a sign that said, 'coastal highway or scenic route.' It gave me an idea.

'Want to take the country road home?' I suggested. 'It'll take an extra hour or two to get home, but I think it's worth it.'

Gordi nodded, and within the hour we were in Ravensthorpe under humid, overcast skies and a warm wind blew. We filled up with gas at the one and only gas station in town with no more than twenty houses, and a country pub. Gordi was a little on edge as no one seemed to be living there except the gas station owner, her partner who was the mechanic, plus the publican and his wife. That is because the government had closed the school and small hospital, so the rest of the townsfolk had left for greener pastures. The quietness unnerved Gordi, and I agreed. I felt sorry for these folks who were clinging onto their livelihood as best they could, despite its being destroyed at the hands of the government's pen pushers, who were making decisions at the stroke of a pen.

THE CUPPA TREE

We continued to Kojonup, stopping for a bathroom break. This tiny thriving township amazed me with its immaculately clean public toilets, inside was handmade lemon scented soaps and pretty hand towels. Well-kept parks and rows of pretty pink roses lining pathways surrounded it while nearby, passionfruit vines grew on trellises in the community park. While waiting for Gordi, I crossed the road to where there were three shops: a small deli, a small post office, and a small, second-hand shop. Outside stood four women eagerly chatting, obviously, locals. I approached them and was welcomed enthusiastically. Through my travels I have learned that just by asking a few questions and listening carefully, most of the time you can discover the whys and wherefores of people and places. I soon found out that women ran the township. It impressed me.

They were all farmers' wives. A well-formed knot of country women who'd taken over the township to keep it running. Otherwise, it would also be on the verge of collapse, like the other small townships we'd just passed through. These ladies were proud of their achievements, and rightly so, as they'd kept the town running, even though the local primary school had only ten pupils. This was a home-schooling project initiated by these women.

I saw their story as a proud one, a large part of the country's spirit that keeps this great land running. I popped a twenty-dollar note into their appeal tin, and they offered me free tea and scones, but what appealed to me most was their clockwork organisation. Every woman knew her job and did it well. Each woman volunteered her time, whether it be at the school-run, a teeny library, a dress up race day or the school-ran second-hand shop, and it all worked. *Now that was a community!*

They'd even posted a timesheet for when the sheep trucks went through town so they could phone their husbands and let them know when the truck was on its way. Their advice to me was, 'Don't pull out in the next ten minutes: two sheep trucks are due to roll through.'

I knew what they meant from experience because following a truck hauling sheep or cows only ever resulted in one's vehicle getting covered in all the crap that flew out the sides. It made me laugh when one woman in the group said, 'You can eat your scones in the middle of the road for the next half hour, but then you have to move.'

My time with these brilliant ladies was certainly an eye-opener about the undying determination and spirit of these small towns, and it was written on all their faces. I could see they'd taken it to the next level of self-sufficiency. Go, Girl Power! I felt empowered just listening to them, their motto written on their faces.

'If you want it badly enough, then go for it.'

CHAPTER 59

The crossroads from the highway to Pinjarra came into view as we coasted along the Highway, rolling on to Mandurah, our last stop before Rockingham. Gordi took hold of my hand.

'Are you ready for this? We can keep this motorhome for one more night if you like.'

I shook my head. 'It's time, Gordi; time we went home to our family.'

My back ached from too much sitting; it was time to stop. We took the turnoff to Rockingham, and suddenly everything looked so familiar; each landmark, sculpture, artwork, road, and tree felt like home to me. I looked out at the views of the Indian ocean, so blue against Rockingham's gold sandy beach. The trees, which had been newly planted when I left were now tall and leafy green.

I'd left Rockingham with Gordi and arrived back with my Kiwi bloke. I had travelled across Australia, covering over fifteen thousand kilometres, but for the first time in a long time, my heart now whispered, *Home.*

What a lovely word that is.

Home was where my family was, ready to make meals together. Home was where my friends were, waiting for me to paint, write and publish my books, make jam with friends, swap seedlings, grow new plants and once more be a part of the art festivals. And home was also community, to simply walk down the main street again and be greeted by name. Home was that place of true satisfaction and contentment, where my cup was filled, that was home to me.

We would soon turn into the driveway of my home in Rockingham. I'd journaled my adventure. I would not forget the memories of my many months on the road and all the twists and turns I'd taken. We rounded the final corner. Just two more turns left until I would see my beautiful family. I would see Jess and hear that familiar, 'Nana.' And I'd hold my granddaughter, Shauna Rae, in my arms. I would hug my daughter Rae and get to know Kane a lot more. While the call of the Outback still sang out to me, I knew there was no greater call than the feeling of being part of your family.

I called Rae. 'Hi, honey, we're two minutes away,'

I felt giddy with excitement. A new chapter was about to begin. This had been an adventure of the heart as much as it had been of life on the road.

'Okay Mum. Jug's on.'

THE END

Till I meet you all once more in my next Adventure / Romance book.

THE TALKING STICK

KEZ.

ACKNOWLEDGMENTS

To all family and friends who look forward to my novels, it means a lot to have others so willing to be of help, sharing their love and confidence in my abilities to tell a good story. Thank you. Without your down-to-earth humour, I couldn't laugh at myself as much as I do.

To Lou, my partner in this life, always willing to get on the road to travel, stopping to take photographs in the most awkward of situations and smile through it all, thank you; it has been a long journey of discovery about each other, with each other. May the spirit of adventure always remain between us.

To my publisher, and the MMH Press Team your encouragement to be not just a Good Author, but a Great Author is a wonderful asset to any writer.

And last but not least our grandson, Jess: without you in my life it would be a dull one. Thank you.

I consider myself one of the lucky ones to sit out in my backyard or here in the outback, surrounded by a universal glory that never fails to show itself. To sit and contemplate, be grateful for all I have, all I've received and all I've experienced. To be so glad that I am alive and healthy. While I am definitely not free of the body's aches and pains within the cage of bones that keep my heart protected, or free of the small heartache that is part and parcel of missing my spiritual home, my family.

I am, however, loved by friends, family, and extended family for without their love in my life I would have floundered. To all of you, thank you for being part of my life and allowing me to be part of yours.

Wishing You All Enough,

Kez

www.ingramcontent.com/pod-product-compliance
Lightning Source LLC
Chambersburg PA
CBHW021358290426
44108CB00010B/288